Jane's
AIRCRAFT
RECOGNITION
GUIDE

David Rendall

HarperCollins*Publishers*

INTRODUCTION

Aircraft recognition is moving away from traditional features such as sweep of wing, number of engines and position of intakes towards small details and modifications. As air forces contract, so many familiar airframes are being tasked with new roles with new systems.

The last all-new fighter to enter service in the West was the F/A-18 in 1980. The latest Russian fighters were designed in the mid 1970s, and although stealth aircraft were only declassified in the late 1980s, the F-117A had been under development for 15 years. New aircraft are being developed but live under the constant threat of cancellation. Deliveries of the Swedish Gripen have just begun and the US Air Force's YF-22 programme continues, but the Rafale is plagued by delays and a question mark stills hangs over the EF2000.

Familiar aircraft are being reborn with new technologies and systems, and this poses problems in recognition. McDonnell Douglas have turned the F-15 into an advanced attack aircraft, the F-15E, and have developed the F/A-18 into the F/A-18E/F. In Russia, Sukhoi has found no end of modifications to the basic Su-27 Flanker airframe, with naval versions, agile versions and the Platypus look-a-like Su-32 FN and SU-34 attack aircraft. These new aircraft can look very similar to their stablemates but have much greater capabilities. All these aircraft can be identified by their small details, 'warts' and 'blisters' that give away which model they are.

A new range of aircraft, included in this book for the first time, are the electronic and signals intelligence aircraft: the Cold War snoopers which are still stretched to the limit gathering information from combat zones around the world. Together with the electronic countermeasures aircraft, which gave Coalition forces the edge over Iraq in 1991, these are now the first aircraft to arrive on the scene and are usually the last to leave.

The digital information age has seen RC-135s and Joint STARS, Israeli Phalcons and Swedish 340AEWs sporting huge arrays of antennas and electro-optical sensors. Russian and US airliners have been turned into flying command posts, shielded against the effects of nuclear war and fitted out with so much electronics they need refrigeration units to stop them melting.

Infomation has become such a major concern for the US Government that after a lapse of three years a small number of SR-71 Blackbirds have been returned to service. Despite its 30-year-old design it remains, along with even older U-2/TR-1s, one of the most effective strategic reconnaissance platforms available.

Despite this move towards standard airframes and mission specified systems, and the end of the Cold War, research and development continues at a ferocious pace. Warfare has dominated the aircraft industry more than anything else this century, spurring development regardless of cost. World War I made aircraft safe and viable; World War II made them fast and popular. The Cold War has made aircraft 'smart' as advanced technologies like composites and electronic avionics allow for a new era in reliability, safety and design. Civil aircraft are using this technology to steal a march on their military cousins. Composite light aircraft and airliners flown by electronic brains are making new markets as the technology brings down the running costs of civil aviation. The Boeing 777 was designed, tested and flown on a computer before the first aircraft was ever built, and the SATIC A300-600T Super Transporter has been made possible through advanced materials.

Once the preserve of British Airways and Air France Concordes, the next century could see new breeds of supersonic or even hypersonic airliners. Several Russian design teams are studying supersonic executive jets, and European companies also see the benefits of high sub-sonic cruising speeds. The only problem these aircraft face is financial, not technological.

Helicopters have started to arrive in new shapes as the first production tilt-rotor nears service and the first 'stealth' helicopters appear. Bell and Boeing's V-22 tilt-rotor is a US Marine Corps priority, and a host of civilian designs are being based on its unique design. Sikorsky and Boeing have built the world's first low-observable helicopter, the RAH-66 Commanche, which has many of the blended shapes and materials seen on the YF-22. Russia has attack helicopters under development, with advanced features like ejection seats and comprehensive electronic countermeasures. Europe is pushing ahead with a range of new-generation helicopters such as the Tiger, NH 90 and EH101. Another new technology is NOTAR (no tail rotor). In an effort to bring down noise and increase safety many helicopter manufacturers are developing alternatives to the conventional helicopter layout. McDonnell Douglas has begun production of the first, the MD Explorer. Perhaps the most modified helicopter is the Sikorsky S-70 Black Hawk. Aside from its utility transport role it can now be seen fitted with wings, radars and in-flight refuelling probes. With these modifications it can be found carrying out special operations, drug interdiction, intelligence gathering and combat search and rescue.

In writing this book I have had to be fairly ruthless in my selection process. A number of aircraft types have had to be omitted. Microlights and homebuilt aircraft were not entered because the sheer number involved would require another 500 pages. A great number of experimental aircraft have been left out along with a number of prototypes, because I have kept to aircraft in service or with strong support. Full details of all these aircraft along with other future concepts can be found in the latest edition of Jane's All the World's Aircraft.

Interest in lighter-than-air aircraft is increasing, but most of the designs are prototypes or non-proven concepts. Only one is included here; the high-endurance Westinghouse Sentinel early warning platform for the US Navy.

To avoid confusion I have entered all aircraft under the company name with which they first flew, and are generally associated. US and European companies have undergone a widespread process of merger and some famous names like General Dynamics, Grumman and Aerospatiale Helicopters are no longer used.

David Alexander Rendall
King's Green, November 1995

ACKNOWLEDGEMENTS

Putting this book together could not have been possible without the help of a number of people: James Goulding for the new silhouettes, and Barrie Compton for modifying many others; Kevan Box for his time and effort on the photograph scanner; Ruth Jowett for her unstinting help and advice and Ian Drury at Harper Collins for making it happen at the other end. For all the support I have had from my colleagues at Jane's, and most of all from my family at home I can only offer my thanks.

CONTENTS

CONTENTS

CONTENTS

CONTENTS

CONTENTS

COMBAT AIRCRAFT

AIDC Ching-Kuo Taiwan

Type: air superiority fighter   **Accommodation:** one pilot

Dimensions:
Length: 43 ft 6 in (13.26 m)
Wingspan: 29 ft 6 in (9 m)
Height: 13 ft 3 in (4.04 m)
(the above are all estimated)

Weights:
Max T/O: 27 000 lb
(12 750kg)

Performance:
Max Speed: approx Mach 1.8
Range: n/a
Powerplant: two ITEC
(Garrett/AIDC) TFE1042-70
turbofans
Thrust: 6025 lb (53.6 kN) –
9460 lb (84.16 kN) with
afterburner

Armament:
one 20 mm M61A1 Vulcan
cannon; seven hardpoints; Sky
Sword I and II AAMs; Hsiung
Feng II ASMs; bombs; rockets

Variants:
Ching-Kuo twin-seat
operational trainer (illustrated)

Notes: Taiwan's first indigenous fighter design, now entering squadron
service. The USA has agreed to sell F-16s to Taiwan, and as a result the
original requirement for 256 Ching-Kuos has been reduced to 130.

AMX Brazil/Italy

Type: close support and reconnaissance fighter   **Accommodation:** one pilot

Dimensions:
Length: 41 ft 2 in (12.55m)
Wingspan: 32 ft 8 ins (9.97m)
Height: 14 ft 11 ins (4.55m)

Weights:
Empty: 14 771 lb (6700 kg)
Max T/O: 28 660 lb (13 000 kg)

Performance:
Max Speed: Mach 0.86
Range: 1000 nm (1852 km)
Powerplant: one Rolls Royce
Spey Mk 807 turbofan
Thrust: 11 030 lb (49.1 kN)

Armament:
one 20 mm M61A1 Vulcan
cannon (Italy); two 30 mm
554 DEFA cannon (Brazil); five
hardpoints; 8377 lb (3800 kg);
AIM-9L Sidewinder or MAA-1
Piranha AAMs; bombs; rockets

Variants:
AMX-T two seat operational
trainer

Notes: Developed as a replacement for Italian G91s by Aeritalia and
Aermacchi in 1977, EMBRAER of Brazil joined the partnership in 1980. The
AMX can also carry out photographic reconnaissance with a Brazilian-made
underfuselage pod.

Atlas Cheetah South Africa

Type: fighter and reconnaissance aircraft   **Accommodation:** one/two pilots

Dimensions:
Length: 51 ft (15.55 m)
Wingspan: 26 ft 11 in (8.22 m)
Height: 14 ft 9 in (4.5 m)

Weights:
Empty: 14 550 lb (6600 kg)
Max T/O: 30 200 lb (13 700 kg)

Performance:
Max Speed: Mach 2.2;
863mph at sea level
Range: unknown

Powerplant: one SNECMA
Atar 9K-50 turbojet (D/C)
Thrust: 15 873 lb (70.6 kN)
with afterburner

Armament:
one 30 mm DEFA cannon; V3B
Kukri, V3C Darter, Python and
Shafrir dogfight AAMs; AS.30
ASMs; bombs; rockets

Variants:
Cheetah D original two-seat

trainer, 'pathfinder' and all-
weather attack a/c, most
converted from Mirage IIIDZ;
Cheetah E original single-
seater based on Mirage IIIEZ;
Cheetah C current service
version (allegedly based on
the Kfir), lengthened, with
ELTA EL2032/M radar and Kfir-
type undercarriage

AVIOANE IAR-93/
Soko J-22 Orao (Eagle) Romania/Former Yugoslavia

Type: ground attack/reconnaissance fighter   **Accommodation:** one pilot

Dimensions:
Length: 42 ft 8 in (13.02 m)
Wingspan: 30 ft 6 in (9.30 m)
Height: 14 ft 10 in (4.52 m)

Weights:
Empty: 12 676 lb (5750 kg)
Max T/O: 24 030 lb (10 900 kg)

Performance:
Max Speed: IAR-93B 665 mph
(1070 km) - J-22 702 mph
(1130km)
Range: IAR-93B 1025 nm
(1900 km) - J-22 712 nm

(1320 km)
Powerplant: Two
Turbomeccanica/Orao Viper
Mk 632-41 turbojets or two
Viper Mk 632-47 with
afterburner
Thrust: 8000 lb (35.58 kN) -
10 000 lb (44.48 kN) with
afterburner

Armament:
two 23mm twin GSh-23L
cannon; five hardpoints;
IAR-93B 5511 lb (2500 kg)
warload - J-22 6173 lb (2800

kg); bombs; rockets

Variants:
J-22A - Yugoslav single-seater
IJ-22 - Yugoslav recce
IAR-93A - Romanian non-
afterburning
IAR-93B - Romanian
afterburning
NJ-22 - Yugoslav trainer
J-22(M) Orao 2 - afterburning
and big external tanks
NJ-22(M) - two-seater

BAe Sea Harrier F/A Mk 2 UK

Type: carrier borne multi-role fighter   **Accommodation:** one pilot

Dimensions:
Length: 46 ft 6 in (14.17 m)
Wingspan: 25 ft 3 in (7.70 m)
Height: 12 ft 2 in (3.71 m)

Weights:
Empty: 14 052 lb (6374 kg)
Max T/O: 26 200 lb (11 880 kg)

Performance:
Max Speed: Mach 1.25; 736 mph (1185 km/h) low level
Range: 800 nm (1500 km)
Powerplant: one Rolls-Royce Pegasus Mk106 vectored Thrust turbofan
Thrust: 21 500lb (95.6kN)

Armament:
two 30 mm ADEN cannon pods; five hardpoints; 8000 lb (3630 kg) warload - 5000 lb (2270 kg) with vertical take off; AMRAAM/AIM-7M Sidewinder AAMs; Sea Eagle SSMs; WE117 nuclear bomb; bombs; rockets

Notes: Essentially a stretched Sea Harrier FRS Mk 1 with new radar and avionics, plus the ability to carry the AIM-120 AMRAAM (the first European fighter so equipped), the F/A Mk 2 has now virtually replaced its predecessor in squadron service in the Royal Navy's Fleet Air Arm.

BAe Sea Harrier FRS Mk 1/51 UK

Type: carrier-borne multi-role fighter   **Accommodation:** one pilot

Dimensions:
Length: 47 ft 7 in (14.50 m)
Wingspan: 25 ft 3 in (7.7 m)
Height: 12 ft 2 in (3.71 m)

Weights:
Empty: 14 052 lb (6374 kg)
Max T/O: 26 200 lb (11 880 kg)

Performance:
Max Speed: Mach 1.25; 736 mph (1185 km/h) low level
Range: 800 nm (1500 km)
Powerplant: one Rolls-Royce Pegasus Mk104 vectored Thrust turbofan
Thrust: 21 500 lb (95.6 kN)

Armament:
two 30 mm ADEN cannon; five hardpoints; 8000 lb (3630 kg) warload - 5000 lb (2270 kg) with vertical take off; Matra Magic AAMs

Notes: In service with Indian Navy only (FRS Mk 51), as virtually all Royal Navy FRS Mk 1s (illustrated) are being converted to the more advanced F/A Mk 2 standard.

BAe Harrier GR Mk 7 UK/USA

Type: ground-attack fighter   **Accommodation:** one pilot

Dimensions:
Length: 47 ft 1 in (14.36 m)
Wingspan: 30 ft 4 in (9.25 m)
Height: 11 ft 7 in (3.55 m)

Weights:
Empty: 15 542 lb (7050 kg)
Max T/O: 31 000 lb (14 061 kg)

Performance:
Max Speed: 661 mph (1065 km/h)
Range: 1190 nm (2202 km)
Powerplant: one Rolls-Royce Pegasus Mk105 vectored Thrust turbofan
Thrust: 21 500 lb (95.63 kN)

Armament:
two 25mm RO cannon; nine hardpoints; 10 800 lb (4899 kg) warload; AIM-9L Sidewinder AAMs; bombs; rockets

Variants:
Harrier TMk 10 twin seat operational trainer; GR 5 earlier version without FLIR

Notes: For USMC Harriers see McDonnell Douglas entries. Has replaced the GR 3 in RAF service, all GR 5s will eventually be upgraded to GR 7 standard.

BAe Hawk 200 UK

Type: multi-role light fighter   **Accommodation:** one pilot

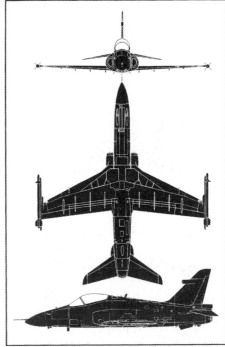

Dimensions:
Length: 37 ft 2 in (11.33 m)
Wingspan: 32 ft 7 in (9.94 m)
Height: 13 ft 8 in (4.16 m)

Weights:
Empty: 9810 lbs (4450 kg)
Max T/O: 20 061 lbs (9100 kg)

Performance:
Max Speed: Mach 1.2

Range: 1400 nm (2594 km)
Powerplant: one RR Turbomeca Adour Mk871 turbofan
Thrust: 5845 lb (26 kN)

Armament:
30/25mm cannon pod; five hardpoints; 6614 lb (3000 kg) warload; AIM-9L Sidewinder AAMs; Sea Eagle SSMs; bombs; rockets

Variants:
none, although designations 203, 208 and 209 are used for various customers as the wing 'dressing' (stores options) differs for Omani, Malaysian and Indonesian jets

Notes: Now entering service with Oman, Malaysia, Indonesia and Saudi Arabia. 80 per cent commonality with basic Hawk trainer.

BAe (Hawker) Hunter UK

Type: ground attack fighter   **Accommodation:** one pilot

Dimensions:
Length: 45 ft 10 in (13.98 m)
Wingspan: 33 ft 8 in (10.26m)
Height: 13ft 2in (4.01 m)

Weights:
Empty: 13 270 lb (6020 kg)
Max T/O: 24 000 lb (10 885 kg)

Performance:
Max Speed: Mach 0.92
Range: 1598 nm (2965 km)
Powerplant: one Rolls-Royce
Avon Mk203 or Mk207
turbojet
Thrust: 10 000 lb (4540 kg)

Armament:
four 30mm ADEN cannon, two

in trainers; four main
hardpoints, plus provision for
outboard rocket rails and
inboard missile pylons; 7400
lb (3357 kg) warload; bombs;
rockets

Variants:
FGA 9 single-seater T 7/T 8
two-seat operational trainer

Notes: The Lebanese Air Force has reactivated part of its stored Hunter fleet, plus acquired additional jets from Oman and the UK. A handful are also still active with the MoD in the UK.

Boeing B-52H USA

Type: long range strategic bomber **Accommodation:** six - pilot; co-pilot; navigator; radar navigator; ECM operator; rear gunner

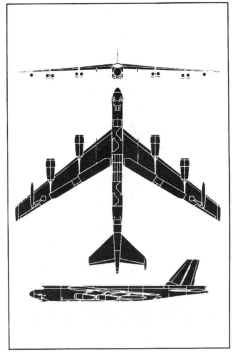

Dimensions:
Length: 160 ft 10 in (49.05 m)
Wingspan: 185 ft (56.39 m)
Height: 40 ft 8 in (12.4 m)

Weights:
Empty: 172 740 lb (78 353 kg)
Max T/O: 505 000 lb
(229 088 kg)

Performance:
Max Speed: 595 mph (957 km/h); 420 mph (819 km/h) low level
Range: 8685 nm (16 093 km) unrefueled
Powerplant: eight Pratt & Whitney TF33-P-3 turbofans
Thrust: 136 000 lb (584.8 kN)

Armament:
20 mm cannon in tail replaced by Stinger AAM launcher
60 000 lb (24 750 kg) warload; 20 AGM-86 cruise missiles

Variants:
Many Variants over its 40 year history only H model remains in service.

Notes: The B-52 entered service in 1955, and continuing upgrades are currently planned to keep it in service well into the 21st century. Bomb bay has a capacity of 1043 cu ft.

CAC J-7II China

Type: fighter and close support aircraft   **Accommodation:** one pilot

Dimensions:
Length: 45 ft 9 in (13.945 kN)
Wingspan: 27 ft 3 in (7.15 m)
- F-7M 23 ft 5 in (8.32 m)
Height: 13 ft 5 in (4.103 m)

Weights:
Empty: 11 629 lb (5275 kg)
Max T/O: 17 967 lb (8150 kg)
- F-7M 16 603 lb (7531 kg)

Performance:
Max Speed: Mach 2.05
Range: 939 nm (1740 km)
Powerplant: one Chengdu
WP7B(BM) turbojet
Thrust: 9700 lb (43.15 kN) -
14 550 lb (59.82 kN) with
afterburner

Armament:
one 23 mm Type 23-2 cannon
(two 30 mm Type 30-1 cannon
F-7M); four hardpoints;
PL-2,2A,5B,7 R.550 Magic

AAMs; bombs; rockets

Variants:
J-7I
J-7II
J-7III - radar-equipped, large
spine, similar to MiG-21M
F-7A
F-7B
F-7BS
F-7M - export version of J-7II
with western avionics
F-7P- Pakistani F-7M

Dassault Rafale France

Type: multi-purpose fighter   **Accommodation:** one pilot

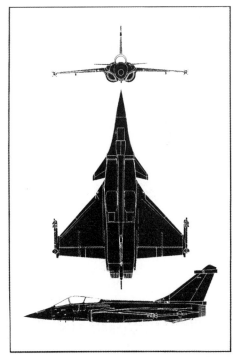

Dimensions:
Length: 50 ft 2 in (15.30 m)
Wingspan: 35 ft 9 in (10.9 m)
Height: 17 ft 6 in (5.34 m)

Weights:
Empty: 19 973 lb (9060 kg);
21 319 lb (9800 kg) Rafale M
Max T/O: 47 399 lb (21 500 kg)

Performance:
Max Speed: Mach 2

Range: 2000 nm (3706 km)
air-to-air; 1180 nm (2186 km)
ground attack
Powerplant: two SNECMA
M88-2 augmented turbofans
Thrust: 21 900 lb (97.4 kN) -
32 800 lb (145.8 kN) with
afterburner

Armament:
one 30 mm DEFA 791B
cannon; Maximum of 14

hardpoints; 13 228 lb (6000
kg) warload; ASMP stand-off
nuclear weapon; Mica AAMs;
Apache stand-off weapon
dispenser; Exocet ASMs; bombs

Variants:
Rafale A proof of concept
demonstrator; Rafale B two-
seat operational trainer;
Rafale C for French Air Force;
Rafale M carrier borne fighter

Notes: 250 planned for French Air Force and 86 for French Navy. In an
attempt to replace the ageing F-8 Crusader as soon as possible, the first naval
aircraft will lack the full avionics suite to bring them into service earlier.

Dassault Mirage 2000C France

Type: multi-role fighter   **Accommodation:** one pilot

Dimensions:
Length: 47 ft 1 in (14.36 m)
Wingspan: 29 ft 11 in (9.13 m)
Height: 17 ft (5.2 m)

Weights:
Empty: 16 534 lb (7500 kg)
Max T/O: 37 480 lb (17 000 kg)

Performance:
Max Speed: Mach 2.2 (Mach 1.2 at sea level)
Range: 2000 nm (3704 km); 1000 nm (1850 km) at low level
Powerplant: one SNECMA M53-P2 turbofans
Thrust: 14 462 lb (21 385 lb with afterburner)

Armament:
two 30 mm DEFA 554 cannon; nine hardpoints; 13 890 lb (6300 kg) warload; Super 530D, 530F, 550 Magic, Magic 2 AAMs; bombs; rockets

Variants:
Mirage 2000 RDM
Mirage 2000 RDI
Mirage 2000-5
Mirage 2000B two-seat operational trainer

Mirage 2000D/N France

Type: strike aircraft   **Accommodation:** pilot and weapons systems officer

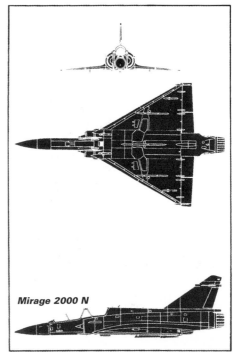

Mirage 2000 N

Dimensions:
Length: 47 ft 9 in (14.55 m)
Wingspan: 29 ft 11 in (9.13 m)
Height: 16 ft 10 in (5.15 m)

Weights:
Empty: 16 775 lb (7600 kg)
Max T/O: 37 480 lb (17 000 kg)

Performance:
Max Speed: Mach 1.4
Range: 800 nm (1480 km);
500 nm (925 km) low level
Powerplant: one SNECMA
M53-P2 turbofan
Thrust: 21 385 lb (95.1 kN)

Armament:
nine hardpoints; 13890 lb
(6300 kg) warload; ASMP
stand-off nuclear weapon
(2000N only); guided
weapons; weapons dispensers;
bombs; rockets

Variants:
2000N nuclear strike aircraft

Notes: Developed from the Mirage 2000, D/Ns have a second crew station,
terrain following radar and optical target acquisition and tracking systems.

Dassault Mirage III France

Type: fighter   Accommodation: one pilot

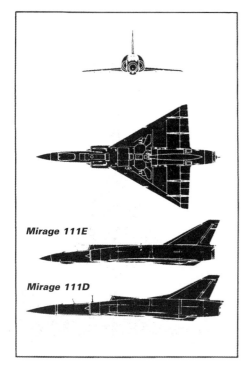

Mirage 111E

Mirage 111D

Dimensions:
Length: 49 ft 3 in (15.03 m);
IIIR 50 ft 10 in (15.50 m)
Wingspan: 26 ft 11 in (8.22 m)
Height: 14 ft 9 in (4.5 m)

Weights:
Empty: 15 540 lb (7050 kg);
IIIR 14 550 lb (6600 kg)
Max T/O: 30 200 lb (13 700 kg)

Performance:
Max Speed: Mach 2.2; 863
mph at sea level
Range: 1294 nm (2400 km)
Powerplant: one SNECMA
Atar 9C turbojet
Thrust: 13 670 lb (60.8 kN)
with afterburner

Armament:
two 30 mm DEFA 552A
cannon; five hardpoints; 8818
lb (4000 kg) warload; Matra
R.530, Magic AAMs; AS.30
ASM; bombs; rockets

Variants:
IIIB/D two-seat ground
attack/training aircraft; IIIR
reconnaissance version

Notes: IIIR has a longer nose with five camera lenses. Brazilian, Swiss and
other upgraded models have canards aft of air intakes.

Dassault Mirage 5 France

Type: multi-role fighter   **Accommodation:** one pilot

Dimensions:
Length: 51 ft (15.55 m)
Wingspan: 26 ft 11 in (8.22 m)
Height: 14 ft 9 in (4.5 m)

Weights:
Empty: 14 550 lb (6600 kg)
Max T/O: 30 200 lb (13 700 kg)

Performance:
Max Speed: Mach 2.2; 863
mph at sea level

Range: 1400 nm (2600 km);
700 nm (1300 km) at low level
Powerplant: one SNECMA
Atar 9C turbojet
Thrust: 13 670 lb (60.8 kN)
with afterburner

Armament:
two 30 mm DEFA 552A
cannon; seven hardpoints;
8818 lb (4000 kg) warload;
Matra R.530, Magic, AIM-9

Sidewinder AAMs; AS.30 ASM;
bombs; rockets

Variants:
5D two-seat ground
attack/training aircraft; 5R
reconnaissance version; 5PA4
Agave radar and Exocet; Elkan
SABCA upgrade with canards
and new avionics fitted into
ex-Belgian aircraft sold to
Chile

Dassault Mirage 50 France

Type: multi-role fighter   **Accommodation:** one pilot

Dimensions:
Length: 51 ft (15.56 m)
Wingspan: 26 ft 11 in (8.22 m)
Height: 14 ft 9 in (4.5 m)

Weights:
Empty: 15 765 lb (7150 kg)
Max T/O: 30 200 lb (13 700 kg)

Performance:
Max Speed: Mach 2.2
Range: 1330 nm (2410 km);
740 nm (1370 km) low level
Powerplant: one SNECMA
Atar 9K-50 turbojet
Thrust: 15 873 lb (70.6 kN)
with afterburner

Armament:
two 30 mm DEFA cannon;
seven hardpoints; Matra
R.530, Magic, AIM-9
Sidewinder AAMs; Exocet,
AS.30 ASM; bombs; rockets

Variants:
operational trainer; Pantera (IAI
upgrade of Chilean Mirage 50)

Notes: Re-engined Mirage 5 with additional fuel and a higher payload, Mirage 50s can be
equipped with Agave radar and Exocet missile. Both Dassault and IAI are offering upgrades, the
latter product featuring a Kfir-style nose plug, whilst the former boasts a Mirage F1-type IFR probe.

Dassault Mirage F1C France

Type: multi-role fighter   **Accommodation:** one pilot

Dimensions:
Length: 49 ft 11 in (15.23 m);
F1C-200 50 ft 2 in (15.30 m)
Wingspan: 27 ft 6 in (8.4 m)
Height: 14 ft 9 in (4.5 m)

Weights:
Empty: 16 314 lb (7400 kg)
Max T/O: 35 715 lb (16 200 kg)

Performance:
Max Speed: Mach 2.2; Mach
1.2 low level
Range: 756 nm (1400 km) low
level

Powerplant: one SNECMA
Atar 9K-50 turbojet
Thrust: 15 873 lb (70.6 kN)
with afterburner

Armament:
two 30 mm DEFA 553 cannon;
seven hardpoints; 8818 lb
(4000 kg) warload; Super 530,
550 Magic, AIM-9 Sidewinder
AAMs; AM 39 Exocet, AS.30L
ASMs; reconnaissance pod;
bombs; rockets

Variants:
F1A attack version without
radar, with undernose laser,
used by South Africa and
Libya; F1B operational trainer;
F1C air defence version with
Cyrano IV radar; F1CR
reconnaissance version; F1C-
200 with in-flight refuelling
boom; F1CT as above,
converted to air-to-ground
role; F1E export version

Dassault Mirage IVP France

Type: supersonic bomber   **Accommodation:** one pilot, one navigator in tandem

Dimensions:
Length: 77 ft 1 in (23.5 m)
Wingspan: 38ft 10 in (11.85 m)
Height: 18 ft 6 in (5.65 m)

Weights:
Empty: 31 965 lb (14 500 kg)
Max T/O: 73 800 lb (33 465 kg)

Performance:
Max Speed: Mach 2.2; Mach
1.8 low level
Range: 1336 nm (2500 km)
Powerplant: two SNECMA
Atar 9K-50 turbojets
Thrust: 31 746 lb (141.22 kN)
with afterburner

Armament:
five hardpoints; 16 000 lb
(7257 kg) warload; semi-
recessed 60Kt nuclear bomb;
IVP – ASMP stand-off nuclear
weapon; Martel ASMs; bombs;
rockets

Variants:
none

Notes: Now used for strategic reconnaissance in operations.

Dassault Super Etendard France

Type: carrier-borne strike fighter   **Accommodation:** one pilot

Dimensions:
Length: 46 ft 11 in (14.31 m)
Wingspan: 31 ft 6 in (9.6 m)
Height: 12 ft 8 in (3.86m)

Weights:
Empty: 14 330 lb (6500 kg)
Max T/O: 26 455 lb (12 000 kg)

Performance:
Max Speed: 733 mph
Range: 920 nm (1700 km)
Powerplant: one SNECMA
Atar 8K-50 turbojet
Thrust: 11 025 lb (4 9kN)

Armament:
two 30 mm DEFA cannon; five
hardpoints; 4630 lb (2100 kg)
warload; 550 Magic AAMs;
AM39 Exocet ASM; bombs;
rockets

Variants:
none

Notes: A few recce versions (IVPs) of the earlier Etendard IVM remain in
service, recognisable by their different nose design. Argentinian jets remain
under Navy command but have not flown from their own carrier for years.

EF2000 Germany/Italy/Spain/UK

Type: multi-role fighter   **Accommodation:** one pilot

Dimensions:
Length: 47 ft 7 in (14.5 m)
Wingspan: 34 ft 5 in (10.5 m)
Height: approx 13 ft 1 in (4 m)

Weights:
Empty: 21 495 lb (9750 kg)
Max T/O: 46 297 lb (21 000 kg)

Performance:
Max Speed: Mach 2
Range: 600 nm (1112 km)
Powerplant: two Eurojet EJ200 advanced turbojets in production models
Thrust: 26 980 lb (120 kN) - 40 500 lb (180 kN) with afterburner

Armament:
one 27 mm Mauser cannon; total of 13 hardpoints; 14 330 lb (6500 kg); AIM-120 AMRAAM, Aspide, ASRAAM AAMs; a range of stand-off weapons; bombs; rockets

Variants:
operational trainer

Notes: The EF2000 continues to suffer from political decision-making concerning its future, particularly in Germany. However, several prototypes are now flying, including a two-seat trainer version.

Fairchild A-10A Thunderbolt USA

Type: close support aircraft   **Accommodation:** one pilot

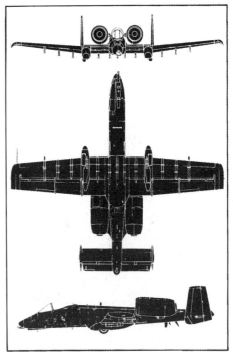

Dimensions:
Length: 53 ft 4 in (16.26 m)
Wingspan: 57 ft 6 in (17.53 m)
Height: 14 ft 8 in (4.47 m)

Weights:
Empty: 23 370 lb (10 710 kg)
Max T/O: 47 400 lb (21 500 kg)

Performance:
Max Speed: 449 mph (722 kmh)
Range: 1080 nm (2000 km)
Powerplant: two General Electric TF34-GE-100 high bypass ratio turbofans
Thrust: 18 130 lb (80.6 kN)

Armament:
one 30 mm GAU-8/A seven-barrelled cannon; 11 hardpoints; 16 000 lb (7257 kg) warload; AGM-65A Maverick; wide range of bombs

Variants:
OA-10A Fast FAC aircraft

Notes: The pilot is protected by a titanium 'bathtub' capable of withstanding 23 mm gun fire.

FMA IA-58 Pucara Argentina

Type: close-support aircraft   **Accommodation:** two pilots in tandem

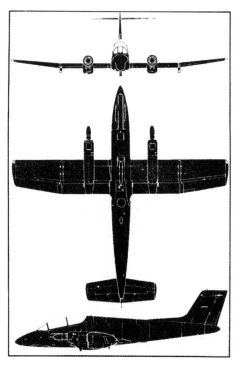

Dimensions:
Length: 46 ft 9 in (14.25 m)
Wingspan: 47 ft 6 in (14.5 m)
Height: 17 ft 1 in (5.36 m)

Weights:
Empty: 8862 lb (4020 kg)
Max T/O: 14 991 lb (6800 kg)

Performance:
Max Speed: 466 mph (750 kmh)
Range: 2002 nm (3710 km)
Powerplant: two Turbomeca Astazou XV1G turboprops
Thrust: 1956 shp (1456 kW)

Armament:
two 20 mm Hispano cannon

and four 7.62 mm FM M2-30 machine guns; three hardpoints; 3307 lb (1500 kg) warload; gun pods; bombs; rockets; mines; torpedoes

Variants:
IA-58C proposed single-seat version

Notes: Several single-seat versions were converted from early models but the programme has been suspended.

General Dynamics F-16 Fighting Falcon USA

Type: multi-role fighter   **Accommodation:** one pilot

Dimensions:
Length: 49 ft 4 in (15.03 m)
Wingspan: 31 ft (9.45 m)
Height: 16 ft 4 in (5.09 m)

Weights:
Empty: GE - 19 517 lb (8853 kg); PW - 18 726 lb (8494 kg)
Max T/O: 37 500 lb (17 010 kg)

Performance:
Max Speed: above Mach 2

Range: 1480 nm (2642 km)
Powerplant: one General Electric F100-GE-100 or one Pratt & Whitney F100-PW-220 turbofan
Thrust: GE - 29 588 lb (131.6 kN); PW - 29 100 lb (129.4 kN)

Armament:
one 20 mm M61A1 Vulcan cannon; six hardpoints, two wingtip rails; 12 000 lb

(5443kg) warload; AIM-120 AMRAAM, AIM-7, AIM-9, Rafael Python 3 AAMs; 30 mm gun pod; AGM-65A; AGM-88 HARM; Harpoon, Penguin; LGBs; bombs; rockets

Variants:
F-16A single-seater; F-16A (ADF); F-16B/D operational trainer; FS-X Japanese licence built derivative

Notes: Specification applies to F-16C. Israeli F-16Ds have a box-like spine fairing housing additional ECM equipment.

33

General Dynamics F-111 Aardvark USA

Type: variable-geometry bomber   **Accommodation:** one pilot, one weapons systems officer side-by-side

Dimensions:
Length: 73 ft 6 in (22.40 m)
Wingspan: spread 63 ft (19.2 m) - swept 31 ft 11 in (9.74 m)
Height: 17 ft 1 in (5.22 m)

Weights:
Empty: 46 172 lb (20 943 kg)
Max T/O: 91 500 lb (41 500 kg)

Performance:
Max Speed: Mach 2.2; Mach 1.2 at sea level
Range: 2750 nm (5093 km)
Powerplant: two Pratt & Whitney TF30 P-3 turbofans
Thrust: 37 000 lb (164.6 kN)

Armament:
one 20 mm M61 Vulcan cannon; four hardpoints, internal bomb bay; 30 000 lb (13 610 kg) warload; guided munitions; bombs

Variants:
F-111E basic tactical strike aircraft; F-111F, new intakes and Pave Tack pod; FB-111A strategic nuclear bomber; F-111G, converted FB-111A; F-111C for RAAF

Grumman EF-111 Raven USA

Type: electronic warfare aircraft   Accommodation: one pilot, one electronic systems officer side-by-side

Dimensions:
Length: 73 ft 6 in (22.40 m)
Wingspan: spread 63 ft (19.2 m) - swept 31 ft 11 in (9.74 m)
Height: 17 ft 1 in (5.22 m)

Weights:
Empty: 46 172 lb (20 943 kg)
Max T/O: 91 500 lb (41 500 kg)

Performance:
Max Speed: Mach 2.2; Mach 1.2 at sea level
Range: 2750 nm (5093 km)
Powerplant: two Pratt & Whitney TF30 P-3 turbofans
Thrust: 37 000 lb (164.6 kN)

Armament:
No fixed armament

Variants:
none

Notes: The principal US Air Force offensive jammer, the Raven is handicapped both by its lack of armament (especially the AGM-88 HARM) and tiny numbers, the latter manifesting itself in astronomical support costs.

Grumman F-14 Tomcat USA

Type: carrier-borne interceptor   **Accommodation:** one pilot, one weapon systems officer in tandem

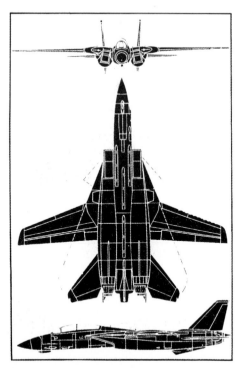

Dimensions:
Length: 62 ft 8 in (19.10 m)
Wingspan: spread 64 ft 1 in (19.54 m) - swept 38 ft 2 in (11.65 m)
Height: 16 ft (4.88 m)

Weights:
Empty: 41 780 lb (18 951 kg)
Max T/O: 74 349 lb (33 724 kg)

Performance:
Max Speed: Mach 1.88
Range: 1600 nm (2965 km)

Powerplant: two General Electric F110-GE-400 turbofans
Thrust: 32 176 lb (143.12 kN) - 54 000 lb (240.2 kN) with afterburner

Armament:
one 20 mm M61A1 Vulcan cannon; four AIM-7 Sparrow or four AIM-54 Phoenix under fuselage; four AIM-9 Sidewinder or two AIM-9 and two AIM-7/AIM-54 on wing pylons

Variants:
F-14A - basic TF30-engined fleet fighter
F-14B - F110 engines by retrofit (originally designated F-14A Plus)
F-14D - new-build and by retrofit with upgraded engines, dual undernose TCS/IRST fairings and strike capability

Grumman A-6E Intruder USA

Type: carrier-borne attack aircraft   **Accommodation:** one pilot, one bombardier side-by-side

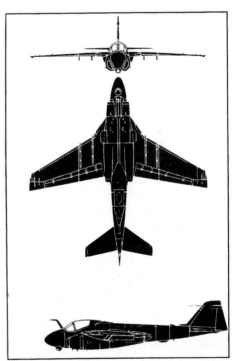

Dimensions:
Length: 54 ft 9 in (16.69 m)
Wingspan: 53 ft (16.15 m)
Height: 16 ft 2 in (4.93 m)

Weights:
Empty: 27 613 lb (12 525 kg)
Max T/O: 58 600 lb (26 580 kg) from catapult

Performance:
Max Speed: 806 mph (1297 kmh) - 644 mph (1037 kmh) at sea level
Range: 878 nm (1627 km)
Powerplant: two Pratt & Whitney J52-P-408 turbojets
Thrust: 18 600 lb (82.2 kN)

Armament:
five hardpoints; 18 000 lb (8165 kg) warload; guided munitions; AGM-88 HARM anti-radiation missile; Harpoon, SLAM ASM

Variants:
KA-6D carrier-borne tanker

Notes: KA-6D can be recognised by five large drop tanks and one refuelling drogue under fuselage. A navalised F-117A with afterburners has been offered to the US Navy as an A-6 replacement.

Grumman EA-6B Prowler USA

Type: carrier-borne electronic countermeasures aircraft

Accommodation: one pilot, one navigator, two electronic systems officers, side-by-side in tandem

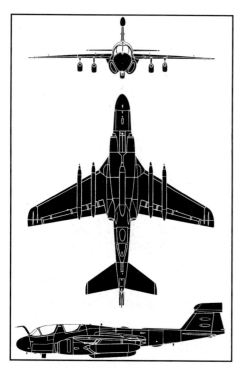

Dimensions:
Length: 59 ft 10 in (18.24 m)
Wingspan: 25 ft 10 in (7.87 m)
Height: 16 ft 3 in (4.95 m)

Weights:
Empty: 31 572 lb (14 321 kg)
Max T/O: 65 000 lb (29 483 kg)

Performance:
Max Speed: 610 mph
Range: 955 nm (1769 km)
Powerplant: two Pratt & Whitney J52-P-408 turbojets
Thrust: 18 600 lb (82.2 kN)

Armament:
four hardpoints can carry AGM-88 HARM anti-radiation missiles

Variants:
ICAP-II/Block 86 - HARM capability
ADVCAP - new avionics
ADVCAP/Block 91 - further improvements
VEP - aerodynamic improvements

IAI Kfir Israel

Type: multi-role fighter   **Accomodation:** one pilot

Dimensions:
Length: 51ft 4 in (15.65 m)
Wingspan: 25 ft 11 in (8.22 m)
Height: 14 ft 11 in (4.55 m)

Weights:
Empty: 16 050 lb (7285 kg)
Max T/O: 36376 lb (16 500 kg)

Performance:
Max Speed: 1516 mph

Range: 419 nm (776 km)
combat radius

Powerplant: one IAI-built
General Electric J79-J1E
turbojet
Thrust: 11 890 lb (52.89 kN)

Armament:
two 30mm DEFA S53 cannon;
nine hardpoints;13 415 lb
(6085 kg) warload; Magic,

AIM-9, Shafrir or Python
AAMs; bombs; rockets

Variants:
Kfir without canards (basically
re-enginned Mirage IIICJ); Kfir
C1 with small fixed canards;
Kfir C2 with large fixed
canards; Kfir TC2/TC7 two-seat
operational trainers; Kfir C10
with enlarged radome

Lockheed F-117A USA

Type: precision attack stealth aircraft   **Accommodation:** one pilot

Dimensions:
Length: 65 ft 11 in (20.08 m)
Wingspan: 43 ft 4 in (13.20 m)
Height: 12 ft 5 in (3.78 m)

Weights: estimated
Empty: 30 000 lb (13 608 kg)
Max T/O: 52 500 lb (23 814 kg)

Performance:
not confirmed by USAF
Max Speed: 646 mph (1040 kmh)
Range: 1200 nm (1112 km) unrefuelled
Powerplant: two General Electric F404-GE-F1D2 non-augmented turbofans

Thrust: 21 600 lb (96 kN)

Armament:
internal weapons bay; precision guided munitions; other potential weapons include the AGM-65 Maverick ASM and AGM-88 HARM anti-radiation missile

Notes: Modernised version being offered as carrier-borne attack aircraft with afterburner. The USAF won't either confirm or deny a weapon's suitability for the F-117, but the ordnance delivered in combat has been limited so far to laser-guided GBU-10 or GBU-27 2000 lb bombs.

Lockheed/General Dynamics/ Boeing F-22 Lightning II USA

Type: advanced tactical fighter   **Accommodation:** one pilot

Dimensions: production
model
Length: 62 ft 1 in (18.92 m)
Wingspan: 43 ft 0 in (13.11 m)
Height: 16 ft 5 in (5 m)

Weights:
Empty: YF-22 30 000 lb
(13 608 kg)
Max T/O: F-22 60 000 lb
(27 216 kg)

Performance: YF-22
Max Speed: supercruise Mach
1.58 - Mach 1.7 with
afterburner
Range: unknown
Powerplant: two Pratt &
Whitney F119-PW-100
advanced technology engines
with vectoring exhaust
nozzles
Thrust: 70 000 lb (310 kN)

Armament:
one long-barrel 20mm gun;
three internal bays, four
external hardpoints for ferry
tanks only; AIM-120
AMRAAM, AIM-9L Sidewinder
AAMs

Variants:
YF-22 prototype and proof of
concept aircraft
F-22A enlarged, refined
production fighter

Lockheed F-104S Starfighter USA

Type: multi-role fighter   **Accommodation:** one pilot

Dimensions:
Length: 54 ft 9 in (16.69 m)
Wingspan: 21 ft 11 in (6.68 m)
Height: 13 ft 6 in (4.11 m)

Weights:
Empty: 14 900 lb (6700 kg)
Max T/O: 31 000 lb (14 060 kg)

Performance:
Max Speed: Mach 2.2 - Mach 1.2 at sea level
Range: 1576 nm (2920 km)
Powerplant: one General Electric J79-GE-19 turbojet
Thrust: 11 870 lb (52.8 kN) - 17 900 lb (79.62 kN) with afterburner

Armament:
one 20 mm M61 Vulcan cannon; maximum of nine hardpoints; 7500 lb (3402 kg) warload; Alenia Aspide AIM-7 Sparrow, AIM-9 Sidewinder AAMs; bombs; rockets

Variants:
F-104G mutli-role fighter-bomber; RF-104G dedicated recce jet; TF-104G operational trainer; RF-104G(T) Taiwanese conversion with LOROP camera in lengthened nose; F-104ASA Alenia-built upgrade of Italian F-104S interceptor

McDonnell Douglas F-15C Eagle USA

Type: air superiority fighter   **Accommodation:** one pilot

Dimensions:
Length: 63 ft 9 in (19.43 m)
Wingspan: 42 ft 9 in (13.05 m)
Height: 18 ft 5 in (5.63 m)

Weights:
Empty: 28 600 lb (12 973 kg)
Max T/O: 68 000 lb (30 845 kg)

Performance:
Max Speed: Mach 2.5+

Range: 2500 nm (4631 km)
Powerplant: two Pratt &
Whittney F100-PW-220
turbofans
Thrust: 47 540 lb (211.4 kN)
with afterburner

Armament:
one 20 mm M61A1 Vulcan
cannon; 11 hardpoints; four
AIM-7 Sparrow or AIM-120

AMRAAM; four AIM-9
Sidewinder

Variants:
F-15D twin-seat operational
trainer
F-15J version for Japan
F-15DJ two-seater for Japan

Notes: Can be configured to carry conformal fuel tanks and extra ECM kit

McDonnell Douglas F-15E Strike Eagle USA

Type: attack/air superiority fighter   **Accommodation:** one pilot, one weapon systems officer in tandem

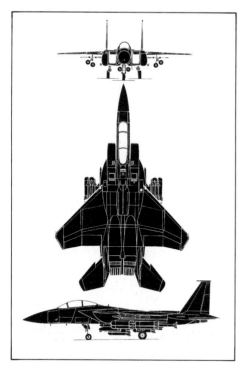

Dimensions:
Length: 63 ft 9 in (19.43 m)
Wingspan: 42 ft 9 in (13.05 m)
Height: 18 ft 5 in (5.63 m)

Weights:
Empty: 32 000 lb (14 515 kg)
Max T/O: 81 000 lb (36 741 kg)

Performance:
Max Speed: Mach 2.5

Range: 2400 nm (4445 km)
Powerplant: two Pratt &
Whitney F100-PW-229s
Thrust: 58 200 lb (258.8 kN)
with afterburner

Armament:
one 20 mm M61A1 Vulcan
cannon; 13 hardpoints; 24
500 lb (11 113 kg) warload;
AIM-7 Sparrow, AIM-120

AMRAAM and AIM-9
Sidewinder AAMs; B57/B61
free fall nuclear weapons;
guided weapons; AGM-65
Maverick; AGM-130 stand-off
bomb; bombs; rockets

Variants:
F-15I for Israel; F-15S for
Saudi Arabia

Notes: Retains full interceptor capability. Israeli F-15Is are almost identical in
capability, while Saudi F-15Ss lack some of the more advanced avionics and
ECM equipment. Similar F-15U proposed for UAE. Early USAF versions had the
same engine as the F-15C.

McDonnell Douglas F/A-18C Hornet USA

Type: multi-role fighter   **Accommodation:** one pilot

Dimensions:
Length: 56 ft (17.07 m)
Wingspan: 37 ft 6 in (11.43 m)
Height: 15 ft 3 in (4.66 m)

Weights:
Empty: 23 050 lb (10 455 kg)
Max T/O: 56 000 lb (25 401 kg)

Performance:
Max Speed: Mach 1.8

Range: 1800 nm (3336 km)
Powerplant: two General Electric F404-GE-400 low bypass turbofans
Thrust: 32 000 lb (142.4 kN) with afterburner

Armament:
one 20 mm M61A1 Vulcan cannon; nine hardpoints; 15 500 lb (7031 kg); AIM-7, AIM-120 AMRAAM, AIM-9; SLAM, Harpoon, AGM-65; AGM-88 HARM; guided weapons; bombs; rockets

Variants:
F/A-18D operational trainer; F/A-18D night attack with FLIR; F/A-18E/F advanced version has new intakes and is larger overall

Notes: Some two-seat F/A-18Ds have been converted for use as forward air control aircraft. The F/A-18E/F can be recognised by its square cut intakes.

45

McDonnell Douglas/
BAe AV-8B Harrier II plus UK/USA

Type: carrier-borne attack aircraft   **Accommodation:** one pilot

Dimensions:
Length: 47 ft 9 in (14.55 m)
Wingspan: 30 ft 4 in (9.25 m)
Height: 11 ft 7 in (3.55 m)

Weights:
Empty: 14 860 lb (6740 kg)
Max T/O: 31 000 lb (14 061 kg)

Performance:
Max Speed: 661 mph (1065 kmh)
Range: 1300nm (2408 km)
Powerplant: one Rolls-Royce F402-RR-408 vectored thrust turbofan
Thrust: 23 800 lb (105.87 kN)

Armament:
one 25 mm GAU-12/U cannon; nine hardpoints; 13 235 lb (6003 kg) warload; AIM-120 AMRAAM, AIM-9 Sidewinder AAMs; guided weapons; bombs; rockets

Variants:
none

Notes: Incorporates an AN/APG-65 radar in redesigned nose. Italy has purchased 16, with an option for eight more, constituting its first carrier based fixed-wing capability.

McDonnell Douglas/
BAe AV-8B Harrier II UK/USA

Type: carrier-borne attack aircraft   **Accommodation:** one pilot

Dimensions:
Length: 46 ft 4 in (14.1 2 m),
TAV-8B 50 ft 3 in (15.32 m)
Wingspan: 30 ft 4 in (9.25 m)
Height: 11 ft 7 in (3.55 m)

Weights:
Empty: 13 968 lb (6336 kg),
TAV-8B 14 223 lb (6451 kg)
Max T/O: 31 000 lb (14 061 kg)

Performance:
Max Speed: 661 mph (1065 kmh)
Range: 1300 nm (2408 km)
Powerplant: one Rolls-Royce F402-RR-408 vectored thrust turbofan
Thrust: 23 800 lb (105.87 kN)

Armament:
one GAU-12/U cannon; nine hardpoints; 13 235 lb (6003 kg) warload; AIM-9 Sidewinder AAMs; guided weapons; bombs; rockets

Variants:
TAV-8B trainer; AV-8B Night Attack with FLIR

Notes: Night Attack aircraft have a bulge at the forward base of the canopy housing the FLIR. Some jets have large 100 per cent LERX.

McDonnell Douglas F-4 Phantom USA

Type: multi-role fighter   **Accommodation:** one pilot, one weapons systems officer

Dimensions:
Length: 63 ft (19.20 m)
Wingspan: 38 ft 7 in (11.77 m)
Height: 16 ft 5 in (5.02 m)

Weights:
Empty: 30 328 lb (13 757 kg)
Max T/O: 61 795 lb (28 030 kg)

Performance:
Max Speed: Mach 2
Range: 1718 nm (3184 km)
Powerplant: two General
Electric J79-GE-17A
Thrust: 35 800 lb (159.2 kN)
with afterburner

Armament:
one 20 mm M61A1 cannon
(not in Wild Weasel); nine
hardpoints; 16 000 lb (7250
kg) warload; AIM-7 Sparrow,
AIM-9 Sidewinder AAMs;
B57/B61 free fall nuclear
weapons; bombs; rockets

Variants:
RF-4C/E tactical
reconnaissance aircraft; F-4E
basic tactical fighter with
undernose cannon; F-4EJ Kai
Japanese update with APG-66
radar and improved RHAWS;
F4F ICE German air defence
update with APG-65 and
AMRAAM; F-4G Wild Weasel
air defence suppression
fighter; Kurnass 2000 Israeli
upgrade with new avionics

McDonnell Douglas A-4 Skyhawk USA

Type: attack aircraft   **Accommodation:** one pilot

Dimensions:
Length: 49 ft 4 in (12.29 m),
TA-4 42 ft 7 in (12.98 m)
Wingspan: 27 ft 6 in (8.38 m)
Height: 15 ft (4.57 m), TA-4
15 ft 3 in (4.66 m)

Weights:
Empty: 10 800 lb (4899 kg)
Max T/O: 24 500 lb (11 113 kg)

Performance:
Max Speed: 654 mph (1052 kmh)
Range: 1740 nm (3225 km)
Powerplant: one Pratt &
Whitney J-52-PW-408
turbojet
Thrust: 11 200 lb (50 kN)

Armament:
two 20 mm M12 cannon; five

hardpoints; 7000 lb warload;
bombs rockets; AIM-9
Sidewinder; AGM-65 Maverick
and guided weapons - A4K;
bombs; rockets

Variants:
TA-4 trainer; New Zealand A-
4K; Singapore A-4S Super
Skyhawk; A-4M dorsal hump,
exported to Argentina

Notes: Singapore re-engined its A-4s with the 10 800 lb (48.04k N) F404-GE
100D engine and new avionics. New Zealand A-4s have received structural
improvements and new avionics including the AN/APG-66(NZ) radar.

Mitsubishi F-1 Japan

Type: close-support fighter   **Accommodation:** one pilot

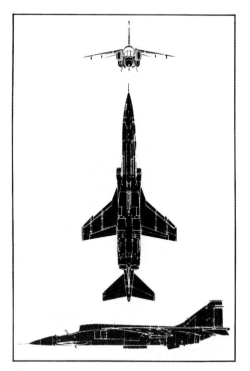

Dimensions:
Length: 56 ft 9 in (17.31 m)
Wingspan: 25 ft 10 in (7.88 m)
Height: 14 ft 8 in (4.48 m)

Weights:
Empty: 14 149 lb (6418 kg)
Max T/O: 30 203 lb (13 700 kg)

Performance:
Max Speed: Mach 1.6
Range: 1402 nm (2600 km)
ferry range
Powerplant: two Rolls-Royce
Turbomeca Adour Mk801A
turbofans
Thrust: 14 610 lb (64.98 kN)

Armament:
one 20 mm JM61 cannon; five
hardpoints; 12 500 lb (2721
kg) warload; AIM-9
Sidewinder; Mitsubishi ASM-1
ASM; bombs; rockets

Variants:
T-2 advanced trainer

Notes: Easily confused with the SEPECAT Jaguar. The F-1 was developed from
the T-2 in 1972.

Mikoyan MiG-17 Fresco Russia

Type: fighter-bomber   **Accommodation:** one pilot

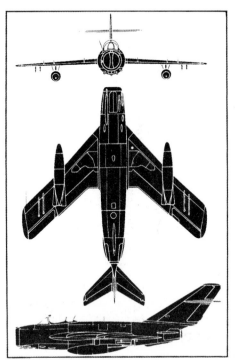

Dimensions:
Length: 37 ft 3 in (11.36 m)
Wingspan: 31 ft 7 in (9.63 m)
Height: 12 ft 5 in (3.8 m)

Weights:
Empty: 8664 lb (3930 kg)
Max T/O: 13 379 lb (6069 kg)

Performance:
Max Speed: 711 mph (1145 kmh)
Range: 755 nm (1400 km)
Powerplant: one Klimov VK-1A turbojet
Thrust: 7605 lb (33.83 kN)

Armament:
one 37 mm Nudelmann-Suranov NS-37 cannon and two 23 mm NR-23 cannon; two hardpoints; bombs; rockets

Variants:
J-5 Chinese built version; JJ-5 Chinese trainer; FT-5 for export; LIM-6 Polish-built with brake chute fairing

Notes: Also built under licence by China, Czechoslovakia and Poland, a total of 9000 are believed to have been produced.

Mikoyan MiG-19 Farmer Russia

Type: interceptor **Accommodation:** one pilot

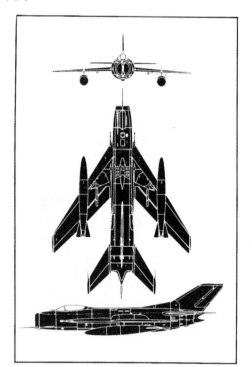

Dimensions:
Length: 37 ft 6 in (11.43 m)
Wingspan: 32 ft (9.75 in)
Height: 12 ft 9 in (3.885 m)

Weights:
Empty: 12 698 lb (5760 kg)
Max T/O: 19 840 lb (9000 kg)

Performance:
Max Speed: Mach 1.4
Range: 370 nm (685 km)
Powerplant: two axial flow turbojets
Thrust: 8818 lb (4000 kg)

Armament:
two 37 mm cannon and two 23 mm cannon; AAMs; air-to-air rockets

Variants:
Shenyang J-6 Chinese-built version; F-6 export version; JJ-6 two-seat trainer; FT-6 for export; various radar-equipped sub-variants

Notes: The Chinese version proved to be more popular. Export success for the F-6 was followed by large exports of the A-5 on which it was based (for A-5 see separate entry).

Mikoyan MiG-21 Fishbed Russia

Type: multi-role fighter   **Accommodation:** one pilot fishbed

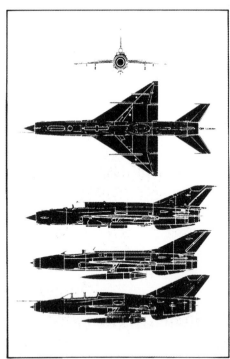

Dimensions:
Length: 51 ft 8 in (15.76 m)
Wingspan: 23ft 5in (7.15 m)
Height: 13 ft 5 ft (4.1 m)

Weights:
Empty: 12 882 lb (5843 kg)
Max T/O: 21 605 lb (9800 kg)

Performance:
Max Speed: Mach 2, Mach 1
at low level
Range: 971 nm (1800 km)
Powerplant: one Tumansky R-
13-300 turbojet
Thrust: 9340 lb (41.55 kN), 14
550 lb (64.73 kN)

Armament:
one twin 23 mm GSh-23
cannon; four hardpoints; K-
13A Atoll, AA-2C Atoll, AAMs;
rockets; bombs

Variants:
MiG-21U/UM trainer

Notes: Fighter versions progressively improved, with increased avionics,
armament and better radar. Characterised by increases in spine, tailfin area
and nose size. Upgrades offered for the hundreds of MiG-21s still in service.

Mikoyan MiG-23 Flogger Russia

Type: multi-role fighter   **Accommodation:** one pilot

Dimensions:
Length: 51 ft 4 in (15.6 m)
Wingspan: spread 45 ft 10 in (13.96 m), swept 25 ft 6 in (7.78 m)
Height: 15 ft 9 in (4.82 m)

Weights:
Empty: 22 485 lb (10 200 kg)
Max T/O: 39 250 lb (17 800 kg)

Performance:
Max Speed: Mach 2.35
Range: 1050 nm (1950 km)

Powerplant: one Soyuz/Khachaturov R-35-300 turbojet
Thrust: 28 660 lb (127.5 kN) with afterburner

Armament:
one 23 mm GSh-23L cannon; six hardpoints; R-23R Apex, R-23T Apex, R-60T Aphid, weapons dispensers, bombs, rockets

Variants:
MiG-23U trainer; MiG-23B series (hybrid fighter-bomber with MiG-27-type nose and MiG-23B intakes); MiG-23ML/MLD lightweight fighter version with improved avionics; MiG-23MS downgraded export version with Jay Bird radar in smaller radome

Mikoyan MiG-27 Flogger-D and -J Russia

Type: ground attack fighter   **Accommodation:** one pilot

Dimensions:
Length: 56 ft (17.076 m)
Wingspan: spread 45 ft 10 in
(13.96 m), swept 25 ft 6 in
(7.78 m)
Height: 15 ft 9 in (4.82 m)

Weights:
Empty: 26 252 lb (11 908 kg)
Max T/O: 44 750 lb (20 300 kg)

Performance:
Max Speed: Mach 1.7
Range: 582 nm (1080 km)
Powerplant: one
Soyuz/Khachaturov R-29B-
300 turbojet
Thrust: 17 625 lb (78.40 kN),
23 335 lb (112.7 kN) with
afterburner

Armament:
one 23 mm GSh-23l cannon;
30 mm GSh-6-30 gun pod;
seven hardpoints; 8818 lb
(4000 kg) warload; tactical
nuclear bombs; R-3S Atoll-D,
R-13M AAMs; Kh-23 Kerry,
Kh-29, AS-14 Kedge ASM;
bombs; rockets

Variants:
numerous sub-variants

Notes: Redesigned MiG-23 for ground attack role, 'Flogger-J' has LERXes,
improved avionics and a laser rangefinder.

Mikoyan MiG-25 Foxbat Russia

Type: interceptor/reconnaissance aircraft   **Accommodation:** one pilot

Dimensions:
Length: 78 ft 1 in (23.82 m)
Wingspan: 45 ft 11 in (14.01 m)
Height: 20 ft (6.1 m)

Weights:
Empty: n\a
Max T/O: 80 950 lb (36 720 kg)

Performance:
Max Speed: Mach 2.83
Range: 675 nm (1250 km)
supersonic; 933 nm (1730 km)
subsonic
Powerplant: two
Soyuz/Tumansky R-12BD-300
single shaft turbojets
Thrust: 49 400 lb (220 kN)

Armament:
four hardpoints; R-23 Apex,
R-73A Archer, R-60T Aphid
AAMs; Kh-58 Kitler ASM -
MiG-25BM

Variants:
MiG-25PU/RU trainer; MiG-
25BM defence suppression;
MiG-25R/RB/RBSh tactical
reconnaissance aircraft

Notes: Designed to intercept high-flying high-speed bombers, the MiG-25
has been adapted to a number of roles mainly tactical high-altitude recce

Mikoyan MiG-29 Fulcrum Russia

Type: multi-role fighter   **Accommodation:** one pilot

Dimensions:
Length: 48 ft 9 in (14.87 m)
Wingspan: 37 ft 3 in (11.36 m)
Height: 15 ft 6 in (4.73 m)

Weights:
Empty: 24 030 lb (10 900 kg)
Max T/O: 40 785 lb (18 500 kg)

Performance:
Max Speed: Mach 2.3
Range: 1133 nm (2100 km)
Powerplant: two
Klimov/Sarkisov RD-33
turbofans
Thrust: 22 220 lb (98.8 kN)

Armament:
one 30 mm GSh-301 cannon;
seven hardpoints; R-77, R-
60MK, R-27R1, AAMs; weapons
dispensers; bombs; rockets

Variants:
MiG-29UB trainer; MiG-29K
carrier borne fighter

Notes: The 'Fulcrum-C' and MiG-29S have a larger curved spine housing an active jammer and fuel. MiG-29M with FBW controls, sharp LERX, new spine, broad-chord tailplanes and PGM capability. The MiG-29K did extensive trials aboard the aircraft carrier Kuznetsov.

MiG-31 Foxhound Russia

Type: interceptor   **Accommodation:** one pilot, one weapons systems officer in tandem

Dimensions:
Length: 74 ft 5 in (22.7 m)
Wingspan: 44 ft 2 in (13.464 m)
Height: 20 ft 2 in (6.15 m)

Weights:
Empty: 48 115 lb (21 825 kg)
Max T/O: 101 850 lb
(46 200 kg)

Performance:
Max Speed: Mach 2.83
Range: 1700 nm (3300 km)
Powerplant: two Aviadvigatel
D-30F6 turbofans
Thrust: 68 340 lb (303.8 kN)

Armament:
one 23 mm GSh-23 cannon;
four R-33 Amos, two R-40T

Acrid, four R-60 Aphid AAMs;
also cleared for R-77
AMRAAMski

Variants:
MiG-31B/D improved variants
with refuelling probes (retractable); MiG-31M new canopy,
frameless windscreen, R-37
missiles, wingtip ESM pods

NAMC Q-5 1A Fantan China

Type: attack aircraft   **Accommodation:** one pilot

Dimensions:
Length: 50ft 7in (15 415m)
Wingspan: 31ft 10in (9.70m)
Height: 14ft 9in (4.5m)

Weights:
Empty: 14 317lb (6494kg)
Max T/O: 26 455lb (12 000kg)

Performance:
Max Speed: Mach 1.1
Range: 1080nm (2000km)
Powerplant: two Shenyang
WP6 turbojets
Thrust: 11464lb (51kN)

Armament:
one 23mm Type 23-2K

cannon; ten hardpoints; PL-
2/2B/7 AIM-9 Sidewinder,
R.550 Magic AAMs; C-801
ASM; bombs; rockets

Variants:
A-5C export version; A-5M
Alenia upgrade

Notes: Some Chinese A-5s are capable of carrying a single 5-20kT nuclear
bomb.

Northrop B-2 Spirit USA

Type: stealth bomber   **Accommodation:** one pilot one mission commander side-by-side

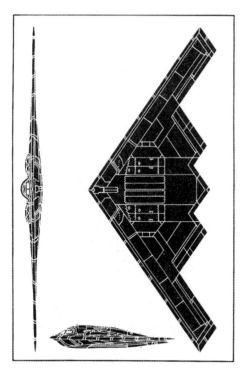

Dimensions:
Length: 69ft (21.03m)
Wingspan: 172ft (52.43m)
Height: 17ft (5.18m)

Weights:
Empty: 110 000lb (49 900kg)
Max T/O: 376 000lb
(170 550kg)

Performance:
Max Speed: n\a
Range: 6600nm (12 223km),
4500nm (8 334km) low level
Powerplant: four General
Electric F118-GE-110 turbofans
Thrust: 76 000lb (169kN)

Armament:
internal bomb bay with rotary

launchers carrying 16 nuclear
weapons or bomb racks
carrying conventional
weapons; 50 000lb (22 680kg)
warload; AGM-131 SRAM II
stand-off nuclear weapon,
AGM-129 nuclear cruise
missile; B61, B83 free fall
nuclear weapons; conventional
bombs and mines

Notes: The most expensive aircraft ever running at $865 million per aircraft.
The USAF originally wanted 133 B-2s, but only 20 had been funded by 1995.
There is provision for a third crew member behind the commander.

Northrop F-5E Tiger II USA

Type: light multi-role fighter   **Accommodation:** one pilot

Dimensions:
Length: 47ft 4in (14.45m), 51ft 4in (15.65m)
Wingspan: 26ft 8in (8.13m)
Height: 13ft 4in (4.07m)

Weights:
Empty: 9723lb (4410kg)
Max T/O: 24 722lb (11 214kg)

Performance:
Max Speed: Mach 1.64
Range: 1340nm (2483km)
Powerplant: two General Electric J85-GE-21B turbojets
Thrust: 10 000lb (44.48kN) with afterburner

Armament:
two 20mm M39A2 cannon;
five hardpoints; 7000lb (3175kg) warload; AIM-9 Sidewinder AAMs; AGM-65 Maverick ASM; bombs; rockets

Variants:
RF-5E TigerEye reconnaissance aircraft, F-5F operational trainer; Tiger III, IAI upgrade (Chile).

Notes: The Tigereye can be distingushed by its longer nose with numerous camera lens'. The earlier F-5A/B Tiger is slightly smaller, with smaller LERXes and no radar

Panavia Tornado IDS Germany/Italy/UK

Type: low-altitude interdictor   **Accommodation:** one pilot one weapons systems officer in tandem

Dimensions:
Length: 54ft 10in (15.72m)
Wingspan: spread 45ft 7in
(13.91m); swept 28ft 2in (8.6m)
Height: 19ft 6in (5.95m)

Weights:
Empty: 30 620lb (13 890kg)
Max T/O: 61 620lb (27 950kg)

Performance:
Max Speed: Mach 2.2; 691mph
(1112km/h) at low level

Range: 2100nm (3890km)
Powerplant: two Turbo-Union
RR199-34R Mk101 turbofans
Thrust: 17 400lb (77.4kN), 29
680lb (132kN) with afterburner

Armament:
two 27mm IWKA-Mauser
cannon; four hardpoints, two
multiple weapon carriage
systems; 19 840lb (9000kg)
warload; WE177 free-fall
nuclear bomb UK only; AIM-9

Sidewinder AAMs; ALARM,
AGM-88 HARM anti-radiation
missiles; AGM-65 Maverick,
Kormoran, Sea Eagle ASMs;
guided munitions; bombs;
rockets

Variants:
Tornado ECR defence
suppression aircraft; GRMk 1A
reconnaissance aircraft;
GRMk 1B maritime strike
aircraft

Notes: Italy is converting an IDS squadron to ECR standard, the UK has converted
some for maritime strike, others for tactical reconnaissance. Some 140 UK GRMk 1s
are to receive a mid-life upgrade to bring it up to GRMk 4 standard.

Panavia Tornado ADV Germany/Italy/UK

Type: interceptor   **Accommodation:** one pilot, one weapon systems officer in tandem

Dimensions:
Length: 61ft 3in (18.68m)
Wingspan: spread 45ft 7in
(13.91m); swept 28ft 2in (8.6m)
Height: 19ft 6in (5.95m)

Weights:
Empty: 31 970lb (14 500kg)

Max T/O: 61 700lb (27 986kg)

Performance:
Max Speed: Mach 2.2
Range: 2000nm (3704km)
Powerplant: two Turbo Union
RB199-34R Mk104 turbofans
Thrust: 18 200lb (81kN)

Armament:
one 27mm IWKA-Mauser
cannon; two hardpoints; four
Skyflash, four Sidewinder
AAMs

Variants:
none

Notes: called F3 in UK service. Italy has leased 24 ex-RAF aircraft as an
interim measure before introduction of the EF2000.

Rockwell B-1B Lancer USA

Type: strategic bomber   **Accommodation:** pilot, co-pilot, ofensive systems officer, defensive systems officer side-by-side in tandem

Dimensions:
Length: 147ft (44.81m)
Wingspan: spread 136ft 8in (41.67m) swept 78ft 2in (23.84m)
Height: 34ft (10.36m)

Weights:
Empty: 192 000lb (87 090kg)
Max T/O: 477000lb (216365kg)

Performance:
Max Speed: Mach 1.25; 600mph (965km/h) low level
Range: 6475nm (12 000km)
Powerplant: four General Electric F101-GE-102 augmented turbofans
Thrust: 123 120lb (547.6kN)

Armament:
three internal bomb bays; 84 000lb warload; eight AGM-86B cruise missiles; 24 AGM-69 SRAM; 12 B28 or 24 B61 free-fall nuclear weapons; conventional bombs or mines; optional six external hardpoints for 12 AGM-86Bs

Notes: Although not a stealth aircraft wing blending and other technology achieved a radar cross section of only one per cent that of the B-52. Externally similar to the Tu-160 Blackjack, but much smaller.

Saab JAS-39A Gripen Sweden

Type: multi-role fighter   **Accommodation:** one pilot

Dimensions:
Length: 46ft 3in (14.1m)
Wingspan: 27ft 6in (8.4m)
Height: 14ft 9in (4.5m)

Weights:
Empty: 14 600lb (6622kg)
Max T/O: 27 560lb (12 500kg)

Performance:
Max Speed: over Mach 2
Range: n\a
Powerplant: one General Electric Volvo Flygmotor RM12 turbofan
Thrust: 12 140lb (54kN); 18 100lb (80.5kN) with afterburner

Armament:
one 27mm BK27 cannon; seven hardpoints; RB74 (Sidewinder), AIM-120 AMRAAM AAMs; RB75 (Maverick), RB15F ASMs; munitions dispensers; bombs; rockets

Variants:
JAS-39B trainer

Notes: Hungary and the Czech republic have shown an interest in the Gripen, and an export version is now being marketed through British Aerospace.

Saab J37 Viggen Sweden

Type: multi-role aircraft   **Accommodation:** one pilot

Dimensions:
Length: 51ft 1in (15.58m)
Wingspan: 34ft 9in (10.6m)
Height: 19ft 4in (5.9m)

Weights:
Empty: 26 014lb (11 800kg)
Max T/O: 37 478lb (17 000kg)

Performance:
Max Speed: above Mach 2;
Mach 1.2 low level
Range: 1080nm (2000km)
Powerplant: one Volvo
Flygmotor RM8B turbofan
Thrust: 16 203lb (72.1kN), 28
108lb (125kN) with
afterburner

Armament:
one 30mm Oerlikon KCA
cannon; seven hardpoints;
RB71 (Skyflash), RB74
(Sidewinder) AAMs; bombs;
rockets

Variants:
SK37 trainer; SF37
reconnaissance aircraft

Notes: The Swedish Viggen fleet is undergoing modernization to create a full multi-role capability with weapons designed for the Gripen.

Saab J35 Draken Sweden

Type: interceptor   **Accommodation:** one pilot

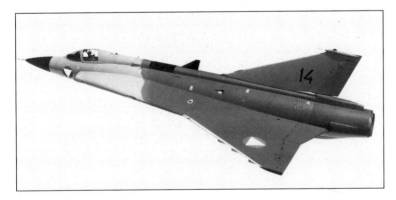

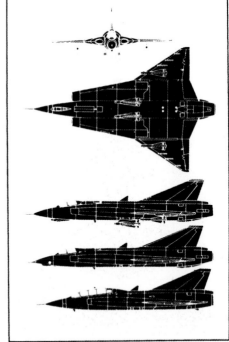

Dimensions:
Length: 50ft 4in (15.35m)
Wingspan: 30ft 10in (9.4m)
Height: 12ft 9in (3.89m)

Weights:
T/O: 23 956lb (10 354kg)

Performance:
Max Speed: Mach 2

Range: 1754nm (3250km)
Powerplant: one licence built
Rolls-Royce Avon 300 turbojet
Thrust: 12 790lb (5800kN);
17 650lb (8000kg) with
afterburner

Armament:
one 30mm ADEN cannon; six
hardpoints; RB27 (Falcon),

RB24 (Sidewinder) AAMs;
bombs; rockets

Variants:
J35C trainer; S35E
reconnaissance version; J35J
upgraded fighter version
(Sweden & Austria)

Notes: To be replaced by Gripen in Swedish service by next century. S35E has
a notch below the nose cone and camera lens' along the side.

Saab J32 Lansen Sweden

Type: ECM and EW aircraft   **Accommodation:** one pilot, one observer

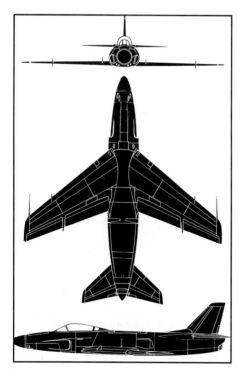

Dimensions:
Length: 48ft (14.65m)
Wingspan: 42ft 8in (13m)
Height: 15ft 6in (4.75m)

Weights:
Empty: 15 400lb (7000kg)
Max T/O: 22 000lb (10 000kg)

Performance:
Max Speed: 700mph
(1100km/h)
Range: 994 miles (1600km)
Powerplant: one Svenska
Flygmotor RM5 (improved
Rolls-Royce Avon) turbojet
Thrust: 9921lb

Armament:
(J32B) four 20mm cannon;
Type 304 ASM; bombs;
rockets; no armament on J32E

Variants:
J32B attack aircraft (used as
trainer); J32D target tug; J-
32E EW and sampling
platform

Notes: Used for 'aggressor' ECM training or offensive jamming. Other versions
are equipped for radioactive air sampling.

SAC J-8 Finback China

Type: multi-role fighter   **Accommodation:** one pilot

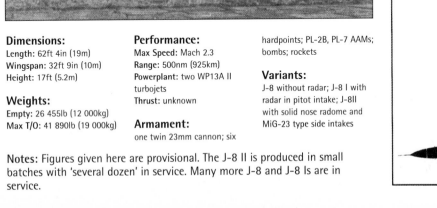

Dimensions:
Length: 62ft 4in (19m)
Wingspan: 32ft 9in (10m)
Height: 17ft (5.2m)

Weights:
Empty: 26 455lb (12 000kg)
Max T/O: 41 890lb (19 000kg)

Performance:
Max Speed: Mach 2.3
Range: 500nm (925km)
Powerplant: two WP13A II
turbojets
Thrust: unknown

Armament:
one twin 23mm cannon; six
hardpoints; PL-2B, PL-7 AAMs;
bombs; rockets

Variants:
J-8 without radar; J-8 I with
radar in pitot intake; J-8II
with solid nose radome and
MiG-23 type side intakes

Notes: Figures given here are provisional. The J-8 II is produced in small
batches with 'several dozen' in service. Many more J-8 and J-8 Is are in
service.

Sepecat Jaguar France/UK

Type: ground-attack aircraft   **Accommodation:** one pilot

Dimensions:
Length: 50ft 11in (15.52m)
Wingspan: 28ft 6in (8.69m)
Height: 16ft (4.89m)

Weights:
Empty: 15 432lb (7000kg)
Max T/O: 34 612lb (15 700kg)

Performance:
Max Speed: Mach 1.6; Mach

1.1 at low-level
Range: 1902nm (3524km)
Powerplant: two Rolls-Royce
Turbomeca Adour Mk804
turbofans
Thrust: 10 640lb (47.4kN); 18
080lb (71.5kN) with
afterburner

Armament:
two 30mm ADEN or DEFA

cannon; five hardpoints; 10
500lb (4763kg) warload; two
overwing AIM-9 Sidewinder or
R.550 Magic AAMs; one AS.37
anti-radar missile; bombs;
rockets

Variants:
Jaguar T Mk 2 and E trainers;
Jaguar International export
version

Notes: To be replaced by the EF2000, the Royal Air Force's Jaguar fleet have
been involved in the Gulf War and Bosnia and operated over Kurdistan. The
many different camouflage schemes they have worn over the past four years
give graphic evidence of their busy life.

Sukhoi Su-7 Fitter A-C Russia

Type: ground-attack aircraft   **Accommodation:** one pilot

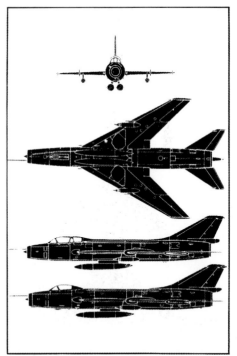

Dimensions:
Length: 55ft 1in (16.8m)
Wingspan: 28ft 9in (8.77m)
Height: 15ft 9in (4.8m)

Weights:
Empty: 18 360lb (8328kg)
Max T/O: 29 630lb (13 440kg)

Performance:
Max Speed: Mach 1.2
Range: 780nm (1450km)
Powerplant: one Lyulka AL-7F-1-100 turbojet
Thrust: 14 980lb (66.64kN)

Armament:
two 30mm NR-30 cannon; four hardpoints; over 2205lb (1000kg) warload; bomb; rockets

Variants:
Su-7BM export version for Algeria and Iraq

Notes: Withdrawn from ex-Warsaw pact inventories, remain in service with North Korea and possibly Algeria.

Sukhoi Su-17/22 Fitter D-K Russia

Type: ground attack aircraft   **Accommodation:** one pilot

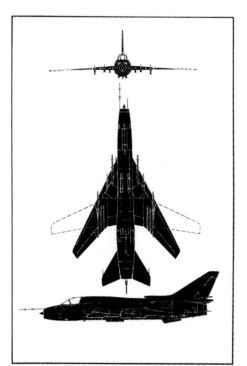

Dimensions:
Length: 61ft 6in (18.75m)
Wingspan: spread 45ft 3in
(13.8m)
Height: 16ft 5in (5m)

Weights:
Empty: 30 864 (14 000kg)
Max T/O: 42 990lb (19 500kg)

Performance:
Max Speed: Mach 2.09
Range: 1240nm (2300km);
755nm (1400km) low level
Powerplant: one Saturn/Lyulka
AL-21F-3 turbojet
Thrust: 17 200lb (76.5kN); 24
700lb (110kN) with
afterburner

Armament:
two 30mm NR-30 cannon; nine
hardpoints; 9370lb (4250kg)
warload; free-fall nuclear
weapons; AS-7 Kerry, AS-9
Kyle, AS-10 Karen ASMs; 23mm
gun pods; bombs; rockets

Variants:
Su-22 export version; Su-17R
reconnaissance aircraft; Su-
17UM-3/Su-22U trainers

Notes: There are a number of different Fitters: some have a bulged fuselage
with a larger engine, others are export models; details given are for standard
Russian aircraft.

Sukhoi Su-24 Fencer Russia

Type: tactical bomber aircraft   **Accommodation:** one pilot one weapons systems officer side-by-side

Dimensions:
Length: 80ft 5in (24.53m)
Wingspan: spread 57ft 10in (17.63m) swept 34ft (10.36m)
Height: 16ft 3in (4.97m)

Weights:
Empty: 41 885lb (19 000kg)
Max T/O: 87 520lb (39 700kg)

Performance:
Max Speed: Mach 2.18; Mach

1.15 low level
Range: 1130nm (2100km)
Powerplant: two Saturn/Lyulka AL-21F-3A turbojets
Thrust: 49 400lb (220kN) with afterburner

Armament:
one 23mm six-barrel cannon; nine hardpoints; 17 635lb (8000kg) warload; TN-1000,

TN-1200 nuclear weapons; Kh-23 Kerry, Kh-25 Karen, AS-11 Kilter, AS-12 Kegler, AS-13 Kingbolt, Kh-29 Kedge ASMs; 23mm gun pods; bombs; rockets

Variants:
Su-24M improved bomber; Su-24MR reconnaissance version; Su-24MP EW aircraft

Notes: A number of Iraqi Su-24s fell into Iranian hands during the 1991 Gulf War. Iran has not returned them and may buy more from Russia.

Sukhoi Su-25 Frogfoot Russia

Type: close-support aircraft   **Accommodation:** one pilot

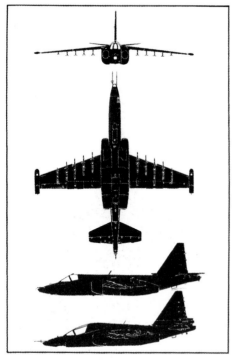

Dimensions:
Length: 50ft 11in (15.53m)
Wingspan: 47ft 1in (14.36m)
Height: 15ft 9in (4.8m)

Weights:
Empty: 20 950lb (9500kg)
Max T/O: 38 800lb (17 600kg)

Performance:
Max Speed: 606mph

(975km/h)
Range: 675nm (1250km);
405nm (750km) low level
Powerplant: two
Soyuz/Tumansky R-195
turbojets
Thrust: 19 842lb (88.36kN)

Armament:
one twin 30mm AO-17A
cannon; eight hardpoints

9700lb (4400kg) warload; R-
3S Atol, R60 Aphid AAMs; Kh-
23 Kerry, Kh-25 Karen Kh-29
ASMs; chemical weapons;
23mm gun pods; bombs;
rockets

Variants:
Su-25UB trainer; Su-39
advanced version

Notes: A number of Su-25UBs were converted to UBP standard to allow for
carrier operations, plans for further conversions have been shelved along with
the Navy's fixed-wing aspirations. The Su-39 incorporates lessons learned
from the Afghan War with new avionics and more fuel.

Sukhoi Su-27 Flanker Russia

Type: interceptor fighter   **Accommodation:** one pilot

Dimensions:
Length: 71ft 11in (21.935m)
Wingspan: 48ft 2in (14.70m)
Height: 19ft 5in (5.932m)

Weights:
Empty: 39 021lb (17 700kg)
Max T/O: 48 500lb (22 00kg)

Performance:
Max Speed: Mach 2.35
Range: 2160nm (4000km)
Powerplant: two Saturn/
Lyulka AL-31F turbofans
Thrust: 55 114lb (245.4kN)

Armament:
one 30mm GSh-301 cannon;
ten hardpoints; R-72R Alamo-

A, R-27T Alamo-B, R-27ER
Alamo-D, R-73A Archer, R-60
Aphid, R-33 Amos; rockets

Variants:
Su-27UB operational trainer;
Su-27K carrier-borne fighter
(now Su-33) with canards and
folding wings; Su-27P
interceptor for PVO

Notes: the Su-27K was the prototype Su-33 which was to be the standard carrier-borne fighter for the Russian Navy. Some 20 Su-33s were delivered and are now used from shore-bases.

Sukhoi Su-30MK Flanker Russia

Type: multi-role fighter   **Accommodation:** one pilot

Dimensions:
Length: 71ft 11in (21.935m)
Wingspan: 48ft 2in (14.70m)
Height: 20ft 10in (5.932m)

Weights:
Empty: unknown
Max T/O: 52 910lb (24 000kg)

Performance:
Max Speed: Mach 2

Range: 1620nm (3000km)
Powerplant: two
Saturn/Lyulka AL-31F
turbofans
Thrust: 55 114lb (245.4kN)

Armament:
one 30mm GSh-301 cannon;
12 hardpoints; 17 635lb
(8000kg) warload; R-72R
Alamo-A, R-27T Alamo-B, R-
27ER Alamo-D, R-73A Archer,
R-60 Aphid, R-33 Amos; Kh-
31 Krypton, Kh-59 Kingbolt,
Kh-59M ASMs; guided
weapons; bombs; rockets

Variants:
Su-30 interceptor; Su-30M
multi-role fighter; Su-30MK
export version

Notes: Based on the Su-27, the Su-30M retains all of its predecessor's air-to-air roles combined with a precision attack capability.

Sukhoi Su-34 Flanker Russia

Type: long-range tactical bomber   **Accommodation:** one pilot, one weapon systems officer side-by-side

Dimensions:
Length: 71ft 11in (21.935m)
Wingspan: 48ft 2in (14.70m)
Height: 20ft 10in (5.932m)

Weights:
Empty:
Max T/O: 97 800lb (44 360kg)

Performance:
Max Speed: Mach 1.8
Range: 2160nm (4000km)
Powerplant: two
Saturn/Lyulka AL-32FM
turbofans
Thrust: 61 730lb (274.6kN)

Armament:
one 30mm GSh-301 cannon;

12 hardpoints; 17 635lb
(8000kg) warload; R-73
Archer, R-77 AMMs; Kh-31
Krypton, Kh-59 Kingbolt, Kh-
59M ASMs; guided weapons;
bombs

Variants:
Su-34FN maritime strike

Notes: Production version of the Su-27B. The long boom between the engines may contain sensors to control rearward firing missiles. The flat nose contains terrain following radar, and the cockpit is shielded by titanium armour.

Sukhoi Su-35 Flanker Russia

Type: multi-role fighter   **Accommodation:** one pilot

Dimensions:
Length: 72ft 2in (22m)
Wingspan: 49ft 2in (15m)
Height: 19ft 8in (6m)

Weights:
Empty: 40 564lb (17 500kg)
Max T/O: 74 956 (34 000kg)

Performance:
Max Speed: Mach 2.35; Mach
1.18 low level
Range: 2160nm (4000km)
Powerplant: two
Saturn/Lyulka AL-32FM
turbofans
Thrust: 61 730lb (274.6kN)

Armament:
one 30mm GSh-301 cannon;
14 hardpoints; 17 635lb
(8000kg) warload; R-27
Alamo, R-40 Acrid, R-60
Aphid, R-73A Archer, R-77
AMRAAMski AAMs; Kh-25ML
Karen Kh-25MP Kegler, Kh-29
Kedge, Kh-31 Krypton ASMs;
guided bombs; bombs, rockets

Tupolev Tu-160 Blackjack Russia

Type: strategic bomber   **Accommodation:** two pilots, two weapons systems officers side-by-side in tandem

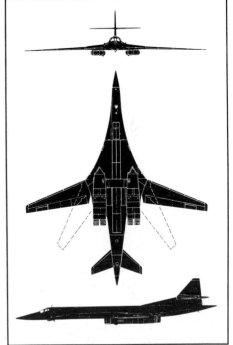

Dimensions:
Length: 177ft 6in (54.1m)
Wingspan: spread 182ft 9in (55.7m), swept 166ft 4in (50.7m)
Height: 43ft (13.10m)

Weights:
Empty: 242 500lb (110 000kg)

Max T/O: 606 260lb (275 000kg)

Performance:
Max Speed: Mach 2.05
Range: 6640nm (12 300km)
Powerplant: four Samara/Trud MK-321 turbofans
Thrust: 202 320lb (900kN)

Armament:
internal bomb bay; 36 000lb (16 300kg) warload; 12 Kh-15P Kickback SRAMs; six Kh-55 Kent cruise missiles; free-fall nuclear weapons; conventional bombs

Notes: With the break-up of the Soviet Union most Tu-160s fell into Ukrainian hands. The aircraft has proved too costly for their air force and discussions are under way to hand them over to Russia in return for a cut in Ukraine's outstanding debts.

Tupolev Tu-95MS Bear Russia

Type: turboprop powered strategic bomber and reconnaissance aircraft

Accommodation: two pilots, radio operator, navigator/defensive systems officer, flight engineer, bombardier/navigator, rear gunner

Dimensions:
Length: 162ft 5in (49.5m)
Wingspan: 167ft 8in (51.1m)
Height: 39ft 9in (12.12m)

Weights:
Empty: 198 415lb (90 000kg)
Max T/O: 414 470lb (188 000kg)

Performance:
Max Speed: 575mph (828km/h); 404mph (650km/h) low level

Range: 3455nm (6400km)
Powerplant: four KKBM Kuznetsov NK-12MV turboprops
Thrust: 59 180ehp (900kN)

Armament:
two 23mm cannon in tail; internal bomb bay; external hardpoints for cruise missiles and ASMs; 16 Kh-55 Kent cruise missiles; other versions carry anti-submarine weapons or Kh-22 Kitchen missiles

Variants:
Tu-95RT maritime recce; Tu-95MR photographic recce; Tu-142 and -142M ASW versions; Tu-95K strategic bomber and cruise missile carrier; Tu-95K-22 missile carrier; Tu-142MR VLF comms platform ELINT/ECM version; Tu-142MR communications aircraft

Tupolev Tu-22M Backfire Russia

Type: medium bomber   **Accommodation:** two pilots, one navigator, one weapon systems officer side-by-side in tandem

Dimensions:
Length: 139ft 3in (42.46m)
Wingspan: spread 112ft 5in (34.28m) swept 76ft 5in (23.3m)
Height: 36ft 3in (11.05m)

Weights:
Empty: 119 048lb (122 000kg)
Max T/O: 273 370lb (124 000kg)

Performance:
Max Speed: Mach 1.88; Mach 0.86 low level
Range: 1300nm (2410km)
Powerplant: two Kuznetsov/ KKBM NK-25 turbofans
Thrust: 110 230lb (490.4kN)

Armament:
one twin 23mm GSh-23 cannon in tail; internal bomb bay plus external hardpoints; 52 910lb (24 000kg) warload; three Kh-22 Kitchen ASM; ten Kh-15P Kickback SRAM; conventional bombs or mines;

Variants:
Tu22M-2 with vertical intakes; Tu-22-M-3 with Tornado-type raised intakes

Notes: An electronic warfare version has been developed but no details are available.

Tupolev Tu-22 Blinder Russia

Type: medium bomber   **Accommodation:** pilot, navigator/systems officer, rear gunner in tandem

Dimensions:
Length: 139ft (42.6m)
Wingspan: 77ft 1in (23.5m)
Height: 32ft 9in (10m)

Weights:
Empty: 88 183lb (40 000kg)
Max T/O: 202 820lb
(92 000kg)

Performance:
Max Speed: Mach 1.52
Range: 2645nm (4900km)
Powerplant: two Dobrynin
RD-7M-2 turbojets
Thrust: 70 350lb (313.8kN)

Armament:
one twin 23mm NR-23
cannon in tail; internal bomb

bay; 26 455lb (12 000kg)
warload; Kh-22 Kitchen ASM;
free-fall nuclear weapons;
conventional bombs

Variants:
Tu-22R reconnaissance
aircraft; Tu-22P electronic
warfare version; Tu-22U
trainer

Notes: Used for maritime strike and ECM by Russia. Only Libya operates them as bombers and they are probably unserviceable.

Vought A-7 Corsair USA

Type: attack aircraft   Accommodation: one pilot

Dimensions:
Length: 46 ft 1 in (14.06 m)
Wingspan: 38 ft 9 in (11.80 m)
Height: 16 ft (4.9 m)

Weights:
Empty: 19 111 lb (8668 kg)
Max T/O: 42 000 lb (19 050 kg)

Performance:
Max Speed: 691 mph
(1112 kmh)
Range: 2485 nm (4604 km)
Powerplant: one Allison TF41-
A-2 (Rolls Royce Spey)
turbofan
Thrust: 15 000 lb (66.7 kN)

Armament:
one 20 mm M61A1 Vulcan
cannon; eight hardpoints;
15 000 lb (6805 kg) warload;
AIM-9 Sidewinder AAMs;
guided munitions; bombs;
rockets

Variants:
TA-7 operational trainer

Notes: No longer in use with US Armed Forces; a number of surplus A-7s are
being supplied to NATO countries like Greece and Portugal. The Thai Navy is
also receiving A-7s, to make up its first fixed-wing strike capability.

Vought F-8E(FN) Crusader USA

Type: carrier-borne fighter   **Accommodation:** one pilot

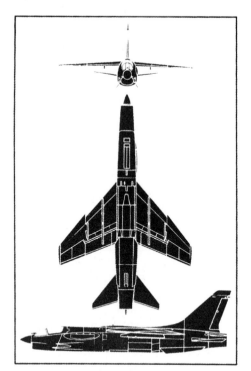

Dimensions:
Length: 54 ft 6 in (16.61 m)
Wingspan: 35 ft 8 in (10.87 m)
Height: 15 ft 9 in (4.8 m)

Weights:
Empty: 19 925 lb (9038 kg)
Max T/O: 34 000 lb (15 420 kg)

Performance:
Max Speed: Mach 2
Range: 1042 nm (1930 km)
Powerplant: one Pratt &
Whitney J57-P-20A turbojet
Thrust: 18 000 lb (80.07 kn)

Armament:
four 20 mm Colt cannon;
Matra 550 Magic, AIM-9
Sidewinder AAMs

Variants:
none still flying

Notes: The entire wing section can be angled up from the fuselage on take-off to provide high angle-of-attack.

LIGHT/STRIKE AIRCRAFT

Aermacchi MB-339 Italy

Type: basic and advanced trainer/ground attack aircraft   **Accommodation:** two pilots in tandem

Dimensions:
Length: 36 ft (11 m)
Wingspan: 35 ft 7in (10.8 m)
Height: 13 ft 1 in (3.4 m)

Weights:
Empty: 6889 lb (3125 kg)
Max T/O: 13 000 lb (5895 kg)

Performance:
Max Speed: 575 mph (926 kmh)

Range: 1140 nm (2110 km)
Powerplant: one licence built
Rolls-Royce Viper Mk632-43
turbojet
Thrust: 4000 lb (17.8 kN)

Armament:
six hardpoints; 4500 lb (2040
kg) warload; Marte Mk2A
ASM (MB-339AM); 30
mm/12.7/7.62 mm gun pods;

AIM-9 Sidewinder, R.550
Magic AAMs; bombs; rockets

Variants:
MB-339AM maritime strike
version; MB-339C more
sophisticated lead-in trainer;
MB-339K single-seat ground
attack aircraft; MB-339RM
EW training aircraft; T-Bird II
unsuccessful JPATS bid

Aermacchi MB-326 Italy

Type: basic and advanced trainer   **Accommodation:** two pilots in tandem

Dimensions:
Length: 35 ft (10.6 m)
Wingspan: 35 ft 7 in (10.8 m)
Height: 12 ft 2 n (3.72 m)

Weights:
Empty: 6885 lb (3123 kg)
Max T/O: 13 000 lb (5897 kg)

Performance:
Max Speed: 539 mph (867 kmh)
Range: 1320 nm (2445 km)
Powerplant: one Rolls-Royce Viper Mk632-42 turbojet
Thrust: 4000 lb (18.9 kN)

Armament:
two 30 mm DEFA cannon

(MB326K); six hardpoints; 4000 lb (1814 kg) warload; 7.62 mm gunpods; R.550 Magic AAMs; AS.11, AS.12 ASMs; bombs; rockets

Variants:
MB326K (Impala I) single-seat operational fighter-bomber

Notes: Known as Impala in South African service and built by Atlas Aviation. Also known as AT-26 Xavante in Brazilian service built by EMBRAER.

Aero L-59 Czech Republic

Type: trainer/ground attack aircraft   **Accommodation:** two pilots in tandem

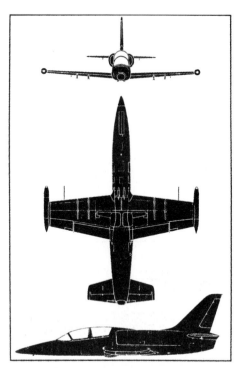

Dimensions:
Length: 40 ft (12.2 m)
Wingspan: 31 ft 3 in (9.54 m)
Height: 15 ft 7 in (4.77 m)

Weights:
Empty: 8885 lb (4030 kg)
Max T/O: 15 432 lb (7000 kg)

Performance:
Max Speed: 537 mph
(865 kmh)
Range: 1079 nm (2000 km)
Powerplant: one Progress DV-
2 turbofan
Thrust: 4850 lb (21.57 kN)

Armament:
one twin 23 mm GSh-23
cannon; four hardpoints; 4000
lb warload; bombs; rockets

Variants:
L-159 advanced single-seater;
L-139 Garrett-engiuned JPATs
contender

Notes: Very similar to the L-39, the only visible difference being the sharper
nose and reconfigured fin cap. It is a much improved aircraft with stronger
airframe, more powerful engine and powered controls.

Aero L-39 Czech Republic

Type: trainer/ground attack aircraft **Accommodation:** two pilots in tandem

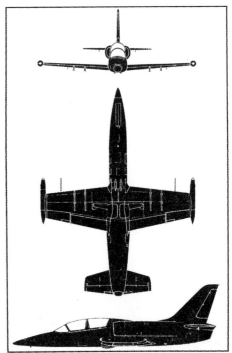

Dimensions:
Length: 39 ft 9 in (12.13 m)
Wingspan: 31 ft (9.46 m)
Height: 15 ft 7 in (4.77 m)

Weights:
Empty: 7617 lb (3455 kg)
Max T/O: 10 362 lb (4700 kg)

Performance:
Max Speed: 466 mph
(750 kmh)
Range: 944 nm (1750 km)
Powerplant: one Progress AI-
TL turbofan
Thrust: 3792 lb (16.87 kN)

Armament:
four hardpoints; 2205 lb
(1000 kg) warload; 23 mm

gun pod; bombs; rockets

Variants:
L-39ZA ground attack aircraft
with ventral gun pod; L-39ZO
weapons trainer with
underwing hardpoints; L-39V
target tug

Aero L-29 Delfin Czech Republic

Type: basic trainer   **Accommodation:** two pilots in tandem

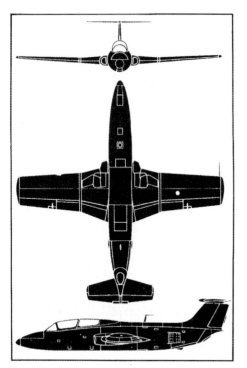

Dimensions:
Length: 35 ft 5 in (10.8 m)
Wingspan: 33 ft 9 in (10.3 m)
Height: 10 ft 3 in (3.13 m)

Weights:
Empty: 5027 lb (2280 kg)
Max T/O: 7804 lb (3540 kg)

Performance:
Max Speed: 407 mph
(655 kmh)
Range: 480 nm (894 km)
Powerplant: one Motorjet
M701c 500 turbojet
Thrust: 1960 lb (8.73 kN)

Armament:
two hardpoints; 600 lb
(272 kg) warload; 7.62 mm
gun pods; bombs; rockets

Variants:
L-29R combat version

Notes: More than 2000 were exported to the former Soviet Union and
Warsaw Pact countries.

90

Aerospatiale CM170 Magister France

Type: basic trainer/ground attack aircraft   **Accommodation:** two pilots in tandem

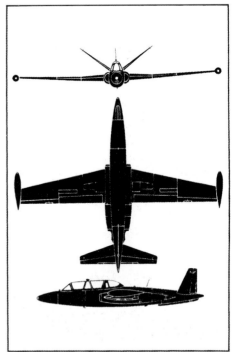

Dimensions:
Length: 33 ft (10 m)
Wingspan: 37 ft 5 in (11.4 m)
Height: 9 ft 2 in (2.8 m)

Weights:
Empty: 5093 lb (2310 kg)
Max T/O: 7182 lb (3260 kg)

Performance:
Max Speed: 435 mph (700 kmh)
Range: 755 nm (910 km)
Powerplant: two Turbomeca Marbore turbojets
Thrust: 1760 lb (800 kg)

Armament:
two 7.62 mm machine guns; two hardpoints; bombs; rockets

Variants:
re-engined Super Magister

Notes: Called Tzukit in Israeli service, it is also used as a ground attack aircraft.

AIDC AT-3 Taiwan

Type: advanced trainer/ground attack aircraft   **Accommodation:** two pilots in tandem

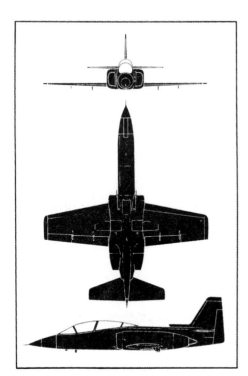

Dimensions:
Length: 42 ft 4 in (12.9 m)
Wingspan: 34 ft 3 in (10.46 m)
Height: 14 ft 3 in (4.36 m)

Weights:
Empty: 8500 lb (3855 kg)
Max T/O: 17 500 lb (7938 kg)

Performance:
Max Speed: 562 mph (904 kmh)
Range: 1230 nm (2279 km)
Powerplant: two Garrett TFE731-2-2L turbojets
Thrust: 3500 lb (15.57 kN)

Armament:
five hardpoints; 6000 lb (2721 kg) warload; machine gun pods; bombs; rockets

Variants:
A-3 Lui-Meng single-seat ground attack aircraft (prototypes only); AT-3P two-seat night attack and weapons trainer (seen in photo)

Notes: Very similar to the CASA Aviojet.

Avioane IAR-99 Soim Romania

Type: advanced trainer/ground attack aircraft   **Accommodation:** two pilots in tandem

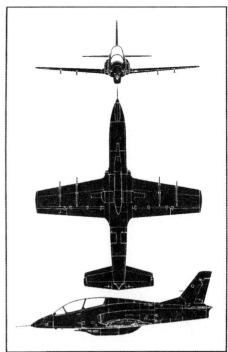

Dimensions:
Length: 36 ft 1 in (11 m)
Wingspan: 32 ft 3 in (9.85 m)
Height: 12 ft 9 in (3.9 m)

Weights:
Empty: 7055 lb (3200 kg)
Max T/O: 9700 lb (4400 kg)

Performance:
Max Speed: 537 mph
(865 kmh)
Range: 593 nm (1100 km)
Powerplant: one licence-built
Rolls-Royce Viper Mk632-41M
turbojet
Thrust: 4000 lb (17.79 kN)

Armament:
removable ventral 23 mm
GSh-23 cannon pack; four
hardpoints; 2204 lb (1000 kg);
7.62 mm gun pod; infra-red
AAMs; warload; bombs;
rockets

Variants:
IAR-109 Swift advanced
version

Notes: IAR-109 first shown in 1992 with expanded avionics and enhanced weapons capability.

BAe Hawk 100 UK

Type: advanced trainer/ground attack aircraft   **Accommodation:** two pilots in tandem

Dimensions:
Length: 40 ft 9 in (12.42 m)
Wingspan: 32 ft 7 in (9.39 m)
Height: 13 ft (3.98 m)

Weights:
Empty: 9700 lb (4400 kg)
Max T/O: 20 061 lb (9100 kg)

Performance:
Max Speed: 622 mph (1001 kmh)
Range: 1360 nm (2519 km)
Powerplant: one Rolls-Royce Turbomeca Adour turbofan
Thrust: 5485 lb (26 kN)

Armament:
removable 30 mm ADEN

cannon pod; five hardpoints; 6614 lb (3000 kg) warload; AIM-9 Sidewinder AAMs; AGM-65 Maverick; bombs; rockets

Variants:
Hawk 108 for Malaysia

Notes: The Hawk 100 has a longer nose than previous versions incorporating FLIR and a laser rangefinder. It also boasts a more powerful version of the Adour turbofan.

BAe Hawk T 1A UK

Type: advanced trainer/ground attack aircraft   **Accommodation:** two pilots in tandem

Dimensions:
Length: 36 ft 7 in (11.2 m)
Wingspan: 30 ft 9 in (9.39 m)
Height: 13 ft (3.9 m)

Weights:
Empty: 8845 lb (4012 kg)
Max T/O: 12 566 lb (5700 kg)

Performance:
Max Speed: 627 mph
(1010 kmh)
Range: 1575 nm (2917 km)
Powerplant: one Rolls-Royce
Turbomeca Adour turbofan
Thrust: 5700 lb (25.35 kN)

Armament:
removable 30 mm gun pod;
five hardpoints; 6614 lb (3000
kg) warload; AIM-9
Sidewinder; bombs; rockets

Variants:
Hawk 100 (described
separately)

Notes: Export versions designated in Hawk 50 and 60 series. T 1As re-wired
for Sidewinders in 1983/86,

95

BAe/McDonnell Douglas T-45A Goshawk UK/USA

Type: carrier-borne advanced trainer   **Accommodation:** two pilots in tandem

Dimensions:
Length: 35 ft 9 in (10.89 m)
Wingspan: 30 ft 9 in (9.39 m)
Height: 13 ft 4 in (4.08 m)

Weights:
Empty: 9834 lb (4460 kg)
Max T/O: 14 081 lb (6387 kg)

Performance:
Max Speed: 625 mph
(1006 kmh)
Range: 826 nm (1532 km)
Powerplant: one Rolls-Royce
Turbomeca F405-RR-401
(navalised Adour Mk 871)
Thrust: 5845 lb (26 kN)

Armament:
five hardpoints for carriage of
training bombs and rockets

Variants:
none

Notes: Studies were carried out at the behest of the US Congress to install a
Garrett F124 turbojet, but the Adour was retained. The T-45A is replacing the
T-2C Buckeye and TA-4J Skyhawk in US Navy service and has reduced
maintenance costs, flight hours and total aircraft numbers.

BAe Strikemaster UK

Type: basic and advanced trainer/ground attack aircraft   **Accommodation:** two pilots side-by-side

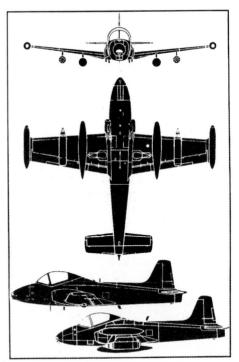

Dimensions:
Length: 33 ft 8 in (10.27 m)
Wingspan: 36 ft 10 in
(11.23 m)
Height: 10 ft 11 in (3.34 m)

Weights:
Empty: 6165 lb (2810 kg)
Max T/O: 11 500 lb (5215 kg)

Performance:
Max Speed: 450 mph
(724 kmh)
Range: 1200 nm (2224 km)
Powerplant: one Rolls-Royce
Bristol Viper Mk535 turbojet
Thrust: 3140 lb (15.2 kN)

Armament:
two 7.62 mm machine gun;
four hardpoints; 2650 lb
(1200 kg) warload; bombs;
rockets

Variants:
Minor sub-variants for
different operators

Notes: Developed from the Royal Air Force's Jet Provost trainer. Striking
similarity with the HAL Kiran.

Canadair CL-41 Tutor Canada

Type: armed trainer   **Accommodation:** two pilots side-by-side

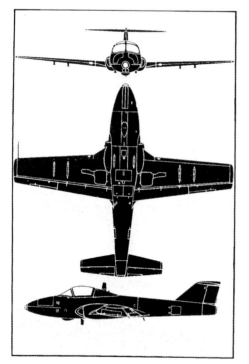

Dimensions:
Length: 32 ft (9.75 m)
Wingspan: 36 ft 5 in (11.13 m)
Height: 9 ft 3 in (2.84 m)

Weights:
Empty: 5296 lb (2400 kg)
Max T/O: 11 000 lb (5000 kg)

Performance:
Max Speed: 470 mph (755 kmh)
Range: 541 nm (1002 km)
Powerplant: one General Electric J85-J4 turbojet
Thrust: 2950 lb (1340 kg)

Armament:
two hardpoints; 3500 lb (1590 kg) warload; AAMs; gunpods; bombs; rockets

Variants:
CL-41G counter insurgency aircraft

Notes: Designated CT-114 in Canadian service. Very similar to Cessna T-37.

CASA C.101 Aviojet Spain

Type: advanced trainer and ground attack aircraft

Accommodation: two pilots in tandem

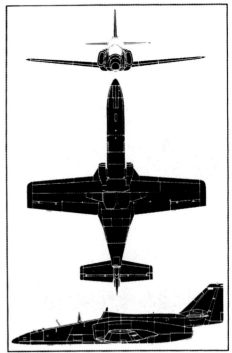

Dimensions:
Length: 41 ft (12.50 m)
Wingspan: 34 ft 9 in (10.6 m)
Height: 13 ft 11 in (4.25 m)

Weights:
Empty: 7650 lb (3470 kg)
Max T/O: 11 023 lb (5000 kg)

Performance:
Max Speed: 510 mph (821 kmh)
Range: 2000 nm (3704 km)
Powerplant: one Garrett TFE-731-5-IJ turbofan
Thrust: 4300 lb (19.13 kN)

Armament:
removable 30 mm/12.7 mm gun pod; six hardpoints; 4960 lb (2250 kg) warload; Sidewinder, R.550 Magic AAMs; AGM-65 Maverick; bombs; rockets

Variants:
C.101EB trainer; C.101CC light attack version; T-36/A-36 Halcon Chilean-built

Notes: Chilean aircraft licence-built by ENAER

Cessna A-37 Dragonfly USA

Type: light attack aircraft   **Accommodation:** two pilots side-by-side

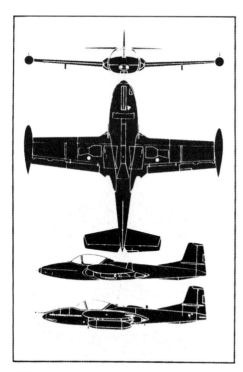

Dimensions:
Length: 28 ft 3 in (8.62 m)
Wingspan: 35 ft 10 in (10.93m)
Height: 8 ft 10 in (2.7 m)

Weights:
Empty: 6211 lb (2817 kg)
Max T/O: 14 000 lb (6350 kg)

Performance:
Max Speed: 507 mph (816 kmh)
Range: 878 nm (1628 km)
Powerplant: two General Electric J85-GE-17A turbojet
Thrust: 2850 lb (12.7 kN)

Armament:
one 7.62 mm GAU-2B chain gun; eight hardpoints; 3800 lb (1723 kg) warload; bombs; rockets

Variants:
T-37 primary trainer (in photo)

Notes: The A-37 was developed out of the T-37 in 1963, the T-37 has less powerful Continental engines and limited weapons capability.

Dassault Dornier Alpha Jet France

Type: advanced trainer and ground attack aircraft   **Accommodation:** two pilots in tandem

Dimensions:
Length: 38 ft 5 in (11.75 m)
Wingspan: 29 ft 10 in (9.11 m)
Height: 13 ft 9 in (4.19 m)

Weights:
Empty: 7374 lb (3515 kg)
Max T/O: 17 637 lb (8000 kg)

Performance:
Max Speed: 621 mph
(1000 kmh)

Range: 2160 nm (4000 km)
Powerplant: two
SNECMA/Turbomeca Larzac
04-C6 turbofans
Thrust: 5952 lb (26.48 kN)

Armament:
removable 27 mm Mauser/30
mm DEFA cannon pod; five
hardpoints; 5510 lb (2500 kg)
warload; provision for
Sidewinder, Magic and

Maverick missiles; bombs;
rockets

Variants:
MS1 close support capable
version assembled in Egypt;
MS2 further improved version;
NGEA new avionics, uprated
engine, Magic AAMs; Lancier
glass cockpit (prototype only)

FMA IA-63 Pampa Argentina

Type: advanced trainer and ground attack aircraft

Accommodation: two pilots in tandem

Dimensions:
Length: 14 ft 1 in (4.29 m)
Wingspan: 31 ft 9 in (9.68 m)
Height: 14 ft 1 in (4.29 m)

Weights:
Empty: 6219 lb (2821 kg)
Max T/O: 8377 lb (3800 kg)

Performance:
Max Speed: 466 mph
(750 kmh)
Range: 809 nm (1500 km)
Powerplant: one Garrett
TFE731-2-2N Turbofan
Thrust: 3500 lb (15.57 kN)

Armament:
five hardpoints; 2557 lb
(1160 kg) warload; 30
mm/7.62 mm gun pods;
bombs; rockets

Variants:
Pampa 2000 International
JPATS

Notes: Pampa 2000 was an unsuccessful bid for the US Joint Primary Training System competition on which export orders were hinged.

GAIC JJ-7 China

Type: advanced trainer   **Accommodation:** two pilots in tandem

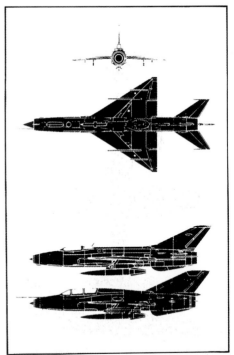

Dimensions:
Length: 48 ft 9 in (14.874 kN)
Wingspan: 23 ft 5 in (8.32 m)
Height: 13 ft 5 in (4.10 m)

Weights:
Empty: 12 167 lb (5519 kg)
Max T/O: 18 860 lb (8555 kg)

Performance:
Max Speed: Mach 2.05
Range: 798 nm (1479 km)
Powerplant: one Chengdu
WP7B(BM) turbojet
Thrust: 9700 lb (43.15 kN) –
14 550 lb (59.82 kN) with
afterburner

Armament:
removable 23 mm gun pod;
two hardpoints; 2617 lb (1187
kg) warload; PL-2/2B AAMs;
bombs; rockets

Variants:
FT-7P export version for
Pakistan

Notes: Pakistani aircraft are slightly lighter and have two extra hardpoints. Very similar to the MiG-21UB.

HAL Kiran India

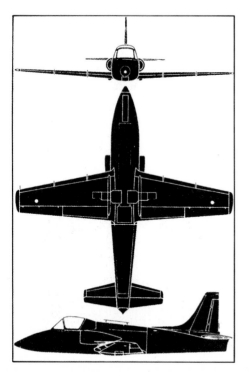

Type: basic trainer   **Accommodation:** two pilots side-by-side

Dimensions:
Length: 34 ft 9 in (10.6 m)
Wingspan: 35 ft 1 in (10.7 m)
Height: 11 ft 11 in (3.63 m)

Weights:
Empty: 5644 lb (2560 kg)
Max T/O: 9336 lb (4235 kg)

Performance:
Max Speed: 432 mph
(688 kmh)
Range: 397 nm (735 km)
Powerplant: one Rolls-Royce
Viper 11 turbojet
Thrust: 2500 lb (11.12 kN)

Armament:
two hardpoints; 7.62 mm gun
pods; bombs; rockets

Variants:
Kiran Mk1A armed trainer;
Kiran MkII advanced version

Notes: Kiran II has a Rolls-Royce Orpheus 701-01 turbojet - 4130 lb (18.4 kN)
- a higher maximum speed and warload, and has nose-mounted cannons.

Kawasaki T-4 Japan

Type: intermediate trainer   **Accommodation:** two pilots in tandem

Dimensions:
Length: 42 ft 8 in (13 m)
Wingspan: 32 ft 7 in (9.94 m)
Height: 15 ft 1 in (4.6 m)

Weights:
Empty: 8356 lb (3790 kg)
Max T/O: 16 535 lb (7500 kg)

Performance:
Max Speed: 645 mph
(1038 kmh)
Range: 900 nm (1668 kmh)
Powerplant: two
Ishikawajima-Harima F3-IHI-
30 turbofans
Thrust: 7320 lb (32.56 kN)

Armament:
two hardpoints; training
bombs; rockets

Variants:

Lockheed T-33 Shooting Star USA

Type: training aircraft   **Accommodation:** two pilots in tandem

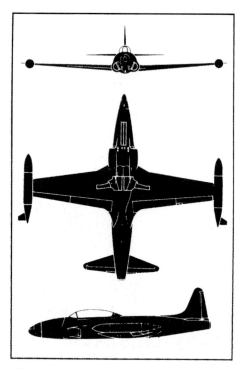

Dimensions:
Length: 37 ft 8 in (11.48 m)
Wingspan: 38 ft 10 in
(11.85 m)
Height: 11 ft 8 in (3.55 m)

Weights:
Empty: 8400 lb (3810 kg)
Max T/O: 11 965 lb (5432 kg)

Performance:
Max Speed: 600 mph
(960 kmh)
Range: 1107 nm (2050 km)
Powerplant: Allison J33-A-23
turbojet
Thrust: 5200 lb (2360 kg)

Armament:
earlier versions had two

12.7 mm machine guns in the
nose, most training versions
are now unarmed

Variants:
many T-33 versions saw
service, but only training, EW
and a handful of RT-33 recce
aircraft remain airworthy

Notes: A development of the US Air Force's first jet fighter, the P-80, the 'T-bird' as it is known was also built under licence in Canada and Japan.

Mikoyan MiG-15UTi Midget Russia

Type: training aircraft   **Accommodation:** two pilots in tandem

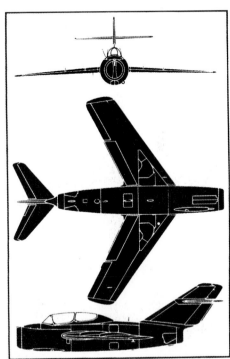

Dimensions:
Length: 36 ft 4 in (11.1 m)
Wingspan: 33 ft 1 in (10.1 m)
Height: 11 ft 2 in (3.4 m)

Weights:
Empty: 8320 lb (3780 kg)
Max T/O: 14 240 lb (6465 kg)

Performance:
Max Speed: 670 mph
(1072 km h)
Range: 367 nm (680 km)
Powerplant: one RD-45
turbojet
Thrust: 5450 lb (2740 kg)

Armament:
no fitted armament but the
fairings for the single 37 mm
and two 23 mm cannon
remain.

Variants:
none

Notes: First flew in 1947 powered by a Rolls-Royce engine. Remains in
widespread service as an advanced trainer.

Mikoyan MiG-AT Advanced Trainer Russia

Type: advanced trainer and light attack aircraft   **Accommodation:** two pilots in tandem

Dimensions:
Length: 37 ft 1 in (11.31 m)
Wingspan: 32 ft 9 in (10 m)
Height: 14 ft 6 in (4.42m)

Weights:
Empty: unknown
Max T/O: 12 037 lb (5460 kg)
Performance:

Max Speed: 528mph (850 kmh)
Range: 1620 nm (3000 km)
Powerplant: two Turbmeca SNECMA Larzac 04-R20 turbofans
Thrust: 6350 lb (28.24 kN)
Armament:
seven hardpoints; 4410 lb (2000 kg) warload; guided missiles; gun pods; bombs; rockets

Variants:
Carrier-capable and single-seat versions planned, plus two-seaters with French or Russian avionics

Notes: Although yet to fly, the MiG-AT is featured because it shows how Russian manufacturers are co-operating with the west in order to make their aircraft more acceptable for export. The MiG-AT is one of two contenders for the Russian air force requirement for 700 advanced trainers.

NAMC/PAC K-8 China/Pakistan

Type: basic trainer and light attack aircraft   **Accommodation:** two pilots in tandem

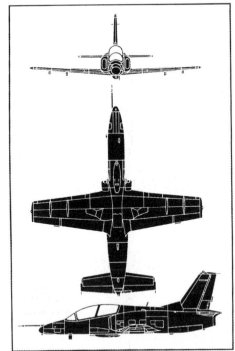

Dimensions:
Length: 38 ft (11.6 m)
Wingspan: 31 ft 7 in (9.63 m)
Height: 13 ft 9 in (4.21 m)

Weights:
Empty: 5924 lb (2687 kg)
Max T/O: 9546 lb (4330 kg)

Performance:
Max Speed: 497 mph (800 kmh)
Range: 1214 nm (2250 km)
Powerplant: one Garrett TFE731-2A-2A turbofan
Thrust: 3600 lb (16.01 kN)

Armament:
one optional 23 mm cannon; four hardpoints 2080 lb (943 kg) warload; PL-7 AAMs; bombs; rockets

Variants:
none

Notes: China has yet to place any orders for the K-8 however, the Pakistan Air Force began deliveries in 1994. The name K-8 refers to the mountain range that separates China and Pakistan.

Northrop T-38A Talon USA

Type: advanced trainer   **Accommodation:** two pilots in tandem

Dimensions:
Length: 46 ft 4 in (14.13 m)
Wingspan: 25 ft 3 in (7.7 m)
Height: 12 ft 10 in (3.92 m)

Weights:
Empty: 7174 lb (3254 kg)
Max T/O: 12 050 lb (5465 kg)

Performance:
Max Speed: Mach 1.23+
Range: 955 nm (1700 km)
Powerplant: two General
Electric J85-GE-5 turbojets
Thrust: 5360 lb (2432 kg);
7700 lb (3496 kg) with
afterburner

Armament:
AT-38 can carry light weapons

Variants:
AT-38 with hardpoints as
lead-in fighter trainer; T-38M
NASA version with radar and
glass cockpit

Notes: Although very similar in appearance to the F-5 Tiger, the Talon is a
completely different aircraft. The T-38 first flew in 1959 and remains the US
Air Force's standard advanced trainer.

Rockwell International T-2 Buckeye USA

Type: carrier-borne advanced trainer   **Accomodation:** two pilots in tandem

Dimensions:
Length: 38 ft 3 in (11.7 m)
Wingspan: 37 ft 10 in (11.5 m)
Height: 14 ft 9 in (4.5 m)

Weights:
Empty: 8474 lb (3844 kg)
Max T/O: 12 500 lb (5670 kg)

Performance:
Max Speed: 530 mph (853 kmh)
Range: 909 nm (1685 km)
Powerplant: two Pratt & Whitney J60-P-6 engine
Thrust: 6000 lb (2720 kg)

Armament:
optional; training bombs; rockets

Variants:
T-2C US Navy version; T-2D used by Venezuela; T-2E Greek advanced trainer

Notes: To be replaced by the T-45A Goshawk, the Buckeye first flew in 1962.

Saab 105 Sweden

Type: training and light attack aircraft

Accommodation: two pilots side-by-side

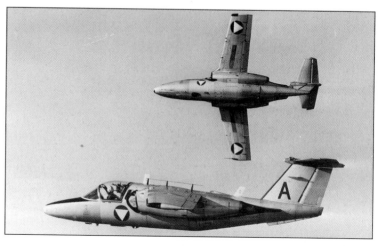

Dimensions:
Length: 35ft 4in (10.8m)
Wingspan: 31ft 2in (9.5m)
Height: 8ft 9in (2.7m)

Weights:
Empty: 6281lb (2849kg)
Max T/O: 10 218lb (4635kg)

Performance:
Max Speed: 603mph (970km/h)
Range: 1242nm (2300km)
Powerplant: one General Electric J85-17B turbojet
Thrust: 1638 lb (7.49 kN)

Armament:
six hardpoints; AAMs; ASMs; gun pods; bombs; rockets;

Variants:
Sk 60D (105D) crew trainer; Sk 60E four-seat liaison aircraft; Sk 60C recce version; 105Ö (105XT) Austrian version

SIAI-Marchetti S.211 Italy

Type: advanced trainer and attack aircraft   **Accommodation:** two pilots in tandem

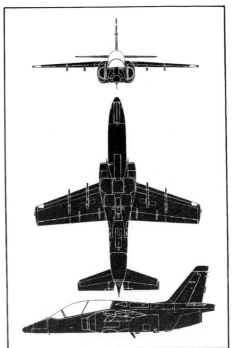

Dimensions:
Length: 31ft 2in (9.5m)
Wingspan: 27ft 8in (8.43m)
Height: 12ft 5in (3.8m)

Weights:
Empty: 4078lb (1850kg)
Max T/O: 6063lb (2750kg)

Performance:
Max Speed: 460mph (740km/h)
Range: 1340nm (2482km)
Powerplant: one Pratt & Whitney Canada JT15D-4C turbofan
Thrust: 2500lb (11.13kN)

Armament:
four hardpoints; 1455lb (660kg) warload; 20mm/12.7mm/7.62mm gun pods; bombs; rockets

Variants:
S.211A updated version

Notes: An updated version was unsuccessfully offered for the US JPATS competiton. The S.211A has a more powerful engine and different wing.

SOKO G-4 Super Galeb Former Yugoslavia

Type: basic/advanced trainer and ground attack aircraft

Accommodation: two pilots in tandem

Dimensions:
Length: 40ft 2in (12.25m)
Wingspan: 32ft 5in (9.88m)
Height: 14ft 1in (4.3m)

Weights:
Empty: 6993lb (3172kg)
Max T/O: 13 889lb (6300kg)

Performance:
Max Speed: 565mph (910km/h)
Range: 1349nm (2500km)
Powerplant: one licence-built Rolls-Royce Viper Mk632-46 turbojet
Thrust: 4000lb (17.8kN)

Armament:
removable 23mm GSh-23L cannon; four hardpoints; 4526lb (2053kg) warload; R-60 Aphid AAMs; bombs; rockets

Variants:
G-4M ugraded version

Notes: The main production plant at Mostar was abandoned during the fighting there in 1992. The G-4 has been extensively used by Croatian Serb and Bosnian Serb forces, four being shot down by USAF F-16s in March 1994.

SOKO G-2 Galeb Former Yugoslavia

Type: armed basic trainer **Accommodation:** two pilots in tandem

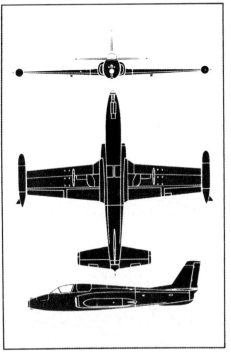

Dimensions:
Length: 33ft 11in (10.34m)
Wingspan: 34ft 4in (10.47m)
Height: 10ft 9in (3.28m)

Weights:
Empty: 5775lb (2620kg)
Max T/O: 9480lb (4300kg)

Performance:
Max Speed: 505mph (756km/h)
Range: 669nm (1240km)
Powerplant: one Rolls-Royce Viper Mk 22-6 turbojet
Thrust: 2500lb (11.12kN)

Armament:
two 12.7mm machine guns; two hardpoints; 660lb (300kg) warload; bombs; rockets

Variants:
G-2AE export version for Libya; J-1 Jastreb single-seat attack aircraft (see profile)

Notes: The Jastreb has a more powerful Viper engine and additional machine guns and hardpoints.

Yakovlev/Aermacchi YAK-AT Russia/Italy

Type: advanced trainer and ground attack aircraft

Accommodation: two pilots in tandem

Dimensions:
Length: 39ft (11.9m)
Wingspan: 34ft 11in (10.64m)
Height: 15ft 5in (4.7m)

Weights:
Empty: unknown
Max T/O: 18 740lb (8500kg)

Performance:
Max Speed: 620mph (1000km/h)
Range: 1185nm (2200km)
Powerplant: two RD-35 turbofans
Thrust: 9700lb (43.2kN)

Armament:
seven hardpoints; gun pods; bombs; rockets

Variants:
none

Notes: Designed for the Russian air force's advanced trainer competition, the Yak-AT is controlled via a fly-by-wire system that allows its performance to be changed to simulate different operational aircraft.

RECCE/PATROL AIRCRAFT

Antonov An-72P Coaler Ukraine

Type: STOL maritime patrol aircraft

Accommodation: two pilots, navigator, flight engineer, radio operator; 40 troops; 20 paratroops

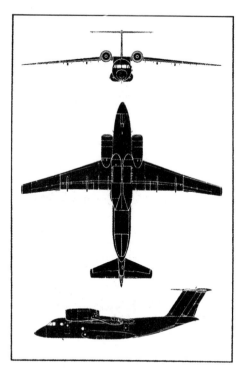

Dimensions:
Length: 92ft 1in (28.1m)
Wingspan: 104ft 7in (31.9m)
Height: 28ft 4in (8.6m)

Weights:
Empty: 42 000lb (19 050kg)
Max T/O: 76 060lb (34 500kg)

Performance:
Max Speed: 438mph

(705km/h)
Endurance: 5 hours 18 minutes
Powerplant: two ZKMB Progress D-36 turbofans
Thrust: 28 660lb (127.48kN)

Armament:
one 23mm gun pod; depth charges; bombs; rockets

Variants:
An-71 Madcap AEW (photo above); An 74 lengthened fuselage and wings; An-72P maritime patroller with gun pod on starboard fuselage and provision for underwing rocket pods and internal weaponry

BAe Nimrod MR 2 UK

Type: anti-submarine patrol aircraft

Accommodation: 11; two pilots, flight engineer, two navigators, two sonic systems operators, radio operator, ESM operator, two loadmasters/observers

Dimensions:
Length: 126ft 9in (38.63m)
Wingspan: 114ft 10in (35m)
Height: 29ft 8in (9m)

Weights:
Empty: 86 000lb (39 000kg)
Max T/O: 177 500lb (80 510kg)

Performance:
Max Speed: 575mph (926km/h)
Range: 4500nm (8340km)
Powerplant: four Rolls-Royce RB168-20 Spey Mk250 turbofans
Thrust: 48 560lb (216kN)

Armament:
internal bomb bay and two hardpoints; 13 500lb (6120kg) warload; Sidewinder AAMs; Harpoon ASMs; ASW torpedos and depth charges; mines

Variants:
Nimrod R I ELINT version (in photo)

Notes: The Nimrod R I can be recognized by the absence of the MAD probe in the tail. All Nimrods now have fixed IFR probes and wingtip ESM pods.

BAe Canberra UK

Type: bomber and multi-role platform   **Accommodation:** one pilot, one navigator

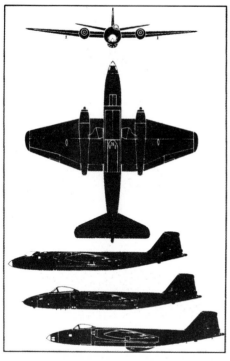

Dimensions:
Length: 66ft 8in (20.32m)
Wingspan: 67ft 10in (20.67m)
Height: 15ft 8in (4.77m)

Weights:
Empty: 27 950lb (12 678kg)
Max T/O: 54 950lb (24 925kg)

Performance:
Max Speed: 517mph

(827km/h)
Range: 3630nm(covert)
(5840km)
Powerplant: two Rolls-Royce
Avon 109 turbojets
Thrust: 14 800lb (6714kg)

Armament (bomber versions only):
internal bomb bay; 6000lb
warload; bombs, rockets

Variants:
Many variants produced but
only the following still in use;
B(I) 8/Mk 56 Peruvian
bombers, Mk 58 Indian; B(2)
ECM version for RAF;
PR 9/Mk 57 RAF photo
recconnaissance aircraft; T 54
operational trainer

Notes: First flew in 1949 and a total of 27 different marks of Canberra have
been in production.

Beechcraft RC-12N Guardrail USA

Type: comms and sensor platform   **Accommodation:** two pilots

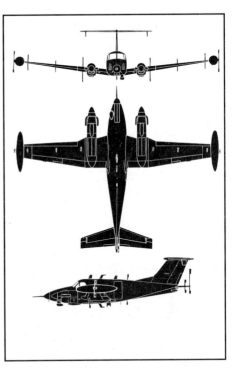

Dimensions:
Length: 43ft 9in (13.34m)
Wingspan: 54ft 6in (16.61m)
Height: 15ft (4.57m)

Weights:
Empty: 8102lb (3675kg)
Max T/O: 12 500lb (5670kg)

Performance:
Max Speed: 339mph (545km/h)
Range: over 1860nm (3445km)
Powerplant: two Pratt & Whitney Canada PT6A-42 turboprops
Thrust: 1700shp (1268kN)

Armament:
none

Variants:
earlier versions RC-12D/H/K Guardrail

Notes: Guardrail provides the most accurate real-time targeting data for the US field commanders. Using ground stations and data links the Guardrail can transmit signals intelligence infomation which is processed to give accurate locations of the transmitters.

Beriev A-40 Mermaid Russia

Type: amphibious anti-submarine patrol aircraft

Accommodation: eight; two pilots; flight engineer; radio operator; navigator; three observers

Dimensions:
Length: 143ft 10in (43.8m)
Wingspan: 135ft 6in (41.62m)
Height: 36ft 3in (11m)

Weights:
Empty: n\a
Max T/O: 189 595lb (86 000kg)

Performance:
Max Speed: 472mph (760km)
Range: 2212nm (4100km)
Powerplant: two Aviadigatel D-30KPV turbofans
Thrust: 52 910lb (235.4kN)

Armament:
internal bomb bay; 14 330lb

(6500kg) payload; ASW torpedoes; depth charges;

Variants:
Be-42 SAR amphibian

Notes: Above each engine pod is an auxiliary booster turbojet each rated at 5510lb (24.5kN). Be-42 lacks the boosters and has no ESM pods on the wing tips.

Beriev Be-12 Mail Russia

Type: amphibious anti-submarine patrol aircraft   **Accommodation:** five; two pilots; flight engineer; two observers

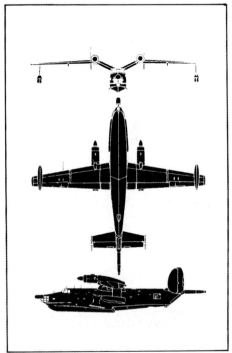

Dimensions:
Length: 99ft (30.2m)
Wingspan: 97ft 8in (29.8m)
Height: 22ft 11in (7m)

Weights:
Empty: 47 840 lb (21 700 kg)
Max T/O: 79 344lb (36 000kg)

Performance:
Max Speed: 342mph (550km/h)
Range: 4050nm (7500km)
Powerplant: two Ivchenko AI-20D turboprops
Thrust: 10 360ehp (7724kN)

Armament:
internal bomb bay and four hardpoints; 22 045lb (10 000kg) payload; ASW torpedoes; depth charges; mines

Variants:
Be-12P airborne firefighter

Notes: First flew in 1960, firefighting versions have been built and operated in Russia.

123

Breguet BR 1050 Alizé France

Type: carrier-borne anti-submarine patrol aircraft   **Accommodation:** pilot and radar operator in tandem, rear operator behind them

Dimensions:
Length: 45ft 5in (13.8m)
Wingspan: 51ft 2in (15.6m)
Height: 16ft 5in (5m)

Weights:
Empty: 12 566lb (5700kg)
Max T/O: 18 078lb (8200kg)

Performance:
Max Speed: 322mph
(518km/h)
Range: 1349nm (2500km)
Powerplant: one Rolls-Royce
Dart RDa7 Mk21 turbofan
Thrust: 2100ehp (1566kW)

Armament:
internal bomb bay and
underwing racks; AS.12 ASMs;
one torpedo; depth charges;
rockets

Variants:
none

Notes: On service list with Indian Navy, although never flown. May continue
in service from the Charles de Gaulle nuclear-powered aircraft carrier.

Boeing E-767 AWACS USA

Type: airborne warning and control aircraft   **Accommodation:** two flight crew; up to 18 mission crew depending on task

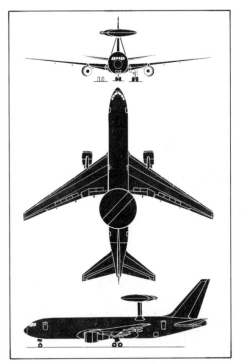

Dimensions:
Length: 159ft 2in (48.5m)
Wingspan: 156ft 1in (47.5m)
Height: 52ft (15.8m)

Weights:
Empty: n/a
Max T/O: 377 000lb (171 004kg)

Performance:
Max Speed: n\a
Range: 4500nm (8334km)
Powerplant: two General
Electric CF6-80C2 turbofans
Thrust: 123 000lb (547.2kN)

Armament:
none

Variants:
none

Notes: The 767 is being offered to the US Air Force as a replacement airframe for the C-135 (Boeing 707/717) in service as AWACS, tankers etc. Japan has ordered four AWACS for delivery in 1998.

Boeing E-3 Sentry USA

Type: airborne warning and control aircraft   **Accommodation:** four flight crew; 13 mission crew

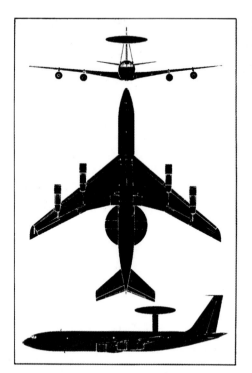

Dimensions:
Length: 152ft 11in (46.6m)
Wingspan: 145ft 9in (44.4m)
Height: 41ft 9in (12.7m)

Weights:
Empty: 180 000lb (81 648kg)
Max T/O: 332 500lb (150 820kg)

Performance:
Max Speed: 530mph (853km/h)
Powerplant: four Pratt & Whitney TF33-PW-100/100A turbofans
Thrust: 84 000lb (186.8kN)
Endurance: 11 hours, 20 with in-flight refueling

Armament:
none but all carry ESM/ECM equipment

Variants:
E-3B/C upgraded versions; RAF E-3D, French E-3F; KE-3 Saudi tanker, no rotodome

Notes: French, Saudi and UK versions are fitted with CFM56-2A2/3 turbofans. UK versions also have in-flight refulling probe and wingtip ESM pods.

Boeing/Northrop Grumman E-8 Joint STARS USA

Type: ground-surveillance aircraft   **Accommodation:** four flight crew; 10 operators

Dimensions:
Length: 152ft 11in (46.6m)
Wingspan: 145ft 9in (44.4m)
Height: 42ft 6in (12.95m)

Weights:
Empty: 171 000lb (77 564kg)
Max T/O: 336 000 (152 407kg)

Performance:
Max Speed: 530mph (853km/h)
Powerplant: four Pratt & Whitney JT3D-3B turbofans
Thrust: 72 000lb (320.4kN)
Endurance: 11 hours; 20 hours with inflight refuelling

Armament:
none

Variants:
E-8A first prototypes; E-8C production versions

Notes: The first two prototypes were rushed into service during the 1991 Gulf war, and proved invaluable to the smooth running of the land war. Converted from civilian Boeing 707-320s.

Boeing RC-135 Rivet Joint USA

Type: signals intelligence platform   **Accommodation:** four flight crew; unknown number of operators

Dimensions:
Length: 164ft (49.9m)
Wingspan: 145ft 9in (44.4m)
Height: 42ft 6in (12.95m)

Weights:
Empty: 171 000lb (77 564kg)
Max T/O: 336 000
(152 407kg)

Performance:
Max Speed: 530mph (853km/h)
Powerplant: four Pratt & Whitney JT3D-3B turbofans
Thrust: 72 000lb (320.4kN)
Endurance: 11 hours; 20 hours with inflight refuelling

Armament:
none

Variants:
RC-135V Rivet Joint, extended thimble nose; RC-135W Rivet Joint, lengthened cheek fairing and no auxiliary intakes on engine pods; TC-135W, single trainer

Notes: Rivet Joint is the workhorse of USAF airborne recce. Using new infra-red and laser equipment, Rivet Joint can reputedly pinpoint a ground-based missile launcher, and direct airstrikes onto it within 15 seconds of launch.

Boeing RC-135 Combat Sent USA

Type: signals intelligence platform   **Accommodation:** four flight crew; unknown number of operators

Dimensions:
Length: 152ft 11in (46.6m)
Wingspan: 145ft 9in (44.4m)
Height: 42ft 6in (12.95m)
Weights:
Empty: 171 000lb (77 564kg)
Max T/O: 336 000 lb (152 407kg)
Performance:

Max Speed: 530mph (853km/h)
Powerplant: four Pratt & Whitney JT3D-3B turbofans
Thrust: 72 000lb (320.4kN)
Endurance: 11 hours; 20 hours with inflight refuelling

Armament:
none

Variants:
none

Notes: Combat Sents collect fine-grain electronic intelligence used to build US radar jammers. The air intake under the nose provides air for cooling the electronics.

Boeing RC-135 Cobra Ball USA

Type: imagery/television intelligence aircraft   **Accommodation:** four flight crew; unknown number of operators

Dimensions:
Length: 164ft (49.9m)
Wingspan: 145ft 9in (44.4m)
Height: 42ft 6in (12.95m)

Weights:
Empty: 171 000lb (77 564kg)
Max T/O: 336 000 (152 407kg)

Performance:
Max Speed: 530mph (853km/h)
Powerplant: four Pratt & Whitney JT3D-3B turbofans
Thrust: 72 000lb (320.4kN)
Endurance: 11 hours; 20 hours with inflight refuelling

Variants:
RC-135X Cobra Eye
TC-135S Telint mission trainer

Notes: Cobra Balls were used to track Russian and Chinese ballistic missile launches during the Cold War. The sole Cobra eye IMINT platform housed even more powerful imagery equipment but has been grounded due to lack of funds – it can be identified by having one black-painted wing to reduce glare.

Boeing E-4B USA

Type: emergency command aircraft   **Accommodation:** crew of 94 on three decks

Dimensions:
Length: 231ft 4in (70.5m)
Wingspan: 195ft 8in (59.6m)
Height: 63ft 5in (19.3m)

Weights:
Empty: 500 000lb (226 800kg) approx
Max T/O: 800 000lb
(362 875kg)

Performance:
Max Speed: 602mph (969km/h)
Powerplant: four General Electric CF6-50E turbofans
Thrust: 208 000lb (934kN)
Endurance: more than 12 hours; Maximum of 72 hours with inflight refuelling

Armament:
none

Variants:
E-4A earlier version

Notes: there are four E-4As and E-4Bs in service and one is always ready for immediate use. They are fitted with cladding to lessen the effects of nuclear blasts. The dorsal bulge on the E-4B houses a 5 mile (8km) long trailing antenna for the communication system.

Dassault Atlantique France

Type: anti-submarine patrol aircraft

Accommodation: 10-12; two pilots, flight engineer, observer, radio-navigator, defensive systems operator, radar operator, tactical co-ordinator, two sonar operators, two additional observers

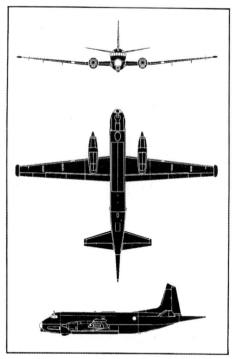

Dimensions:
Length: 110ft 4in (33.63m)
Wingspan: 122ft 9in (37.42m)
Height: 35ft 9in (10.9m)

Weights:
Empty: 56 659lb (25 700kg)
Max T/O: 101 850lb
(46 200kg)

Performance:
Max Speed: 402mph
(648km/h); 368mph (592km/h)
low level
Range: 4900nm (9075km)
Powerplant: two Rolls Royce
Tyne RTy.20 Mk 21 turboprops
Thrust: 12 206ehp (9098kW)

Armament:
internal bomb bay; four
hardpoints; 13 227lb (6000kg)
warload; R.550 MAgic AAMs;
AM 39 Exocet, AS 37 Martel
ASMs; ASW toepedos; depth
charges; bombs

Variants:
Jet Atlantique aimed at RAF;
Peace Peek German Elint type

Notes: Atlantique 2 is second generation ASW version with new avionics and no fin-tip 'football'. It is being offered as a common European patrol aircraft.

Dornier Do 228 ASW Germany

Type: maritime patrol aircraft   **Accommodation:** two pilots, radar operator, observer

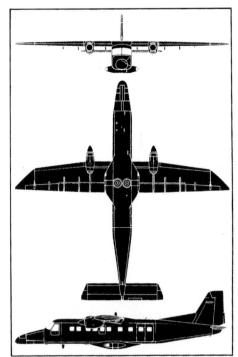

Dimensions:
Length: 54ft 4in (16.5m)
Wingspan: 55ft 9in (16.9m)
Height: 15ft 11in (4.86m)

Weights:
Empty: 7183lb (3258kg)
Max T/O: 14 110lb (6400kg)

Performance:
Max Speed: 256mph (413km/h)
Range: more than 1400nm (2500km)
Powerplant: two Garrett TPE331-5-252D turboprops
Thrust: 1552shp (1157.4kW)

Armament:
four hardpoints; bombs; rockets

Variants:
228 Maritime Polution Surveillance aircraft

Notes: India plans to upgrade a number of their aircraft to carry anti-ship missiles. The Do 228 is mainly used for EEZ patrol and search and rescue.

Grob/E-Systems Egrett/Strato Germany/USA

Type: high-altitude surveillance aircraft   **Accommodation:** one pilot

Dimensions:
Length: 39ft 4in (12m)
Wingspan: 108ft 3in (33m)
Height: 18ft 7in (5.68m)

Weights:
Empty: 6754lb (3063kg)
Max T/O: 10 362lb (4700kg)

Performance:
Max Speed: 176mph
(284km/h)
Powerplant: one Garrett
TPE331-14F-801L turboprop
Thrust: 750shp (559kW)
Endurance: 13 hours

Armament:
none; 12 payload bays for
sensors and radio relay kit

Variants:
G-500 Egrett II, retractable
gear, longer span; G-500
Strato I, Egrett II equipped for
comms relay; G-520T two-seat
trainer

Fokker Maritime Enforcer The Netherlands

Type: maritime surveillance and anti-submarine/ship aircraft

Accommodation: two pilots, tactical co-ordinator, sonar operator, two radar electronic systems operators, two observers

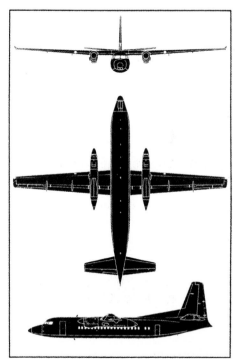

Dimensions:
Length: 82ft 10in (25.2m)
Wingspan: 95ft 1in (29m)
Height: 27ft 3in (8.3m)

Weights:
Empty: 32 620lb (14 796kg)
Max T/O: 47 500lb (21 545kg)

Performance:
Max Speed: 298mph

(480km/h)
Powerplant: two Pratt &
Whitney Canada PW125B
turboprops
Thrust: 5000shp (3728kW)
Endurance: 14 hours

Armament:
eight hardpoints; AGM-84
Harpoon ASMs; ASW
torpedos; depth charges

Variants:
Kingbird AEW, Sentinel border
surveillance aircraft and
Maritime Enforcer 2 based on
Fokker 50; Black Crow 2
comms/elint versions also
Fokker 50-based, with longer
fuselage and five-bladed
props

Grumman S-2 Tracker USA

Type: carrier-borne anti-submarine aircraft   **Accommodation:** two pilots, radar operator, MAD operator

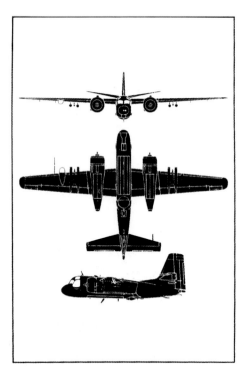

Dimensions:
Length: 43ft 6in (13.3m)
Wingspan: 72ft 7in (22.1m)
Height: 16ft 7in (5m)

Weights:
Empty: 18 750lb (8505kg)
Max T/O: 29 150lb (13 222kg)

Performance:
Max Speed: 265mph
(426km/h)
Powerplant: two Wright R-
1820-82 nine cylinder radial
engines
Thrust: 3050hp
Endurance: nine hours

Armament:
internal bomb bay; six
hardpoints; 4810lb (2182kg)
warload; ASW torpedoes;
depth charges; rockets

Variants:
Firecat aerial firefighter; S-2T
turboprop-powered version

Notes: Only Brazil has a carrier capability, other users operating them from
shore bases. Taiwan and Argentina use updated turboprop version.

Grumman HU-16 Albatros USA

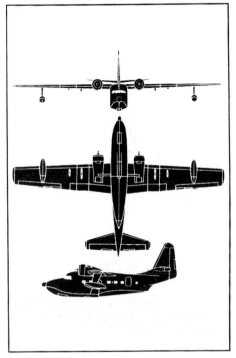

Type: utility amphibian   **Accommodation:** five crew up to 22 passengers

Dimensions:
Length: 62ft 10in (19.2m)
Wingspan: 96ft 8in (29.5m)
Height: 25ft 10in (7.9m)

Weights:
Empty: 22 883lb (10 380kg)
Max T/O: 37 500lb (17 010kg)

Performance:
Max Speed: 236mph (379km/h)
Range: 2477nm (4587km)
Powerplant: two Wright R-1820-76A radial engines
Thrust: 2850hp

Armament:
unarmed

Variants:
most versions withdrawn from service

Notes: Used for search and rescue, remains in service with the Greek navy.

Grumman OV-1D Mohawk USA

Type: observation reconnaissance aircraft   **Accommodation:** two pilots side-by-side

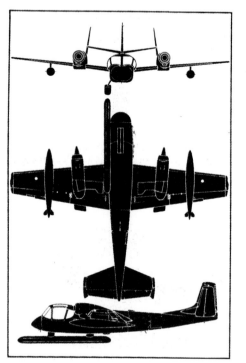

Dimensions:
Length: 41ft (12.5m)
Wingspan: 48ft (14.6m)
Height: 12ft 8in (3.8m)

Weights:
Empty: 12 054lb (5467kg)
Max T/O: 18 109lb (8214kg)

Performance:
Max Speed: 305mph
(491km/h)
Range: 878nm (1627km)
Powerplant: two Lycoming
T53-L-701 turboprops
Thrust: 2800hp

Armament:
none

Variants:
RV-1D EW aircraft
EV-1E Quick Look III elint
version

Notes: OV-1Ds can be fitted with a Sideways Looking Airborne Radar (SLAR) or an infra-red reconnaissance package. Mohawks will eventually be replaced by Joint Stars in the tactical radar recce role and may be withdrawn from US service soon. Ex-US aircraft will remain in use with Argentina.

Grumman E-2C Hawkeye USA

Type: carrier-borne AEW aircraft   **Accommodation:** five; two pilots; radar operator, air control officer, combat infomation centre officer

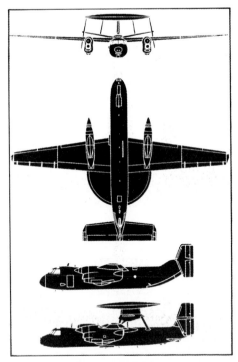

Dimensions:
Length: 57ft 6in (17.5m)
Wingspan: 80ft 7in (24.6m)
Height: 18ft 3in (5.6m)

Weights:
Empty: 39 373lb (17 859kg)
Max T/O: 53 267lb (24 161kg)

Performance:
Max Speed: 389mph (626km/h)
Powerplant: two Allison T56-A-427 turboprops
Thrust: 10 200ehp (7606kW)
Endurance: 6 hours 15 min

Armament:
none

Variants:
TE-2C operational trainer;
E-2T for Taiwan; C-2
Greyhound carrier transport

Notes: Israeli Hawkeyes have an inflight refueling probe above the cockpit. Only the US Navy operates them from carriers at the moment, but the French Navy is to acquire up to four for service on the CVN Charles de Gaulle.

HAMC SH-5 China

Type: maritime patrol amphibian   **Accommodation:** eight; two pilots; navigator; flight engineer; radio operator; three mission operators

Dimensions:
Length: 127ft 7in (38.9m)
Wingspan: 118ft 1in (36m)
Height: 32ft 2in (9.8m)

Weights:
Empty: 58 422lb (26 500kg)
Max T/O: 99 208lb (45 000kg)

Performance:
Max Speed: 345mph (556km/h)
Powerplant: four Dongan WJ5A turboprops
Thrust: 12 620ehp (9396kW)
Endurance: 15 hours

Armament:
dorsal 23mm gun turret; four hardpoints; 13 228lb (6000kg warload; C-101 ASMs; ASW torpedos; depth charges; mines; bombs

Variants:
firefighter; SAR

Notes: intended for a wide range of duties including aerial firefighting, which is becoming a very popular way of dealing with large-scale forest fires.

IAI Phalcon Israel

Type: airborne early warning aircraft   **Accommodation:** four flight crew; 13 mission crew

Dimensions:
Length: 152ft 11in (46.6m)
Wingspan: 145ft 9in (44.4m)
Height: 42ft 6in (12.95m)

Weights:
Empty: 171 000lb (77 564kg)
Max T/O: 336 000 (152 407kg)

Performance:
Max Speed: 530mph (853km/h)
Powerplant: four Pratt & Whitney JT3D-3B turbofans
Thrust: 72 000lb (320.4kN)
Endurance: 10 hours

Armament:
none

Variants:
none

Notes: Using phased array technology the Phalcon radar and equipment can be installed in a variety of airframes. Parts of the Phalcon systems are said to have been installed in South Africa's Boeing 707 tankers.

Ilyushin Il-86 'Maxdome' Russia

Type: airborne command post   **Accommodation:** six flight crew, unknown number of mission crew

Dimensions:
Length: 195ft 4in (59.54m)
Wingspan: 157ft 8in (48.06m)
Height: 51ft 10in (15.81m)

Weights:
Empty: n\a
Max T/O: 458 560lb (208 000kg)

Performance:
Max Speed: 590mph
(950km/h)
Range: 2480nm (4600km)
Powerplant: four KKBM NK-86 turbofans
Thrust: 114 640lb (510kN)

Armament:
none

Variants:
none

Notes: Shielded against the effects of nuclear blasts, hence the absence of cabin windows. The dorsal fin carries satellite comms equipment and there is a drogue housing for VHF trailing wire antenna. The underwing pods appear to be electricity generators. 'Maxdome' is not a real ASCC codename.

Ilyushin/Beriev A-50 Mainstay Russia

Type: airborne early warning aircraft   **Accommodation:** crew of 15

Dimensions:
Length: 152ft 10in (46.59m)
Wingspan: 165ft 8in (50.5m)
Height: 48ft 5in (14.76m)

Weights:
Empty: n/a
Max T/O: 418 875lb
(190 000kg)

Performance:
Max Speed: 528mph
(850km/h)
Range: 3940nm (7300km)
Powerplant: four Aviadvigatel
D-30KP turbofans
Thrust: 105 820lb (470.9kN)

Armament:
none has wingtip ECM pods
and self-defence flares

Variants:
Il-76VKP command post with
dorsal canoe over flight deck;
Il-76M(PP) EW version with
thimble nose; Adnan I Iraqi
AEW with rotodome and rear
fuselage strakes; Baghdad I
Iraqi AEW with radome
replacing rear ramp

143

Ilyushin Il-38 May Russia

Type: maritime patrol aircraft   **Accommodation:** 12; two pilots, flight engineer, around nine mission crew

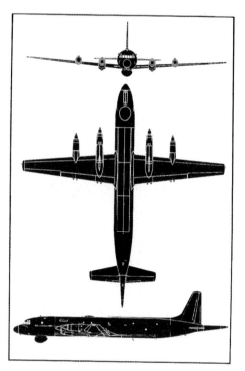

Dimensions:
Length: 129ft 10in (39.6m)
Wingspan: 122ft 9in (37.4m)
Height: 33ft 4in (10.2m)

Weights:
Empty: 79 367lb (36 000kg)
Max T/O: 140 000lb
(63 500kg)

Performance:
Max Speed: 448mph
(722km/h)
Powerplant: four ZMKB
Progress/Ivchenko AI-20M
turboprops
Thrust: 16 760ehp (12 504kW)
Endurance: 12 hours

Armament:
two internal bomb bays; ASW
torpedos; depth charges

Variants:
none

Notes: Development of the Il-18 airliner with new fuselage that houses tandem weapons bays, has a MAD stinger and relocated wings.

Ilyushin Il-20 Coot-A Russia

Type: electronic intelligence aircraft   **Accommodation:** two pilots, flight engineer unknown number of mission crew

Dimensions:
Length: 79ft (24m)
Wingspan: 122ft 9in (37.4m)
Height: 33ft 4in (10.2m)

Weights: 28 417 lb (11 890 kg)
Empty: 28 417lb (11 890kg)

Max T/O: 141 100lb (64 000kg)

Performance:
Max Speed: 419mph 675km/h)
Range: 3508nm (6500km)
Powerplant: four ZMKB Progress/Ivchenko AI-20M

turboprops
Thrust: 16 760ehp (12 504kW)

Armament:
none

Variants:
Il-22 Coot-B Elint version;
Il-22 Coot-C upgraded version

Notes: Operated by the Russian Air Force and Navy, the Il-20 has a sideways looking radar and other sensors housed in the underfuselage canoe and side fairings.

Lockheed S-3 Viking USA

Type: carrier-borne anti-submarine aircraft   **Accommodation:** two pilots, two electronic systems officers

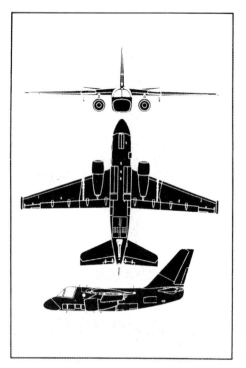

Dimensions:
Length: 53ft 4in (16.3m)
Wingspan: 68ft 8in (20.9m)
Height: 22ft 9in (6.9m)

Weights:
Empty: 24 150lb (10 954kg)
Max T/O: 47 602lb (21 592kg)

Performance:

Max Speed: 518mph (834km/h)
Range: 3230nm (6085km)
Powerplant: two General Electric TF34-GE-2 high bypass ratio turbofans
Thrust: 18 550lb (82.5kN)

Armament:
internal bomb bay and two hardpoints; B57 nuclear depth charges; AGM-84 Harpoon, AGM-84E SLAM ASMs; ASW torpedoes; depth charges; rockets

Variants:
S-3B ASW version; ES-3A EW version; KS-3A carrier-borne tanker (prototype only); US-3A carrier transport

Notes: S-3B can be equipped with aerial refuelling pods. Various special missions configurations are under development for OTH targeting, surveillance and Elint.

Lockheed P-3 Orion USA

Type: anti-submarine patrol aircraft

Accommodation: 10; two pilots, flight engineer, navigator, tactical co-ordinator, two sonar operators, MAD operator, ordnance technician, flight technician

Dimensions:
Length: 116ft 10in (35.61m)
Wingspan: 99ft 8in (30.37m)
Height: 33ft 8in (10.2m)

Weights:
Empty: 61 491lb (27 890kg)
Max T/O: 142 000lb
(64 410kg)

Performance:
Max Speed: 473mph (761km)
Powerplant: four Allison T56-A-14 turboprops
Thrust: 19 640ehp (14 644kW)
Endurance: 17 hours 12 min

Armament:
internal bomb bay and 10 hardpoints; 20 000lb (9071kg)

warload; B57 nuclear depth charges; AIM-9 Sidewinder AAMs; AGM-85 Harpoon ASMs; ASW torpedos; depth charges; mines; rockets

Variants:
ELINT and AEW versions (see separate entry)

Notes: Up to 13 relief crew or passengers can be carried. Canadian versions designated CP-140 Aurora/-140A Arcturus. Most popular ASW aircraft today – over 700 in service and still in production under licence in Japan.

Lockheed EP-3E Aries II USA

Type: electronic intelligence aircraft   **Accommodation:** two pilots, flight engineer, navigator, unknown number of mission crew

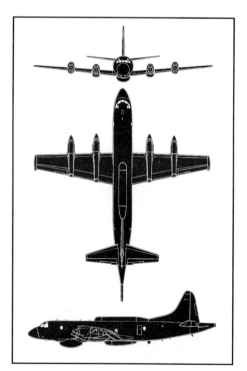

Dimensions:
Length: n/a
Wingspan: 99ft 8in (30.37m)
Height: 33ft 8in (10.2m)

Weights:
Empty: 61 491lb (27 890kg)
Max T/O: 142 000lb
(64 410kg)

Performance:
Max Speed: 473mph (761km)
Powerplant: four Allison T56-A-14 turboprops
Thrust: 19 640ehp (14 644kW)
Endurance: 17 hours 12 min

Armament:
none

Variants:
EP-3J operational trainer; RP-3D reconnaissance version

Notes: Japan has also developed ELINT versions designated EP-3C and UP-3C (the latter used for training only). Used for signals interception and analysis with two squadrons based in Guam and Spain.

Lockheed P-3 AEW&C USA

Type: airborne early warning and control   **Accommodation:** two pilots, flight engineer, navigator, unknown number of mission crew

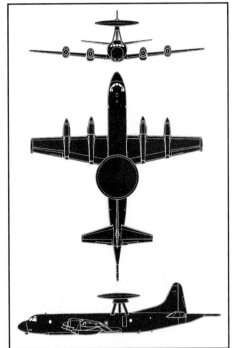

Dimensions:
Length: 116ft 10in (35.61m)
Wingspan: 99ft 8in (30.37m)
Height: 33ft 8in (10.2m)

Weights:
Empty: 61 491lb (27 890kg)

Max T/O: 142 000lb (64 410kg)

Performance:
Max Speed: 473mph (761km)
Powerplant: four Allison T56-A-14 turboprops
Thrust: 19 640ehp (14 644kW)

Endurance: 17 hours 12 min

Armament:
none

Variants:
none

Notes: Developed as a private venture and orginally offered to the RAF, the P-3 AEW&C is in service with the US Customs Service and is used to cover the Gulf of Mexico primarily in search of drug smugglers.

Lockheed SR-71 USA

Type: high-speed high-altitude reconnaissance aircraft   **Accommodation:** one pilot, one navigator in tandem

Dimensions:
Length: 103ft 8in (31.6m)
Wingspan: 55ft 6in (16.9m)
Height: 18ft 5in (5.6m)

Weights:
Empty: 67 500lb (30 618kg)
Max T/O: 172 000 (78 019kg)

Performance:
Max Speed: above Mach 3
Range: classified
Powerplant: two Pratt &
Whitney J58 turbojets
Thrust: 65 000lb (29 484kg)

Armament:
none fitted, however trials
were carried out with nuclear
weapons and AAMs

Variants:
SR-71B two-seat operational
trainer

Notes: Brought back into limited service after having been put in storage as a cost-saving measure. The US Air Force now keeps at least three operational to cover gaps in the US aerial reconnaissance field. The SR-71 holds six world records sustained altitude, speed over distance, absolute speed and two cross-Atlantic timed crossings.

Lockheed U-2/TR-1A USA

Type: high-altitude reconnaissance aircraft   **Accommodation:** one pilot

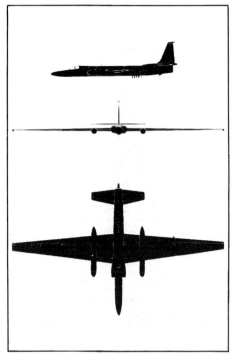

Dimensions:
Length: 63ft (19.2m)
Wingspan: 103ft (31.4m)
Height: 16ft (4.8m)

Weights:
Empty: 10 000lb (4535kg)
Max T/O: 40 000lb (18 144kg)

Performance:
Max Speed: 430mph (693km/h)
Powerplant: one Pratt & Whitney J75-PW-13B turbojet
Thrust: 17 000lb (75.6kN)
Endurance: 12 hours

Armament:
none

Variants:
U-2RT/TR-1B two-seat trainer; U-2S re-engined versions; ER-2 NASA earth survey aircraft

Notes: Still the official backbone of US tactical reconnaissance after 40 years of service, the U-2 can carry a variety of cameras and electronic surveillance equipment to an altitude of 90 000ft (27 430m). Several U-2Rs fitted with dorsal pods for carrying extra equipment but one was lost on take-off in 1995.

Lockheed EC-130E Rivet Rider USA

Type: psychological warfare aircraft   **Accommodation:** four flight crew; numerous mission specialists

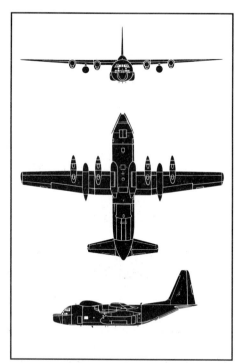

Dimensions:
Length: 97ft 9in (29.7m)
Wingspan: 132ft 7in (40.41m)
Height: 38ft 3in (11.6m)

Weights:
Empty: more than 76 500lb
(34 700kg)
Max T/O: 175 000lb (79 380kg)

Performance:
Max Speed: 374mph
(602km/h)
Range: very high endurance
Powerplant: four Allison T56-A-15 turboprops
Thrust: 9016shp (6724kW)

Armament:
none

Variants:
EC-130E (ABCCC) command
post version; EC-130E (CC)
Elint version; EC-130E
Compass Call; MC-130E
Combat Talon I special
operations aircraft;
HC-130N/P Combat Shadow

Notes: Rivet Rider used to broadcast doctored TV pictures over the entire frequency range, and send out radio messages on civilian networks. Compass Call works with ground stations to jam radar and comms and Combat Talon covers a variety of functions being equipped with TFR and ECM/ESM self-protection kit.

Myasishchev M-55 Mystic Russia

Type: high-altitude reconnaissance aircraft   **Accommodation:** one pilot

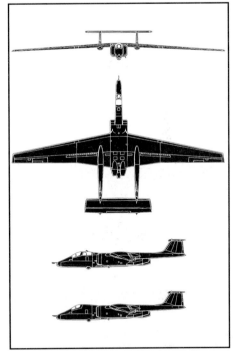

Dimensions:
Length: 75ft (22.8m)
Wingspan: 122ft 11in (37.4m)
Height: 15ft 5in (4.7m)

Weights:
Empty: n/a
Max T/O: more than 44 000lb
(19 950kg)

Performance:
Max Speed: 466mph
(750km/h)
Powerplant: two Aviadvigadel
PS-30-V12 turbojets
Thrust: 22 050lb (98kN)
Endurance: 6 hours 30 min

Armament:
none

Variants:
M-17 Stratosphere single-
engined version

Notes: The M-17 was used for many record-breaking flights and is also used
for enviromental research flights. Maximum altitude is 65 000ft (20 000m).

Piaggio P.166-DL3SEM Italy

Type: offshore patrol aircraft   **Accommodation:** two pilots plus mission crew

Dimensions:
Length: 39ft (11.8m)
Wingspan: 48ft 2in (14.6m)
Height: 16ft 5in (5m)

Weights:
Empty: 5926lb (2688kg)
Max T/O: 9480lb (4300kg)

Performance:
Max Speed: 248mph (400km/h)
Range: 1150nm (2130km)
Powerplant: two Lycoming LTP 101-700 turboprops
Thrust: 1200shp (895kW)

Armament:
no fitted armament

Variants:
special patrol/observation and transport versions offered

Notes: Used by the Italian Custom Service, Navy, Air Force and Ministry of Merchant Marine.

Piaggio PD-808 ECM Italy

Type: electronic warfare aircraft   **Accommodation:** two pilots, three ECM operators

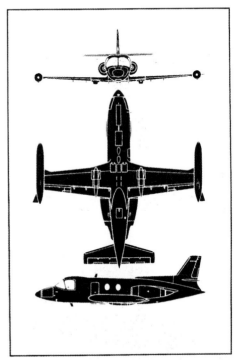

Dimensions:
Length: 42ft 2in (12.8m)
Wingspan: 43ft 3in (13.2m)
Height: 15ft 9in (4.8m)

Weights:
Empty: 10 650lb (4830kg)
Max T/O: 18 000lb (8165kg)

Performance:
Max Speed: 529mph
(852km/h)
Range: 1148nm (2128km)
Powerplant: two Rolls-Royce
Viper turbojets Mk526
turbojets
Thrust: 6720lb (3048kg)

Armament:
none

Variants:
PD-808VIP transport;
PD-808TA navigation trainer;
PD-808RM radio calibration
aircraft; PD-808GE EW aircraft

Notes: A utility design first flown in 1964 which can be adapted to a number of roles including medical transport and survey.

Pilatus Britten-Norman Maritime Defender UK

Type: short range maritime patrol aircraft   **Accommodation:** two pilots, radar operator, up to 10 passengers

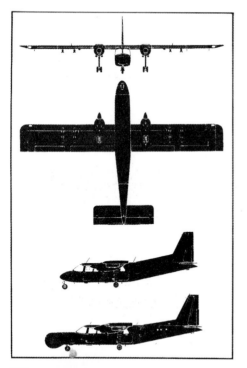

Dimensions:
Length: 35ft 7in (10.8m)
Wingspan: 49ft (14.9m)
Height: 13ft 8in (4.2m)

Weights:
Empty: 4244lb (1925kg)
Max T/O: 6600lb (2993kg)

Performance:
Max Speed: 170mph (274km/h)
Range: 1216nm (2252km)
Powerplant: two Allison 250-B17C truboprops
Thrust: 800shp (596kW)

Armament:
four hardpoints; depth charges; gun pods; bombs; rockets

Variants:
Defender utility version; Battlefield Surveillance Defender reconnaissance version; ELINT version

Notes: The Defender series of STOL aircraft can be adapted for a variety of battlefield and patrol functions. The new Defender 4000 series offers greater payload with no loss in performance.

Rockwell OV-10 Bronco USA

Type: observation/close support aircraft   **Accommodation:** two pilots in tandem, up to five paratroops can be carried

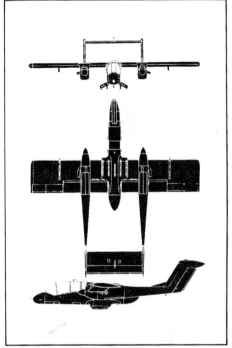

Dimensions:
Length: 41ft 7in (12.6m)
Wingspan: 40ft (12.2m)
Height: 15ft 2in (4.6m)

Weights:
Empty: 6893lb (3127kg)
Max T/O: 14 444lb (6552kg)

Performance:
Max Speed: 288mph (463km/h)
Range: 1200nm (2224km)
Powerplant: two Garrett T76-G-416/417 turboprops
Thrust: 1430ehp (1066kW)

Armament:
five hardponts; AIM-9 Sidewinder AAMs; 20mm/7.62mm gun pods; bombs; rockets

Variants:
OV-10D night surveillance version

Notes: Now out of service with the US armed forces, the Bronco remains in use as a counter-insurgency aircraft in Indonesia, Thailand, Venezuela, Morocco and the Philippines. The OV-10D can be recognised by its long nose and FLIR ball.

157

Saab 340 AEW Sweden

Type: airborne early warning aircraft   **Accommodation:** three flight crew, plus mission crew

Dimensions:
Length: 64ft 8in (19.7m)
Wingspan: 70ft 4in (21.4m)
Height: 22ft 10 in (6.9m)

Weights:
Empty: 17 945lb (8140kg)
Max T/O: 29 000lb (13 155kg)

Performance:
Max Speed: 288mph (463km/h)
Range: n\a
Powerplant: two General Electric CT7-9B turboprops
Thrust: 3500shp (2610kW)

Armament:
none

Variants:
none

Notes: The dorsal pod houses an Ericsson PS-890 Erieye Sideways looking radar.

ShinMaywa Industries US-1 Japan

Type: anti-submarine patrol aircraft   **Accommodation:** two pilots, flight engineer, navigator and up to 20 survivors

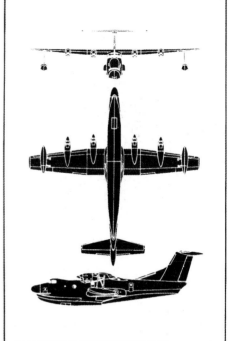

Dimensions:
Length: 109ft 9in (33.5m)
Wingspan: 108ft 9in (33.1m)
Height: 32ft 7in (9.9m)

Weights:
Empty: 56 218lb (25 500kg)
Max T/O: 99 200lb (45 000kg); 94 800lb (43 000kg) from water

Performance:
Max Speed: 325mph (522km/h)
Range: 2060nm (3815km)
Powerplant: four Ishikawajima (General Electric) T64-IHI-10J turboprops
Thrust: 13 972ehp (10 420kW)

Armament:
ASW torpedos; depth charges

Variants:
US-1 SAR version; firefighting amphibian; PS-1 ASW version

Notes: First flown in 1967, the PS-1 version has a dipping sonar which it operates during brief water landings.

Tupolev Tu-16 Badger Russia

Type: maritime strike/reconnaissance aircraft

Accommodation: six; two pilots; navigator/bombardier; tail gunner; two observers

Dimensions:
Length: 114ft 2in (34.8m)
Wingspan: 108ft 3in (32.9m)
Height: 34ft (10.4m)

Weights:
Empty: 82 000lb (37 200kg)
Max T/O: 165 350lb (75 000kg)

Performance:
Max Speed: 652mph (1050mk/h)
Range: 3885nm (7200km)
Powerplant: two RD-3M-500 turbojets
Thrust: 41 840lb (186.1kN)

Armament:
six 23mm AV-23 cannon in tail, dorsal and ventral turrets; 19 800lb (9000kg) warlaod; AS-6 Kingfish ASMs; bombs

Variants:
Tu-16R electronic reconnaissance aircraft; Tu-16PP ECM aircraft

Notes: There are 18 different versions of the Tu-16, most coming under the three broad areas of anti-ship strike, reconnaissance and ECM escort-the main versions are listed above. Other versions include aerial tanker, meterological laboratory and fast transport.

TRANSPORT AIRCRAFT

Aerospatiale N 262 Frégate France

Type: light military transport   **Accommodation:** two pilots; 29 troops; 18 paratroops

Dimensions:
Length: 63ft 2in (19.2m)
Wingspan: 71ft 8in (21.9m)
Height: 20ft 4in (6.2m)

Weights:
Empty: 6175lb (13 613kg)
Max T/O: 23 370lb (10 600kg)

Payload: 6834lb (3100kg)

Performance:
Max Speed: 260mph
(418km/h)
Range: 1295nm (1490km);
565nm (650km) with Max
payload

Powerplant: two Turbomeca
Bastan VIIA turboprops
Thrust: 2260ehp (1685.2KW)

Variants:
short-haul civil commuter

Notes: The French Air Force still operates the Frégate in a utility transport
and training role, the civil version is rare.

Airtech (CASA/IPTN) CN-235M Spain/Indonesia

Type: light military transport   **Accommodation:** two pilots, loadmaster, 48 troops, 46 paratroops

Dimensions:
Length: 70ft 2in (21.4m)
Wingspan: 84ft 8in (25.8m)
Height: 26ft 10in (8.2m)

Weights:
Empty: 19 400lb (8800kg)
Max T/O: 36 376lb (16 500kg)

Payload: 13 227lb (6000kg)

Performance:
Max Speed: 276mph
(445km/h)
Range: 1974nm (3656km);
957nm (1773km) with Max
payload

Powerplant: two General
Electric CT7-9C turboprops
Thrust: 3500hp (2610kW)

Variants:
CN-235MPA Persuader
maritime patrol aircraft

Notes: The CN-235MPA can carry a 7716lb (3500kg) warload (including Exocets) and has an endurance of over 8 hours. It can be recognised by its longer nose containing an air search radar, as yet no orders have been placed.

163

Alenia G222 Italy

Type: light military transport   **Accommodation:** two pilots, loadmaster, 46 troops, 40 paratroops

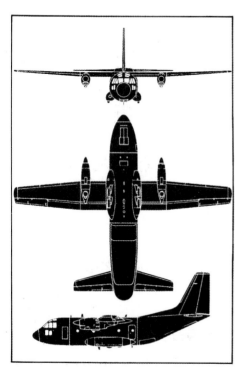

Dimensions:
Length: 74ft 5in (22.7m)
Wingspan: 94ft 2in (28.7m)
Height: 34ft 8in (10.5m)

Weights:
Empty: 34 610lb (9000kg)
Max T/O: 61 730lb (28 000kg)
Payload: 19 840lb (9400kg)

Performance:
Max Speed: 303mph (487km/h)
Range: 2530nm (4685km); 680nm (1260km) with Max payload
Powerplant: two Fiat built General Electric T64-GE-P4D turboprops

Thrust: 6800hp (5070kW)

Variants:
G222SAA firefighter; G222VS EW version; G222T Tyne-engined version for Libya; G222RM radio and navaid calibration variant

Notes: US Air Force aircraft are designated Chrysler C-27As (Chrysler being the prime contractor) and are used only in Panama and South America.

Antonov An-225 Mriya (Cossack) Ukraine

Type: very heavy transport aircraft   **Accommodation:** two pilots, two flight engineers, Navigator, radio operator, 60-70 passengers in cabin

Dimensions:
Length: 275ft 7in (84m)
Wingspan: 290ft (88.4m)
Height: 59ft 8in (18.2m)

Weights:
Empty: n\a
Max T/O: 1 322 750lb (600 000kg)

Payload: 551 150lb (250 000kg)

Performance:
Max Speed: 528mph (850km/h)
Range: 8310nm (15 400km); 2425nm (4500km) with Max payload

Powerplant: six ZMKB Progress D-18T turbofans
Thrust: 309 540lb (1377kN)

Variants:
only a single aircraft so far built

Antonov An-124 Condor Ukraine

Type: heavy military transport   **Accommodation:** two pilots, two flight engineers, navigator, radio operator

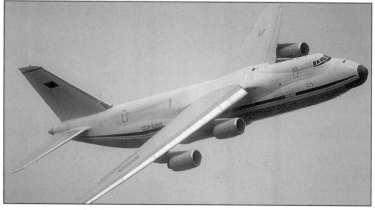

Dimensions:
Length: 226ft 8in (69.1m)
Wingspan: 240ft 5in (73.3m)
Height: 68ft 2in (20.8m)

Weights:
Empty: 385 800lb (175 000kg)
Max T/O: 892 872lb

(405 000kg)
Payload: 330 693lb
(150 000kg)

Performance:
Max Speed: 537mph
(865km/h)
Range: 8900nm (16 500km);

2430nm (4500km) with Max
payload
Powerplant: four ZKMB
Progress D-18T turbofans
Thrust: 206 360lb (918kN)

Variants:
An-124-100 civil version

Notes: The largest aircraft in production. Air Foyle, the only non-Russian civil operator, has set two world records with the An-124.

Antonov An-72/74 Coaler Ukraine

Type: light STOL military transport   **Accommodation:** pilot, co-pilot/navigator, flight engineer, 68 troops, 57 paratroops, 24 stretchers

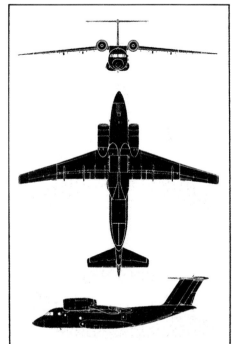

Dimensions:
Length: 92ft 1in (28.1m)
Wingspan: 104ft 7in (31.9m)
Height: 28ft 4in (8.6m)

Weights:
Empty: 42 000lb (19 050kg)
Max T/O: 76 060lb (34 500kg)
Payload: 22 045lb (10 000kg)

Performance:
Max Speed: 438mph (705km/h)
Range: 2590nm (4800km); 430nm (800km) with max payload
Powerplant: two ZKMB Progress D-36 turbofans
Thrust: 28 660lb (127.48kN)

Variants:
An-72A basic version; An-72AT freighter; An-72S executive transport; An-72P dedicated maritime patrol version with cannon on starboard side and underwing hardpoints; An-74 blister windows, nose radome, increased fuel, provision for skis; An-74-200 all-weather version

Antonov An-70 Ukraine

Type: medium military transport   **Accommodation:** two pilots, flight engineer, 170 troops

Dimensions:
Length: 132ft (40.2m)
Wingspan: 144ft 6in (44m)
Height: 52ft (16.1m)

Weights:
Max T/O: 286 600lb
(130 000kg)

Payload: 103 615lb (47 000kg)

Performance:
Max Speed: 497mph
(800km/h)
Range: 3910nm (7250km)
Powerplant: four ZKMB
Progress D-27 propfans

Thrust: 55 200shp (41 160kW)

Variants:
An-70T commercial version

Notes: The first all-propfan aircraft to be flown, the An-70 has very low running costs for its size. A version called An-77 was unsuccessfully offered to the Royal Air Force as a C-130 replacement.

Antonov An-32 Cline Ukraine

Type: light STOL military transport   **Accommodation:** two pilots, navigator, 50 troops, 42 paratroops, 24 stretchers

Dimensions:
Length: 78ft (23.78m)
Wingspan: 95ft 9in (29.2m)
Height: 28ft 1in (8.6m)

Weights:
Empty: 37 038lb (16 800kg)
Max T/O: 59 525lb (27 000kg)
Payload: 14 770lb (6700kg)

Performance:
Max Speed: 329mph
(530km/h)
Range: 1360nm (2520km);
647nm (1200km) with Max
payload
Powerplant: two ZKMB
Progress AI-20D turboprops
Thrust: 10 084ehp (7520kW)

Armament:
Peruvian aircraft can carry
bombs on four bomb racks

Variants:
An-32P Firekiller (in photo)

Notes: The An-32P Firekiller can be recognised by very large under-fuselage tanks. The An-32 is very similar to the An-26 on which it was based, the main difference being the position of the engines above the wings.

Antonov An-30 Clank Ukraine

Type: aerial survey aircraft

Accommodation: two pilots, flight engineer, navigator, radio operator, two surveyors

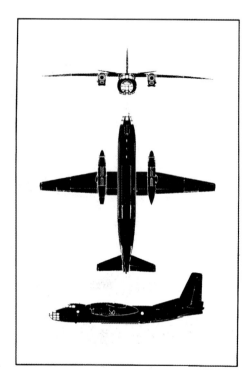

Dimensions:
Length: 79ft 7in (24.26m)
Wingspan: 95ft 9in (29.2m)
Height: 27ft 3in (8.3m)

Weights:
Empty: 34 370lb (15 590kg)
Max T/O: 50 706lb (23 000kg)

Performance:
Max Speed: 335mph (540km/h)
Range: 1420nm (2630km)
Powerplant: two AI-24A turboprops, plus one RU 19A-300 auxiliary turbojet
Thrust: 5100ehp (3804kW)

Variants:
An-30M Sky Cleaner; An-30 dedicated photographic survey platform

Notes: the An-30M carries carbon dioxide containers which when released above clouds can create rain, it is used over arable land, to increase snow cover or to fight forest fires.

Antonov An-26 Curl Ukraine

Type: light military transport   **Accommodation:** two pilots, flight engineer, navigator, radio operator, 40 troops, 24 stretchers

Dimensions:
Length: 78ft 1in (23.8m)
Wingspan: 95ft 9in (29.2m)
Height: 28ft 1in (8.6m)

Weights:
Empty: 33 113lb (15 020kg)
Max T/O: 52 911lb (24 000kg)
Payload: 12 125lb (5500kg)

Performance:
Max Speed: 273mph (440km/h)
Range: 1376nm (2550km); 594nm (1100km) with Max payload
Powerplant: two Ivchenko AI-24VT turboprops, plus one RU 19A-300 auxiliary turbojet
Thrust: 5640ehp (4206kW);

auxiliary 1765lb (7.85kN)

Armament:
provision for bomb rack

Variants:
An-24 Coke earlier version;
An-26RT Elint variant Curl-B;
An-26Sm calibration version

Notes: An-24 smaller with less powerful engines. Built as Y-7 in China.

Antonov An-22 Antheus (Cock) Ukraine

Type: heavy military transport   **Accommodation:** two pilots, flight engineer, navigator, radio operator, 28 passengers in cabin

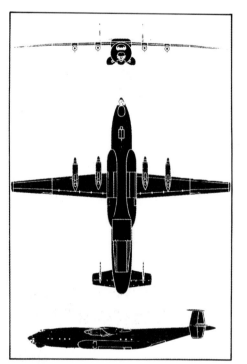

Dimensions:
Length: 190ft (57.9m)
Wingspan: 211ft 4in (64.4m)
Height: 41ft 1in (12.5m)

Weights:
Empty: 251 325lb (114 000kg)
Max T/O: 551 160lb
(250 000kg)

Payload: 176 350lb
(80 000kg)

Performance:
Max Speed: 460mph
(740km/h)
Range: 5905nm (10 950km);
2692nm (5000km) with Max
payload

Powerplant: four Kuznetsov
NK-12MA turboprops
Thrust: 60 000shp (44 740kW)

Variants:
none

Notes: Some An-22s have been fitted with fuselage pylons for carrying
piggy-back loads.

Antonov An-12 Cub Ukraine

Type: medium military transport **Accommodation:** two pilots, flight engineer, navigator, radio operator, tail gunner

Dimensions:
Length: 108ft 7in (33.1m)
Wingspan: 124ft 8in (38m)
Height: 34ft 6in (10.5m)

Weights:
Empty: 61 730lb (28 000kg)
Max T/O: 134 480lb
(61 000kg)
Payload: 44 090lb (20 000kg)

Performance:
Max Speed: 482mph
(777km/h)
Range: 3075nm (5700km);
1942nm (3600km)
Powerplant: four Ivchenko AI-20K turboprops
Thrust: 15 776ehp (11 768kW)

Armament:
two 23mm NR-23 cannon in
tail turret

Variants:
An-12PS Cub-B SAR version;
An-12BK-IS and An-12BK-PP
Cub-D EW/ECM platforms

Notes: ECM Cubs carry large electric generators to jam up to five wavebands simultaneously – a large number of antennae and bulges visible on the underside of the fuselage of these aircraft, and some lack a gun turret.

BAe VC10 UK

Type: aerial tanker and transport aircraft   **Accommodation:** two pilots, flight engineer, up to 151 passengers

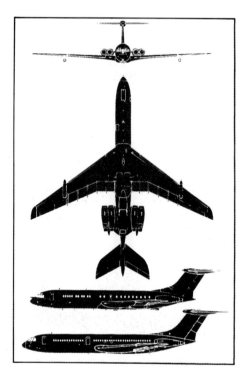

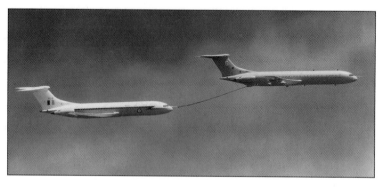

Dimensions:
Length:158ft 8in (48.3m)
Wingspan: 146ft 2in (44.5m)
Height: 39ft 6in (12m)

Weights:
Empty: 146 979lb (86 668kg)
Max T/O: 312 000lb

(141 520kg)
Payload: 39 769lb (18 039kg)

Performance:
Max Speed: 589mph
(914km/h)
Range: 9765 miles (9765km);
5040miles (8115km) with Max

payload
Powerplant: four Rolls-Royce
Conway RCo. 42 turbofans
Thrust: 84 000lb (19 050kg)

Variants:
super VC10 stretched version

Notes: Some 25 VC10s remain in service with the Royal Air Force as
tanker/transports, the tanker versions are to be fitted with Joint Tactical
Information Distribution Systems to enable them to work as a link between
AWACS and ground stations.

Boeing KC-135R Stratotanker USA

Type: strategic flight-refuelling tanker/transport aircraft   **Accommodation:** two pilots, navigator, boom operator

Dimensions:
Length: 136ft 3in (41.5m)
Wingspan: 130ft 10in (39.8m)
Height: 38ft 4in (11.7m)

Weights:
Empty: 98 466lb (44 663kg)
Max T/O: 297 000lb
(134 715kg)

Performance:
Max Speed: 532mph
(856km/h)
Powerplant: four CFM56-2B-1
turbofans
Thrust: 88 000lb (391.6kN)
Endurance: 5 Hours 30
minutes

Variants:
KC-135R(RT) fitted with
refuelling receptacle; KC-135E
reserve aircraft with JT3D-3B
engines; KC-135T former KC-
135Qs used to support F-117s;
KC-135FR French tankers (in
photo)

Notes: Compared with the KC-135A, the R-model can offload up to 150 per
cent more fuel. Having one refuelling boom, US Air Force KC-135Rs cannot
refuel US Navy or NATO aircraft equipped with probes. Conversions for basic
Boeing 707s offer hose and drogue type equipment.

CASA C 212 Aviocar Spain

Type: light military transport   **Accommodation:** two pilots; loadmaster; 25 troops; 24 paratroops

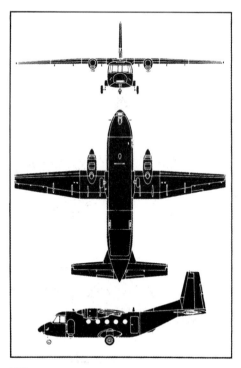

Dimensions:
Length: 52ft 11in (16.2m)
Wingspan: 66ft 6in (20.2m)
Height: 21ft 7in (6.60m)

Weights:
Empty: 9700lb (4400kg)
Max T/O: 17 857lb (8100kg)
Payload: 6217lb (2820kg)

Performance:
Max Speed: 230mph (370kmh)
Range: 1447nm (2680km);
450nm (835km) with Max
payload
Powerplant: two Garrett
TPE331-10R-513C
Thrust: 1800 shp (1342kW)

Armament:
two optional hard points;
1102lb (500kg) warload;
machine-gun pods; rockets;
(ASW version) ASW torpedoes;
Sea Skua ASMs

Variants:
300ASW anti-submarine
version; 300DE ELINT/ECM

Notes: Maritime patrol versions can be identified by a square cut nose randome and ESM pods on top of the tailfin. A civil airliner version seats 26 passengers. ASW versions accommodate seven mission specialists.

de Havilland Canada DHC-4A Caribou Canada

Type: light STOL military transport   **Accommodation:** two pilots; loadmaster; 32 troops; 26 paratroops; 22 stretchers.

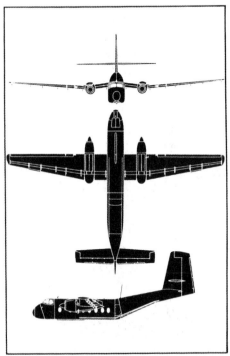

Dimensions:
Length: 72ft 7in (22.1m)
Wingspan: 95ft 7in (29.2m)
Height: 31ft 9in (9.7m)

Weights:
Empty: 18 260lb (8283kg)
Max T/O: 28 500lb (12 928kg)

Payload: 8740lb (3965kg)

Performance:
Max Speed: 216mph (347kmh)
Range: 1135nm (2103km); 210nm (390km) with Max payload

Powerplant: two Pratt & Whitney R-2000-7M2 radial engines
Thrust: 2900Hp (2162kW)

Variants:
see Notes

Notes: First flew in July 1958, remains in service in Australia, Malaysia and Africa. Many versions of the Caribou were built, including specialist communications aircraft for the US Air Force. Standard utility version is the only one in service today.

de Havilland Canada DHC-5 Buffalo Canada

Type: light STOL military transport   **Accommodation:** two pilots; crew chief; 41 troops; 35 paratroops; 24 stretchers

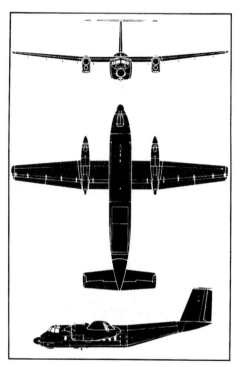

Dimensions:
Length: 79ft (24m)
Wingspan: 96ft (29.3m)
Height: 28ft 8in (8.7m)

Weights:
Empty: 25 160lb (11 412kg)
Max T/O: 49 200lb (22 316kg)

Payload: 18 000lb (8164kg)

Performance:
Max Speed: 261mph (420km/h)
Range: 3300nm (6115km); 600nm (1112km) with Max payload

Powerplant: two General Electric CT64-820-4 turboprops
Thrust: 6266shp (4672kW)

Variants:
DHC-5 sub-variants with different engines

Notes: A stretched, turboprop development of the Caribou the Buffalo was adopted by 20 air forces. The Buffalo can be fitted with Low Altitude Parachute Extraction System, which allow it to drop up to 5000lb (2268kg) onto almost any surface.

Transall C-160 France/Germany

Type: medium military transport   **Accommodation:** two pilots; loadmaster; 93 troops; 68 paratroops; 62 stretchers

Dimensions:
Length: 106ft 3in (32.4m)
Wingspan: 131ft 3in (40m)
Height: 38ft 2in (11.6m)

Weights:
Empty: 61 730lb (28 000kg)
Max T/O: 112 435lb (51 000kg)

Payload: 35 275lb (16 000kg)

Performance:
Max Speed: 319mph (593km/h)
Range: 2750nm (5095km); 1000nm (1853km) with Max payload
Powerplant: two Rolls-Royce Tyne RTy.20 Mk22 turboprops
Thrust: 12 200ehp (9098kW)

Variants:
C-160NG improved avionics, IFR probe; C-160G Gabriel Elint platform with IFR probe and HDU; C-160SE electronic surveillance version

Notes: Four French C-160 H Astarté aircraft are equipped as communication relay stations to support the nation's nuclear deterrence – fitted with Very Low Frequency radio equipment. C-160SE equipped with a SLAR and FLIR or a ventral retractable 360 deg radar.

IAI 202 Arava Israel

Type: light military transport　　　　**Accommodation:** one or two pilots; 24 troops; 16 paratroops; 12 stretchers

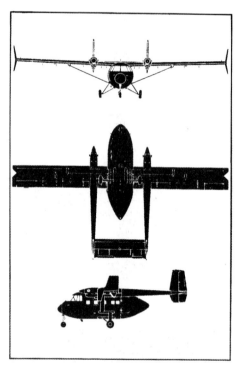

Dimensions:
Length: 44ft 23in (13.5m)
Wingspan: 70ft 11in (21.6m)
Height: 17ft 1in (5.2m)

Weights:
Empty: 9063lb (4111kg)
Max T/O: 17 000lb (7711kg)
Payload: 5500lb (2495kg)

Performance:
Max Speed: 203mph (326km/h)
Range: 860nm (1594km/h); 340nm (630km) with Max payload
Powerplant: two Pratt & Whitney Canada PT6A-34 turboprops
Thrust: 1500shp (1118kW)

Armament:
optional; 12.7mm gun pods; rockets

Variants:
100 civil version; 200 early military version

Notes: The Israeli air force operates a number of special mission Aravas including ELINT and ESM versions. The tail cone of the central fuselage is hinged to move sideways to allow carriage of light vehicles.

Ilyushin Il-76 Candid Russia

Type: heavy-lift military transport   **Accommodation:** two pilots; flight engineer; navigator; tail gunner; two loadmasters;

Dimensions:
Length: 152ft 10in (46.6m)
Wingspan: 165ft 8in (50.5m)
Height: 48ft 5in (14.7m)

Weights:
Empty: n\a
Max T/O: 374 785lb
(170 000kg)
Payload: 88 185lb (40 000kg)

Performance:
Max Speed: 528mph
(850km/h)
Range: 3940nm (7300km);
1970nm (3650km) with Max
payload
Powerplant: four Aviadvigatel
D-30KP turbofans
Thrust: 105 820lb (470.8kN)

Armament:
two 23mm GSh-23L cannon in
tail

Variants:
Il-76MF stretched version;
Il-76TD up-engined version;
Il-76DMP firebomber

Notes: The Il-76MF flew in September 1995 and is 21ft 8in (6.6m) longer in
the fuselage. The Il-76TD has D-30KP-2 engines and can carry an extra
22 046lb (10 000kg).

Kawasaki C-1A Japan

Type: medium-lift military transport   **Accommodation:** two pilots; flight engineer; navigator; loadmaster; 60 troops; 45 paratroops; 36 stretchers

Dimensions:
Length: 95ft 1in (29m)
Wingspan: 101ft 8in (31m)
Height: 32ft 9in (10m)

Weights:
Empty: 50 706lb (23 000kg)
Max T/O: 39 000lb (85 980kg)

Payload: 17 638lb (8000kg)

Performance:
Max Speed: 507mph (815km/h)
Range: 1800nm (3336km); 700nm (806km) with Max payload

Powerplant: two Pratt & Whitney JT8D-9 turbofan
Thrust: 29 000lb (13 150kg)

Variants:
C-1Kai ECM version

Notes: Only one C-1Kai was built and can be recognized by its flat radome in the nose and tail for its ECM equipment.

Lockheed C-5B Galaxy USA

Type: heavy-lift military transport

Accommodation: two pilots; flight engineer; two loadmasters; up to 345 troops

Dimensions:
Length: 247ft 10in (75.5m)
Wingspan: 222ft 8in (67.8m)
Height: 65ft 1in (19.8m)

Weights:
Empty: 374 000lb (169 643kg)
Max T/O: 837 000lb (379 657kg)

Performance:
Max Speed: 571mph (919km/h)
Range: 5618nm (10 411km); 2982nm (5526km) with Max payload

Powerplant: four General Electric TF39-GE-1C turbofans
Thrust: 172 000lb (764.8kN)

Variants:
C-5A early version

Notes: The C-5B Galaxy can carry two M1A2 Main Battle Tanks or six AH-64 Apache helicopters. When it first flew it was the largest aircraft in the world: the Wright Brothers' first flight could have taken place inside the cargo hold!

Lockheed C-141 Starlifter USA

Type: heavy-lift military transport   **Accommodation:** two pilots; flight engineer; navigator; 154 troops; 123 paratroops; 80 stretchers

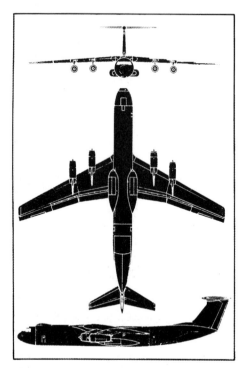

Dimensions:
Length: 168ft 3in (51.3m)
Wingspan: 159ft 11in (48.7m)
Height: 39ft 3in (11.9m)

Weights:
Empty: 148 120lb (67 168kg)
Max T/O: 343 000lb
(155 580kg)

Payload: 90 880lb (41 222kg)

Performance:
Max Speed: 566mph
(910km/h)
Range: 5550nm (10 280km);
2550nm (4725km) with Max
payload
Powerplant: four Pratt &

Whitney TF33-P-7 turbofans
Thrust: 84 000lb (38 100kg)

Variants:
C-141A early version; C-141B
stretched conversion of A-
model

Notes: The narrow fuselage of the C-141 meant it often 'bulked-out' before it reached Maximum take-off weight. A fuselage extension increased its capacity but it remains too narrow for many modern armoured fighting vehicles.

Lockheed C-130 Hercules USA

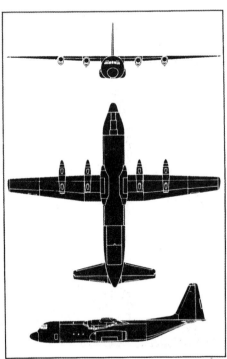

Type: medium-lift military transport   **Accommodation:** two pilots; flight engineer; navigator; 92 troops; 64 paratroops; 74 stretchers

Dimensions:
Length: 97ft 9in (29.8m)
Wingspan: 132ft 7in (40.4m)
Height: 38ft 3in (11.7m)

Weights:
Empty: 76 469lb (34 686kg)
Max T/O: 155 000lb (70 310kg)

Performance:
Max Speed: 374mph (602km/h)
Range: 4250nm (7876km); 2046nm (3791km) with Max payload
Powerplant: four Allison T56-A-15 turboprops
Thrust: 18 032shp (13 448kW)

Armament:
usually unarmed, except for AC-130.

Variants:
C-130H-30 stretched version;
HC-130 search and rescue;
KC-130 tanker version;
DC-130 drone controller
AC-130 gunship

Notes: Over 70 Variants are in service. The stretched version can carry up to 124 troops. C-130s have been fitted with skis and offered with floats. Versions carry out maritime patrol, drone release and control, communications relay, satellite recovery, photographic survey and airborne early warning.

McDonnell Douglas C-17 Globemaster II USA

Type: heavy-lift military transport   **Accommodation:** two pilots; loadmaster; 208 troops; 102 paratroops

Dimensions:
Length: 174ft (53m)
Wingspan: 165ft (50.3m)
Height: 55ft 1in (16.8m)

Weights:
Empty: 269 00lb (122 016kg)
Max T/O: 580 000lb

(263 083kg)
Payload: 169 000lb (76 657kg)

Performance:
Max Speed: 403mph
(648km/h)
Range: 4700nm (8704km);
2400nm (4445km/h) with Max

payload
Powerplant: four Pratt &
Whitney F117-PW-100
turbofans
Thrust: 162 800lb (724kN)

Variants:
none

Notes: The C-17 will replace C-141s in the tactical airlift role delivering heavy cargoes direct to unpaved airstrips in the battle zone.

McDonnell Douglas KC-10 Extender USA

Type: strategic tanker/transport   **Accommodation:** two pilots; navigator; boom operator

Dimensions:
Length: 182ft 7in (55.4m)
Wingspan: 165ft 4in (50.4m)
Height: 58ft 1in (17.7m)

Weights:
Empty: 241 027lb (109 328kg)
Max T/O: 590 000lb
(267 620kg)

Payload: 169 409lb (76 843kg)

Performance:
Max Speed: 610mph
(982km/h)
Range: 9993nm (18 507km);
3797nm (7032km) with Max
payload
Powerplant: three General
Electric GE CF6-50C2
turbofans
Thrust: 157 500lb (700.59kN)

Variants:
KDC-10 conversion of civil
DC-10 for Netherlands air
force

Notes: Developed from the commercial DC-10, the Extender can transfer a total of 200 000lb (90 718kg) of fuel. Can also refuel USMC and Navy aircraft with built-in hose and drogue.

Douglas DC-3/C-47 USA

Type: light military transport   **Accommodation:** two pilots; navigator; loadmaster; 21 troops

Dimensions:
Length: 64ft 5in (19.6m)
Wingspan: 95ft (28.9m)
Height: 16ft 11in (5.2m)

Weights:
Empty: 16 865lb (7657kg)
Max T/O: 25 200lb (11 441kg)
Payload: 8784lb (3784kg)

Performance:
Max Speed: 229mph (368km/h)
Range: 1306nm (2420km/h)
Powerplant: two Wright Cyclone GR-1820-G102A radial engines
Thrust: 2400hp (1790 kW)

Variants:
several turboprop upgrades are available

Notes: First flew in 1935, production ceased after 10 926 had been built in the USA and over 2000 more in Japan and Russia. More than 200 remain in service with 31 air forces. Some aircraft have Pratt & Whitney Twin Wasp engines. Also known as the Dakota.

Myasishchev VM-T Atlant Russia

Type: special-purpose heavy-lift transport   **Accommodation:** two pilots; two flight engineers; navigator

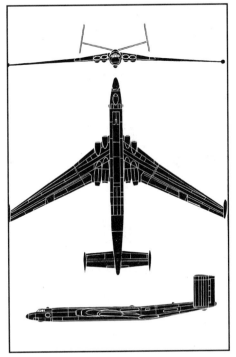

Dimensions:
Length: 167ft 11in (51.2m)
Wingspan: 174ft 5in (53.6m)
Height: 34ft 9in (10.6m)

Weights:
Empty: 166 975lb (75 740kg)
Max T/O: 423 208lb (192 000kg)

Payload: 110 320lb (50 000kg)

Performance:
Max Speed: 310mph
(500km/h)
Range: 810nm (1500km)
Powerplant: four
RKBM/Koliesov VD-7MD

turbojets
Thrust: 94 800lb (421.6kN)

Variants:
none

Notes: Developed from the Bison-C bomber, the two Atlants are used to carry outsize loads such as Energia rocket sections from manufacturing plants to Baikonur cosmodrome.

189

SAC Y-8 China

Type: medium-lift military transport   **Accommodation:** two pilots; flight engineer; navigator; radio operator

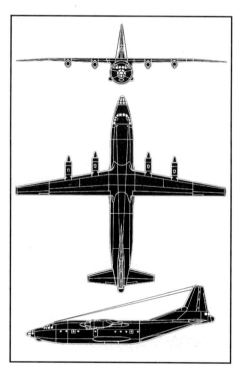

Dimensions:
Length: 111ft 7in (34m)
Wingspan: 124ft 8in (38m)
Height: 36ft 7in (11.2m)

Weights:
Empty: 78 264lb (35 500kg)
Max T/O: 134 480lb (61 000kg)

Payload: 44 090lb (20 000kg)

Performance:
Max Speed: 425mph (685km/h)
Range: 3088nm (5720km); 687nm (1273km) with Max payload
Powerplant: four Zhuzhou

(SMPMC) WJ6 turboprops
Thrust: 17 040ehp (12 708kW)

Variants:
Y-8E drone launch vehicle; Y-8H survey version; Y-8X maritime patrol version

Notes: A Chinese redesign of the Russian An-12 Cub, the Y-8 has also been built for civil operators including a specialised livestock carrier with 500 sheep/goat pens, and an export version with western avionics. The maritime patrol version is under development and may be capable of carrying armament.

Shorts Sherpa C-23A UK

Type: light military transport   **Accommodation:** two pilots; loadmaster

Dimensions:
Length: 58ft (17.7m)
Wingspan: 74ft 10in (22.8m)
Height: 16ft 5in (5m)

Weights:
Empty: 16 040lb (7276kg)
Max T/O: 25 600lb (11 612kg)

Payload: 7280lb (3302kg)

Performance:
Max Speed: 223mph
(359km/h)
Range: 1031nm (1912km);
446nm (827km) with Max
payload

Powerplant: two PT6A-65AR
turboprops
Thrust: 2848shp (2122kW)

Variants:
C-23B US National Guard
version

Notes: The military version of the Shorts 330 airliner, the Sherpa has
strengthened wings and undercarriage, new avionics and more powerful
engines. The US Army operates the C-23B in a utility transport role with full
passenger capacity. The C-23A can be recognised by the lack of passenger
windows, and is used by the US Air Force for transporting high priority cargo
around Europe.

191

XAC Y-7H China

Type: light military transport   **Accommodation:** two pilots; flight engineer; 38 troops; 24 stretchers

Dimensions:
Length: 79ft 9in (24.3m)
Wingspan: 95ft 9in (29.2m)
Height: 29ft 2in (8.9m)

Weights:
Empty: 33 950lb (15 400kg)
Max T/O: 52 910lb (24 000kg)

Payload: 12 125lb (5500kg)

Performance:
Max Speed: 276mph (445km/h)
Range: 1187nm (2200km); 560nm (1038km) with Max payload

Powerplant: two Doingan (DEMC) WJ5A I(M) turboprops
Thrust: 5580shp (4162kW)

Variants:
Y-7H-500 civil cargo version

Notes: A military version of the Y-7 and development of the Russian An-26. Underwing stores can carry up to 4409lb (2000kg) of airdrop containers and could also be used to carry bombs.

TRAINER AIRCRAFT

AIDC T-CH-1 Taiwan

Type: trainer/ground attack aircraft   **Accommodation:** two pilots in tandem

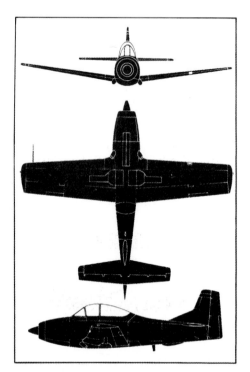

Dimensions:
Length: 33ft 8in (10.3m)
Wingspan: 40ft (12.2m)
Height: 12ft (3.7m)

Weights:
Empty: 5750lb (2608kg)
Max T/O: 11 150lb (5057kg)

Performance:
Max Speed: 368mph
(592km/h)
Range: 1085nm (2010km)
Powerplant: one Lycoming
T53-L-701 turboprop
Thrust: 1450ehp (1081kW)

Armament:
underwing stores points;
machine gun pods; rockets;
bombs

Variants:
A-CH-1 light attack/FAC;
R-CH-1 recce version

Notes: Very similar to the T-28 Trojan, the T-CH-1 was designed and built in Taiwan for training and ground attack duties.

BAe Bulldog UK

Type: primary trainer/ground attack aircraft   **Accommodation:** two pilots side-by-side

Dimensions:
Length: 23ft 3in (7.1m)
Wingspan: 33ft (10.1m)
Height: 7ft 5in (2.3m)

Weights:
Empty: 1430lb (649kg)
Max T/O: 2350lb (1066kg)

Performance:
Max Speed: 150mph (241km/h)
Range: 540nm (1000km)
Powerplant: one Avco Lycoming IO-360-A1B6 piston engine
Thrust: 200hp (149kW)

Armament:
four hardpoints; 640lb (290kg) warload; 7.62mm machine gun pods; grenade launchers; bombs; rockets

Variants:
Beagle Pup civil version

Notes: Designed by Scottish Aviation before it was incorporated into BAe, the Bulldog first flew in 1969 and is in service with six air forces. Armament is optional and not fitted to Royal Air Force aircraft.

Beechcraft T-34 Mentor USA

Type: basic trainer/ground attack aircraft   **Accommodation:** two pilots in tandem

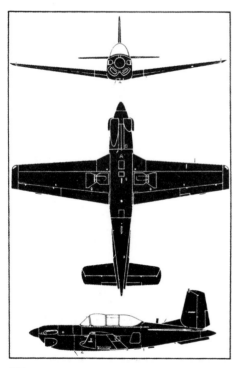

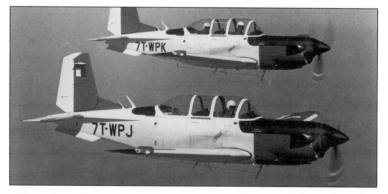

Dimensions:
Length: 28ft 8in (8.7m)
Wingspan: 33ft 3in (10.2m)
Height: 9ft 7in (2.9m)

Weights:
Empty: 2960lb (1342kg)
Max T/O: 4300lb (1950kg)

Performance:
Max Speed: 246mph (396km/h)
Range: 708nm (1311km)
Powerplant: one Pratt & Whitney Canada PT6A-25 turboprop
Thrust: 715shp (533kW)

Armament:
(T-34-C-1) four hardpoints; 600lb (272kg) warload; SUU-11 Minigun pods; AGM-22A guided missiles; bombs; rockets

Variants:
T-34C-1 armed trainer

Notes: Production ended in 1990 and they remain in service with the US Navy and nine other air forces. In US Navy service the T-34 established the lowest accident rate of any aircraft in the fleet.

Daewoo DHI KTX-1 Korea

Type: basic trainer   **Accommodation:** two pilots in tandem

Dimensions:
Length: 33ft 9in (10.3m)
Wingspan: 33ft 2in (10.1m)
Height: 12ft 3in (3.7m)

Weights:
Empty: 3153lb (1430kg)
Max T/O: 5470lb (2481kg)

Performance:
Max Speed: 357mph (574km/h)
Range: 900nm (1668km)
Powerplant: one Pratt & Whitney Canada PT6A-25A turboprop
Thrust: 550shp (410kW)

Armament:
none fitted as standard

Variants:
none

Notes: First flew in December 1991, development continues and it should enter full-scale production in 1997.

de Havilland Canada DHC-1 Chipmunk Canada

Type: primary trainer   **Accommodation:** two pilots in tandem

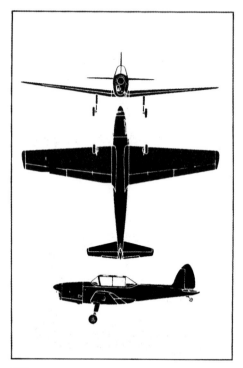

Dimensions:
Length: 25ft 5in (7.7m)
Wingspan: 34ft 4in (10.5m)
Height: 7ft (2.2m)

Weights:
Empty: 1158lb (526kg)
Max T/O: 1930lb (875kg)

Performance:
Max Speed: 139mph
(223km/h)
Range: 780nm (485km)
Powerplant: one DH Gypsy
Major piston engine
Thrust: 145hp (108.1kW)

Armament:
none

Variants:
T 10 RAF/Army Air Corps
designation

Notes: First flew in 1946, the Chipmunk is only now being replaced in Royal Air Force service. Very similar to the HAL HT-2. Retired Chipmunks are finding roles with flying clubs and as a glider tug.

EMBRAER EMB-312 Tucano Brazil

Type: basic trainer and ground attack aircraft **Accommodation:** two pilots in tandem

Dimensions:
Length: 32ft 4in (9.86m)
Wingspan: 36ft 6in (11.14m)
Height: 11ft 1in (3.4m)

Weights:
Empty: 4123lb (1870kg)
Max T/O: 7000lb (3175kg)

Performance:

Max Speed: 278mph (448km/h)
Range: 995nm (1843km)
Powerplant: one Pratt & Whitney Canada PT6A-25C turboprop
Thrust: 750shp (559kW)

Armament:
four hardpoints; 2205lb (1000kg) warload; machine gun pods; bombs; rockets

Variants:
Shorts built S312 for RAF; EMB-312H Super Tucano, stretched re-engined version; EMB-312H ALX attack aircraft

Notes: the Brazilian Government has just signed a contract for the delivery of ALX attack aircraft to operate in inhospitable Amazon basin region.

ENAER T-35DT Turbo Pilan Chile

Type: basic trainer   **Accommodation:** two pilots in tandem

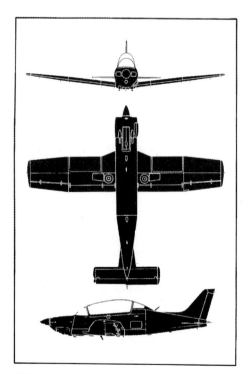

Dimensions:
Length: 28ft 2in (8.6m)
Wingspan: 29ft (8.8m)
Height: 8ft 8in (2.6m)

Weights:
Empty: 2080lb (943kg)
Max T/O: 2950lb (1338kg)

Performance:
Max Speed: 264mph (426km/h)
Range: 410nm (759km)
Powerplant: one Allison 250-B17D turboprop
Thrust: 420shp (313kW)

Armament:
none fitted as standard

Variants:
T-35 Pilan (Devil) earlier piston-engined version

Notes: The T-35DT is a conversion of the earlier T-35 incorporating a turboprop engine. Over 140 T-35s were built before production ceased in 1991.

Fuji T-5 (KM-2Kai) Japan

Type: primary trainer   **Accommodation:** two pilots side-by-side

Dimensions:
Length: 27ft 8in (8.4m)
Wingspan: 32ft 11in (10m)
Height: 9ft 8in (2.9m)

Weights:
Empty: 2385lb (1082km)
Max T/O: 3979lb (1805kg)

Performance:
Max Speed: 222mph (357km/h)
Range: 510nm (945km)
Powerplant: one Allison 250-B17D turboprop
Thrust: 350shp (261kW)

Armament:
none fitted as standard

Variants:
KM-2 earlier piston engined version; T-5U utility version

Notes: Deliveries of the KMKai to the Japanese Self-Defence Forces began in 1988. The original KM-2 is no longer in service.

Fuji KM-2B Japan

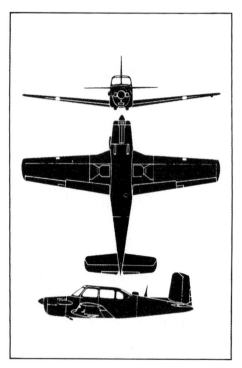

Type: primary trainer **Accommodation:** two pilots in tandem

Dimensions:
Length: 26ft 4in (8m)
Wingspan: 32ft 10in (10m)
Height: 9ft 11in (3m)

Weights:
Empty: 2469lb (1120kg)
Max T/O: 3329lb (1510kg)

Performance:
Max Speed: 234mph (377km/h)
Range: 520nm (965km/h)
Powerplant: one Lycoming IGSO-480-A1A6 piston engine
Thrust: 340hp (254kW)

Armament:
none

Variants:
KM-2BKai turboprop (see separate entry)

Notes: The KM-2B incorporated the cockpit layout of the T-34 with the Powerplant and fuselage of the KM-2, hence its similarity to the Mentor.

HAL HPT-32 Deepak India

Type: primary trainer   **Accommodation:** two pilots side-by-side, one passenger

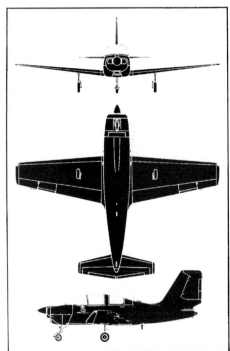

Dimensions:
Length: 25ft 4in (7.7m)
Wingspan: 31ft 2in (9.5m)
Height: 9ft 7in (2.9m)

Weights:
Empty: 2280lb (1034kg)
Max T/O: 2915lb (1322kg)

Performance:
Max Speed: 175mph
(281km/h)
Range: 755nm (1400km)
Powerplant: one Lycoming
AEO-540-D4B5 piston engine
Thrust: 260hp (194kW)

Armament:
four hardpoints; 562lb (255kg)
warload; machine gun pods;
bombs; rockets

Variants:
civilian version
HTT-34 turboprop version

Notes: The Deepak is also used for observation, liaison and target towing.

NAMC PT-6A China

Type: primary trainer   **Accommodation:** two pilots in tandem

Dimensions:
Length: 27ft 9in (8.4m)
Wingspan: 33ft 6in (10.2m)
Height: 10ft 8in (3.3m)

Weights:
Empty: 2414lb (1095kg)
Max T/O: 3086lb (1400kg)

Performance:
Max Speed: 185mph (297km/h)
Range: 372nm (690km)
Powerplant: one Zhuzhou (SMPMC) HS6A radial engine
Thrust: 285hp (213kW)

Armament:
(CJ-6B) weapons stations under wings; bombs; rockets

Variants:
CJ-6B armed version

Notes: First flown in 1960, over 2000 have been built in China. Export versions have been sold to Albania, Bangladesh, Cambodia, North Korea, Tanzania and Zambia.

Neiva N621 Universal Brazil

Type: basic training/ground attack aircraft　　　　**Accommodation:** two pilots side-by-side

Dimensions:
Length: 28ft 9in (8.8m)
Wingspan: 36ft 1in (11m)
Height: 9ft 9in (3m)

Weights:
Empty: 2535lb (1150kg)
Max T/O: 3747lb (1700kg)

Performance:
Max Speed: 199mph
(320km/h)
Range: 277nm (515km)
Powerplant: one Lycoming
IO-720 piston engine
Thrust: 400hp (298kW)

Armament:
two hardpoints; 7.62mm
machine gun pods; bombs;
rockets

Variants:
called T-25 in Brazilian
service; AT-25 armed version

Notes: Designed as a replacement for the T-6 Texan and Fokker S-11/S-12, the Universal was also adopted as a counter-insurgency aircraft. Being replaced by the Tucano in the both the training and attack roles.

Neiva L-42 Regante Brazil

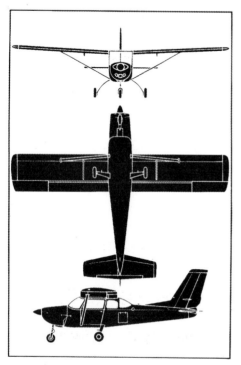

Type: primary trainer   **Accommodation:** two pilots, two passengers, side-by-side in tandem

Dimensions:
Length: 23ft 1in (7m)
Wingspan: 29ft 11in (9.1m)
Height: 9ft 7in (2.9m)

Weights:
Empty: 1410lb (640kg)
Max T/O: 2293lb (1040kg)

Performance:
Max Speed: 137mph (220km/h)
Range: 482nm (896km)
Powerplant: one Lycoming O-30-A1D engine
Thrust: 180hp (134kW)

Armament:
none fitted as standard

Variants:
L-42 observation aircraft

Notes: A civil version was built but never enterd full scale production. The L-42 can be recognised by its stepped down rear cabin windows for better visability for the observer.

PAC Airtrainer CT4 New Zealand

Type: primary trainer   **Accommodation:** two pilots side-by-side

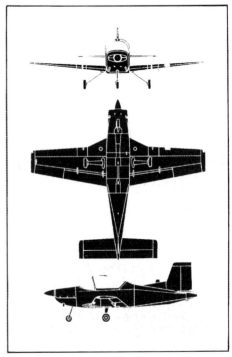

Dimensions:
Length: 23ft 2in (7m)
Wingspan: 26ft (7.9m)
Height: 8ft 6in (2.6m)

Weights:
Empty: 1720lb (780kg)
Max T/O: 2650lb (1202kg)

Performance:
Max Speed: 264mph (426km/h)
Range: 600nm (1112km)
Powerplant: one Teledyne Continental IO-360-HB9 piston engine
Thrust: 210hp (157kW)

Armament:
none

Variants:
CT4C turboprop version; CT4CR development

Notes: A re-design of a re-design, the Airtrainer's lineage is based on the Victa Aircruiser, itself a version of the Victa Airtourer.

Pilatus PC-9 Switzerland

Type: basic trainer   **Accommodation:** two pilots in tandem

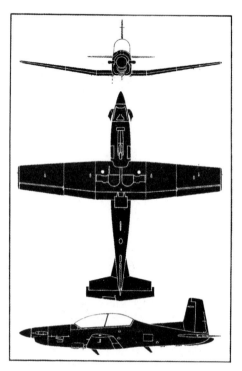

Dimensions:
Length: 33ft 4in (10.2m)
Wingspan: 33ft 2in (10.3m)
Height: 10ft 8in (3.3m)

Weights:
Empty: 3715lb (1685kg)
Max T/O: 7055lb (3200kg)

Performance:
Max Speed: 368mph
(593km/h)
Range: 887nm (1642km/h)
Powerplant: one Pratt &
Whitney Canada PT6A-62
turboprop
Thrust: 1150shp (857kW)

Armament:
none fitted as standard

Variants:
PC-9 MkII JPATS version;
PC-9/A Australian trainer;
PC-9B German target tug

Notes: The PC-9 MkII was the successful candidate in the US Air Force/US
Navy Joint Primary Air Training System competition. Pilatus teamed with
Raytheon/Beech and redesigned 70 per cent of the PC-9 with a pressurised
cockpit, greater range and more powerful engine.

Pilatus PC-7 Turbo Trainer Switzerland

Type: basic trainer   **Accommodation:** two pilots in tandem

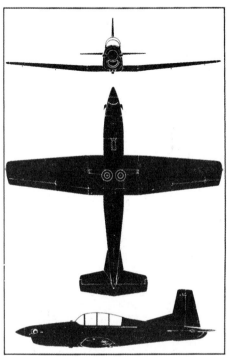

Dimensions:
Length: 33ft 2in (10.1m)
Wingspan: 33ft 2in (10.1m)
Height: 10ft 8in (3.3m)

Weights:
Empty: 3682lb (1670kg)
Max T/O: 5952lb (2700kg)

Performance:
Max Speed: 288mph (463km/h)
Range: 730nm (1352km)
Powerplant: one Pratt & Whitney Canada PT6A-25C turboprop
Thrust: 700shp (522kW)

Armament:
six hardpoints; bombs; rockets

Variants:
PC-7 Mk 2 Astra for South Africa with stepped cockpits

Notes: The Mk 2 was developed for the South African Air Force to replace AT-6G Harvards, and due to UN restrictions was fitted with two hardpoints for drop tanks only.

Raytheon/Beech JPATS PC-9 Mk II Switzerland/USA

Type: basic trainer   **Accommodation:** two pilots in tandem

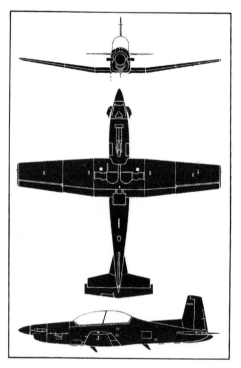

Dimensions:
Length: 33ft 4in (10.2m)
Wingspan: 33ft 2in (10.1m)
Height: 10ft 8in (3.26m)

Weights:
Empty: 3715lb (1685kg)
Max T/O: 7055lb (3200kg)

Performance:
Max Speed: 414mph
(667km/h)
Range: 887nm (1642km)
Powerplant: one Pratt &
Whitney Canada PT6A-68
turboprop
Thrust: 1708shp (1274kW)

Armament:
none fitted

Variants:
none

Notes: Derived from the Pilatus PC-9 the Mk II has all-digital avionics and zero/zero ejection seats, together with a more powerful engine.

RFB Fantrainer Germany

Type: basic trainer   **Accommodation:** two pilots in tandem

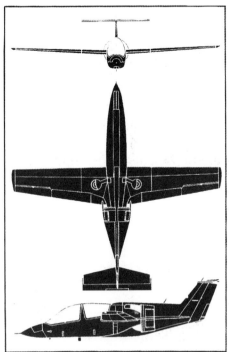

Dimensions:
Length: 30ft 2in (9.2m)
Wingspan: 31ft 11in (9.7m)
Height: 10ft 4in (3.2m)

Weights:
Empty: 2456lb (1114kg)
Max T/O: 3968lb (1800kg)

Performance:
Max Speed: 288mph (463km/h)
Range: 1250nm (2316km)
Powerplant: one ducted Allison 250-C30 turboshaft
Thrust: 650hp (484.5kW)

Armament:
none

Variants:
Fantrainer 400 stretched fuselage, metal wings; Fantrainer 800 upgraded version

Notes: A unique design, the Fantrainer's ducted prop design gives it the appearance of a jet. The Thai Air Force use them as lead-in trainers with student pilots going directly to F-5s. The Fantrainer 800 has an uprated 250-C30 engine rated at 800hp (597kW) with no increase in weight or size.

SIAI-Marchetti SF.260W Warrior Italy

Type: primary trainer/ground attack aircraft   Accommodation: two pilots side-by-side

Dimensions:
Length: 23ft 3in (7.1m)
Wingspan: 27ft 4in (8.3m)
Height: 7ft 11in (2.4m)

Weights:
Empty: 1830lb (830kg)
Max T/O: 2866lb (1300kg)

Performance:
Max Speed: 190mph
(305kmh)
Range: 890nm (1650km)
Powerplant: one Textron
Lycoming O-540-E4A5 piston
engine
Thrust: 260hp (194kW)

Armament:
two or four hardpoints; 661lb
(300kg) warload; 7.62mm gun
pods; bombs; rockets

Variants:
SF.260A, B, C, D civil version

Notes: The Warrior is an armed version of the earlier SF.260 trainer which
was also built for the civil market. SF.260TP turboprop used by Sri Lanka.

Slingsby T-3A Firefly UK

Type: primary trainer   **Accommodation:** two pilots side-by-side

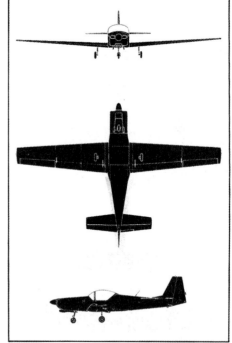

Dimensions:
Length: 24ft 10in (7.6m)
Wingspan: 34ft 9in (10.6m)
Height: 7ft 9in (2.4m)

Weights:
Empty: 1780lb (807kg)
Max T/O: 2525lb (1145kg)

Performance:
Max Speed: 175mph (281km/h)
Range: 408nm (755km)
Powerplant: one Textron Lycoming AEIO-540-D4A5 piston engine
Thrust: 260hp (194kW)

Armament:
none

Variants:
T-67M military trainer with AEIIO-320-D1B engine

Notes: The T-3A was selected as the US Air Force's flight grading trainer, and a total of 113 will be built, mainly by Northrop Grumman.

SOCATA TB30 Epsilon France

Type: primary trainer .   **Accommodation:** two pilots in tandem

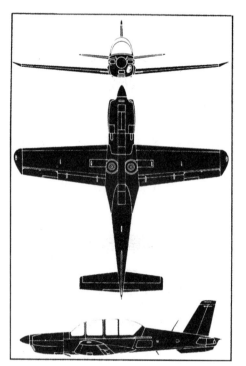

Dimensions:
Length: 24ft 10in (7.6m)
Wingspan: 25ft 11in (7.9m)
Height: 8ft 8in (2.7m)

Weights:
Empty: 2055lb (932kg)
Max T/O: 2755lb (1250kg)

Performance:
Max Speed: 236mph
(530km/h)
Powerplant: one Textron
Lycoming AEIO-540L1B5D
piston engine
Thrust: 330hp (224kW)
Endurance: 3 hours 45 mins

Armament:
four hardpoints; 1056lb
(480kg) warload; machine gun
pods; bomb; rockets

Variants:
Armed sub-variant for Togo`

Notes: Portuguese aircraft were assembled by OGMA. French aircraft are not armed and lack hardpoints. Formed the basis of the TB31 Omega turboprop trainer currently under development.

UTVA-60/-66 Former Yugoslavia

Type: light utility aircraft   **Accommodation:** pilot; three passengers/observers

Dimensions:
Length: 27ft 6in (8.4m)
Wingspan: 37ft 5in (11.4m)
Height: 10ft 6in (3.2m)

Weights:
Empty: 2756lb (1250kg)
Max T/O: 4000lb (1814kg)

Performance:
Max Speed: 143mph (230km/h)
Range: 404nm (750km/h)
Powerplant: one Lycoming GSO-480-B1J6 piston engine
Thrust: 270hp (202kW)

Armament:
none fitted as standard

Variants:
UTVA 66AM air ambulance;
UTVA 66H with floats;
UTVA 66V with provision for underwing armament

Notes: UTVA-66 derived from UTVA-56 of 1959 vintage. UTVA-66 introduced fixed leading-edge slats and larger tail. It is no longer in production, and a number of them fell into Slovenian and Croatian hands during the civil war.

UTVA-75 Former Yugoslavia

Type: primary trainer   **Accommodation:** two pilots, two passengers side-by-side in tandem

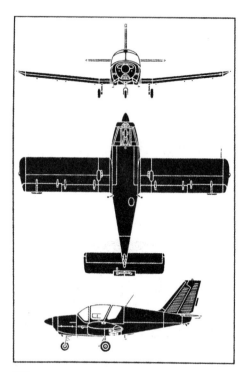

Dimensions:
Length: 23ft 4in (7.1m)
Wingspan: 31ft 11in (9.7m)
Height: 10ft 4in (3.2m)

Weights:
Empty: 1587lb (720kg)
Max T/O: 2513lb (1140kg)

Performance:
Max Speed: 118mph (190km/h)
Range: 755nm (1400km)
Powerplant: one Textron Lycoming IO-360-B1F piston engine
Thrust: 180hp (134kW)

Armament:
two hardpoints; 440lb (200kg) warload; machine gun pods; bombs; rockets

Variants:
glider tug and civil versions

Notes: In service with the Slovenian and Croatian Air Forces as a trainer/light attack aircraft as well as the Yugoslav Air Force.

Valmet L-90TP Redigo Finland

Type: primary trainer/liaison aircraft   **Accommodation:** two pilots side-by-side

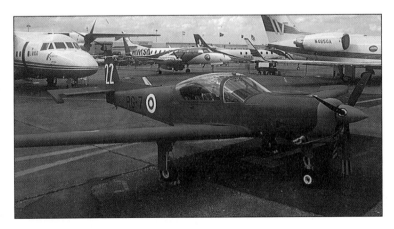

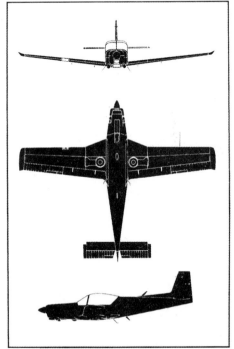

Dimensions:
Length: 27ft 11in (8.5m)
Wingspan: 34ft 9in (10.6m)
Height: 10ft 6in (3.2m)

Weights:
Empty: 2183lb (990kg)
Max T/O: 4189lb (1900kg)

Performance:
Max Speed: 289mph (465 km/h)
Range: 755nm (1400km)
Powerplant: one Allison 250-B17F turboprop
Thrust: 500shp (373kW)

Armament:
none

Variants:
none

Notes: Derived from the L-70 Miltrainer, or Vinka, the Redigo is used by the Finnish Air Force. L-90TP also used by Mexico.

PZL Mielec M-26 01 Iskierka Poland

Type: primary trainer   **Accommodation:** two pilots in tandem

Dimensions:
Length: 27ft 2in (8.3m)
Wingspan: 28ft 2in (8.6m)
Height: 9ft 8in (2.9m)

Weights:
Empty: 2072lb (940kg)
Max T/O: 3086lb (1400kg)

Performance:
Max Speed: 205mph (400km/h)
Range: 874nm (1620km)
Powerplant: one Textron Lycoming AEIO-540-L1B5D piston engine
Thrust: 300hp (224kW)

Armament:
none fitted as standard

Variants:
M-26 01 with PZL-F engine

Notes: The PZL-powered M-26 00 has slightly less power than the Lycoming. There are two avionics options, Polish or Bendix/King.

PZL Warszawa PZL-130TB Turbo Orlik Poland

Type: basic trainer   **Accommodation:** two pilots in tandem

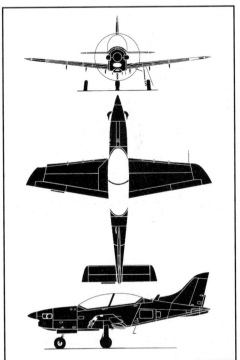

Dimensions:
Length: 29ft 6in (9m)
Wingspan: 29ft 6in (9m)
Height: 11ft 7in (3.5m)

Weights:
Empty: 3527lb (1600kg)
Max T/O: 5952lb (2700kg)

Performance:
Max Speed: 316mph (508km/h)
Range: 1242nm (2300km)
Powerplant: one Motorlet M601E turboprop
Thrust: 750shp (560kW)

Armament:
six hardpoints; 1764lb (800kg) warload; Strela AAMs; 7.62mm gun pods; bombs; rockets

Variants:
130TC/TD/TE export versions

Notes: The export versions come with Bendix/King avionics a Pratt & Whitney engine or with limited `ecomony' equipment. Deliveries to the Polish Air Force began in 1992. The aircraft was demonstrated in Israel and South Africa.

CIVIL
AIRCRAFT

AIRLINERS

Airbus A300 France/Germany/UK/Spain

Type: large-capacity, long-haul airliner   **Accommodation:** two pilots: 330 passengers

Dimensions:
Length: 177 ft 11 in (54.08 m)
Wingspan: 147 ft 1 in (44.84m)
Height: 54 ft 6 in (16.62 m)

Weights:
Empty: 197 686 lb (89 670 kg)
Max T/O: 375 885 lb (170 500 kg)
Payload: 65 500 lb (29 710 kg)

Performance:
Cruising speed: Mach 0.80

Range: 4664 miles (7505 km)
Power plant: two General Electric CF6-80 C2A1 turbo fans
Thrust: 59 000 lb (262.4 kN)

Variants:
A300B2 basic version
A300B4 leading edge flaps
A300-600 increased capacity
A300-600R increased range

Airbus A310 France/Germany/UK/Spain

Type: medium-capacity, long-haul airliner   **Accommodation:** two pilots; 280 passengers

Dimensions:
Length: 153 ft 1 in (46.66m)
Wingspan: 144 ft 0in
(43.89 m)
Height: 51 ft 10 in (15.80 m)

Weights:
Empty: 176 685 lb (80 142 kg)
Max T/O: 313 050 lb

(142 000 kg)
Payload: 72 443 lb
(32 860 kg)

Performance:
Cruising Speed: mach 0.80
Range: 3600 nm (6667 km)
Power plant: two General-
Electric CF6-80C2A2

turbofans
Thrust: 107 000 lb (476 kN)

Variants:
A310-200C convertible
passenger/freighter;
A310-200F pure freighter;
A310-300 extended range

Notes: First flew in 1982, the first extended range version flew in 1985. Wingtip fences were introduced as standard in 1986. The Airbus A310 was the first western-built aircraft to achieve Russian State Aviation Register certification, granted in October 1991. Winglets from 1986.

Airbus A320/A319/A321 France/Germany/UK/Spain

Type: medium-capacity, short-haul airliner   **Accommodation:** two pilots; 179 passengers

Dimensions:
Length: 123 ft 3 in (37.57 m)
Wingspan: 111 ft 3 in (33.91 m)
Height: 38 ft 9 in (11.80 m)

Weights:
Empty: 93 112 lb (41 782 kg)

Max T/O: 162 040lb (73 500kg)
Payload: 42 372 lb (19 220 kg)

Performance:
Cruising speed: 515 mph (903 kmh)
Range: 2650 nm (4970 km)

Power plant: two CFM56-5Al turbofans
Thrust: 50 000 lb (222.4 kN)

Variants:
A319 shortened version
A321-200 extended version

Notes: A320 is the first subsonic commercial aircraft equipped for fly-by-wire (FBW) control throughout the entire normal flight regime, and the first to have sidestick controller (one for each pilot) instead of a control column and aileron wheel. The A319 first flew in September 1995 and already has orders for 51. Launched in 1989, the A321 is a stretched variant of the A320, designed to take more passengers and have a longer range.

Airbus A330 France/Germany/UK/Spain

Type: large-capacity long-haul airliner   **Accommodation:** two pilots; 440 passengers

Dimensions:
Length: 208 ft 10 in (63.65 m)
Wingspan: 197 ft 2 in (60.3 m)
Height: 52 ft 11 in (16.23 m)

Weights:
Empty: 265 175 lb

(120 285 kg)
Max T/O: 467 375 lb (212 000 kg)
Payload: 102 958 lb (46 715 kg)

Performance:

Cruising speed: 547 mph (880

kmh)
Range: 4500 nm (8334 km)
Power plant: two General Electric CF6-80E1A2 turbofans
Thrust: 135 000 lb (600.6 kN)

Variants:
longer range A330-300

Notes: The Airbus A330 was developed simultaneously with the four engined Airbus A340.

Airbus A340 France/Germany/UK/Spain

Type: large-capacity, long-haul airliner   **Accommodation:** two pilots; 335 passengers

Dimensions:
Length: 194 ft 10 in (59.39 m)
Wingspan: 197 ft 10 in (60.3 m)
Height: 54 ft 11 in (16.74 m)

Weights:
Empty: 271 350 lb (123 085 kg)

Max T/O: 566 575 lb (257 000 kg)
Payload: 101 225 lb (45 915 kg)

Performance:
Cruising speed: Mach .82
Range: 7450 nm (13 343 km)

Power plant: four CFM56-5C4 turbofans
Thrust: 124 800 lb (551 kn)

Variants:
A340-200, A340-300, A340 AARGOS

Notes: This variant of the Airbus A330 was launched in 1987, and differs mainly in the number of engines and related systems. Variants include the shorter A340-200, and the larger A340-300. The A340 AARGOS is a dedicated platform for investigating climatic changes.

Aerospatiale/BAe Concorde France/UK

Type: supersonic transport aircraft

Accommodation: two pilots; flight engineer; 128 passengers

Dimensions:
Length: 203 ft 9 in (62.10 m)
Wingspan: 83 ft 10 in (25.56 m)
Height: 37 ft 5 in (11.4 m)

Weights:
Empty: 173 000 lb (78 000 kg)

Max T/O: 408 000 lb (185 065 kg)
Payload: 28 000 lb (12 700 kg)

Performance:
Cruising speed: Mach 2.04
Range: 3550 nm (6580 km)

Power plant: four Rolls-Royce/SNECMA Olympus 593 Mk 610 turbojets
Thrust: 152 200 lb (677 kN)

Variants:
none

Notes: With the exception of the SR-71, Concorde is the only aircraft in the world to fly routinely at Mach 2. First flown in 1969, it remains the only supersonic passenger aircraft in service.

BAe RJ Avroliner (BAe 146) UK

Type: short-haul airliner **Accommodation:** two pilots; 70 passengers

Dimensions:
Length: 93 ft 11 in (26.20 m)
Wingspan: 86 ft (26.21 m)
Height: 28 ft 3 in (8.6 m)

Weights:
Empty: 51 700 lb (23 451 kg)

Max T/O: 25 000 lb (11 340 kg)
Payload: 22 000 lb (10 070 kg)

Performance:
Cruising speed: 447 mph (767 kmh)
Range: 1600 nm (2963 km)

Power plant: four AlliedSignal LF 507 turbofans
Thrust: 28 000 lb (124.56 kN)

Variants:
QT Quiet Trader cargo aircraft; Combi

Notes: Developed from BAe 146, RJ Avroliner features digital avionics and uprated engines. Three fuselage lengths; short fuselage RJ70, medium length RJ85 and long fuselage RJ100, equivalent to BAe 146-100, -200 and -300.

BAC One-Eleven UK

Type: short-haul airliner   **Accommodation:** two pilots; 119 passengers

Dimensions:
Length: 93 ft 6 in (28.5 m)
Wingspan: 93 ft 6 in (28.5 m)
Height: 24 ft 6 in (7.47 m)

Weights:
Empty: 51 731 lb (23 646 kg)

Max T/O: 92 000 lb (41 730 kg)
Payload: 21 269 lb (9 647 kg)

Performance:
Cruising speed: 541 mph (857 kmh)
Range: 1997 nm (3700 km)

Power plant: two Rolls-Royce Spey Mk 512 turbofans
Thrust: 25 100 lb (11 384 kg)

Variants:
series 200, 300, 400, 475, 485, 500 and 525

Notes: Also built under licence in Romania as the Rombac One-Eleven, three complete series 525s and one 485 were delivered as training models for Romanian production. The One-Eleven went through several upgrades during its life but only the 500 was stretched.

Boeing 707 USA

Type: long-haul passenger aircraft   **Accommodation:** two pilots; flight engineer; 219 passengers

Dimensions:
Length: 152 ft 11 in (46.61 m)
Wingspan: 145 ft 9 in (44.42 m)
Height: 42 ft 5 in (12.93 m)

Weights:
Empty: 146 400 lb (66 406 kg)

Max T/O: 333 600 lb (151 315 kg)
Payload: 88 900 lb (40 324 kg)

Performance:
Cruising speed: 627 mph (1010 kmh)
Range: 5000 nm (9265 km)

Power plant: four Pratt & Whitney JT3P turbojets
Thrust: 38 000 lb (17 200 kg)

Variants:
720; cargo; combi; tanker; 320 increased capacity; 420 increased capacity

Notes: One of the most popular commercial passenger aircraft, the 707 has numerous variants, both civil and military. Upgrades are available to re-engine, reduce noise and convert to cargo/combi transport. The original prototype first flew in 1954, and the last commercial delivery was made in 1982, after more than 1000 had been built.

Boeing 727 USA

Type: medium-haul airliner **Accommodation:** two pilots; flight engineer; 189 passengers

Dimensions:
Length: 153 ft 2 in (46.69 m)
Wingspan: 108 ft (32.92 m)
Height: 34 ft (10.36 m)

Weights:
Empty: 100 000 lb (45 360 kg)
Max T/O: 184 000 lb

(83 820 kg)
Payload: 63 102 lb (28 622 kg)

Performance:
Cruising speed: 622 mph (1001 kmh)
Range: 2370 nm (4392 km)
Power plant: Three Pratt &

Whitney JT8D-9A turbofans
Thrust: 43 500 lb (193.5 kN)

Variants:
100, 200 airliners; 100C, 100QC and 200F cargo versions

Notes: First flown in 1963, the last version, a 727-200 was delivered in 1984. Over 1800 aircraft were built in total.

Boeing 737-100/-200 USA

Type: short-haul airliner   **Accommodation:** two pilots; 130 passengers

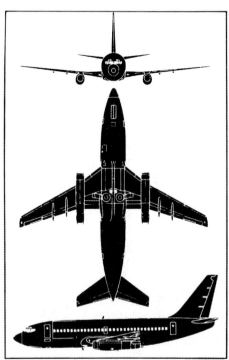

Dimensions:
Length: 96 ft 11 in (29.5 m)
Wingspan: 93 ft (28.3 m)
Height: 37 ft (11.3 m)

Weights:
Empty: 60 507 lb (27 445 kg)
Max T/O: 115 500 lb
(52 390 kg)

Payload: cargo 34 966 lb
(15 860 kg)

Performance:
Cruising speed: 532 mph
(856 kmh)
Range: 2255 nm (4179 km)
Power plant: two Pratt &
Whitney JT8D-15A turbofans

Thrust: 31 000 lb (137.8 kN)

Variants:
-100 original 115-seater;
-200 130-seater available in
corporate, cargo, combi,
Surveiller; T-43A trainers

Notes: Several versions of JT8D engine are available for different range/cargo
configurations. Corporate version fitted out with executive seating and
additional fuel. The T-45A used for navigation training, and three Surveillers
built for Indonesian Air Force recognised by large square dorsal fairing.

Boeing 737-300 -400/-500 USA

Type: short-haul airliner   **Accommodation:** two pilots; 149 passengers

Dimensions:
Length: 109 ft 7 in (33.4 m)
Wingspan: 94 ft 9 in (28.8 m)
Height: 36 ft 6 in (11.1 m)

Weights:
Empty: 70 320 lb (31 895 kg)

Max T/O: 124 500 lb (56 472 kg)
Payload: 20 000 lb (9072 kg)

Performance:
Cruising speed: 565 mph (908 kmh)

Range: 2850 nm (5278 km)
Power plant: two CFM56-3C-1 turbofans
Thrust: 44 000 lb (195.7 kN)

Variants:
stretched 400; shortened 500

Notes: The three developments of the basic 737 incorporate modern engine and avionics technology and are designed for different roles. The 400 carries more passengers, the 500 is designed to replace the 200 series.

Boeing 747 USA

Type: long-haul widebody airliner   **Accommodation:** two pilots; flight engineer; 516 passengers

Dimensions:
Length: 231 ft 10 in (70.7 m)
Wingspan: 195 ft 8 in (59.6 m)
Height: 63 ft 5 in (19.3 m)

Weights:
Empty: 358 100 lb (162 431 kg)
Max T/O: 710 000 lb
(322 050 kg)

Payload: 200C cargo 225 000 lb (102 058 kg)

Performance:
Cruising speed: 610 mph (981 kmh)
Range: 7900 nm (14 630 km)
Power plant: four Pratt & Whitney, General Electric or Rolls Royce turbofans
Thrust: 219 000 lb (974 kN) highest rating

Variants:
747SP short fuselage long range version; heavier 200; extended 300; F freighter; M combi; C convertable

Notes: The original wide-bodied passenger transport, the Jumbo first flew in 1969. A total of 720 were produced before production switched to the 747-400. Engine choice is dependent on model and role. The 300 can be recognized by the extended upper fuselage.

Boeing 747-400 USA

Type: long-haul widebody airliner   **Accommodation:** two pilots; option for two extra pilots; 448

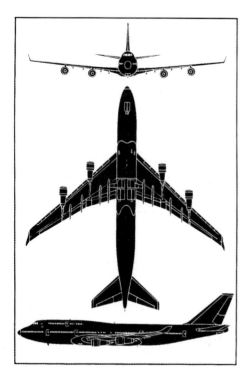

Dimensions:
Length: 231 ft 10 in (70.6 m)
Wingspan: 211 ft 5 in (64.4 m)
Height: 63 ft 8 in (19.4 m)

Weights:
Empty: 399 000 lb
(180 985 kg)

Max T/O: 800 000 lb
(362 875 kg)
Payload: 249 122 b (113 00 kg)

Performance:
Cruising speed: 583 mph (976 kmh)
Range: 7230 nm (13 390 km)

Power plant: four Pratt &
Whitney, General Electric or
Rolls-Royce turbofans
Thrust: 121 200 lb (1080 kN)
max rating
Variants:
400F freighter; Combi; high-
density 400 Domestic

Notes: An advanced version of the 747, the 400s can be recognised by the winglets and extended upper deck. The Domestic is used in Japan for high density routes, it has no winglets and lower engine rating.

Boeing 757 USA

Type: medium-haul airliner   Accommodation: two pilots; 239 passengers

Dimensions:
Length: 155 ft 3 in (47.3 m)
Wingspan: 124 ft 10 in (38 m)
Height: 44 ft 6 in (13.6 m)

Weights:
Empty: 126 060 lb (57 180 kg)
Max T/O: 230 000 lb

(104 325 kg)
Payload: freighter 72 210 lb
(32 754 kg)

Performance:
Cruising speed: Mach 0.86
Range: 4000 nm (7408 km)
Power plant: two Rolls Royce

or Pratt & Whitney turbofans
Thrust: 83 400 lb (371 kN)

Variants:
PF freighter; M combi;
freighter

Notes: The first of Boeings new generation of airliners, the 757 was the first
Boeing to be offered with non-US engines. Boeing has a modified 757 used
as a testbed for the F-22s avionics. The 757PF was designed specifically for
United Parcel Service.

Boeing 767 USA

Type: medium-haul widebody airliner   **Accommodation:** two pilots; optional third flight crew; 242 passengers

Dimensions:
Length: 159 ft 2 in (48.5 m)
Wingspan: 156 ft 1 in (47.6 m)
Height: 52 ft (15.8 m)

Weights:
Empty: 184 500 lb (83 688 kg)
Max T/O: 387 000 lb

(175 540 kg)
Payload: 36 540 lb (16 574 kg)

Performance:
Cruising speed: mach 0.8
Range: 6805 nm (12 603 km)
Power plant: two Pratt &
Whitney, General Electric or

Rolls-Royce turbofans
Thrust: 12 000 lb (539.2 kN)

Variants:
ER extended range; 300
stretched version; freighter;
300ER extended range and
stretched fuselage

Notes: The 767-300 has a 10 ft 1 in (3 m) extension in the fuselage. United Parcel Service has ordered the freighter version for delivery in late 1995. The 767 airframe is being offered as a replacement airframe for the 707/717 military tanker/AWACS/SIGINT platforms.

Boeing 777 USA

Type: long-haul widebody airliner   **Accommodation:** two pilots; 440 passengers

Dimensions:
Length: 209 ft 1 in (63.7 m)
Wingspan: 199 ft 11 in (60.9 m)
Height: 60 ft 9 in (18.5 m)

Weights:
Empty: 304 500 lb (138 120 kg)

Max T/O: 590 000 lb (267 620 kg)
Payload: 120 500 lb (54 660 kg)

Performance:
Cruising speed: mach 0.87
Range: 7380 nm (13 667 km)
Power plant: two Pratt &t Whitney, General Electric or Rolls-Royce turbofans
Thrust: 168 000 lb (747.2 kN)

Variants:
A, market standard version; B, market heavier version

Notes: The latest airliner from Boeing, the 777 is also their first fly-by-wire. The outer 21 ft 3 in (6.5 m) of each wing can be folded upwards to reduce width at airport gates. The launch customer, United Airlines, took delivery of the first 777 in mid-1995.

Fokker 100 The Netherlands

Type: short-haul airliner

Accommodation: two pilots; 79 passengers

Dimensions:
Length: 116 ft 6 in (35.5 m)
Wingspan: 92 ft 1 in (28.1 m)
Height: 27 ft 10 in (8.5 m)

Weights:
Empty: 54 217 lb (24 593 kg)
Max T/O: 95 000 lb (43 090 kg)

Payload: 24 486 lb (11 108 kg)

Performance:
Cruising speed: 532 mph
(856 kmh)
Range: 1290 nm (2389 km)
Power plant: two Rolls Royce
Tay Mk620 turbofans

Thrust: 27 700 lb (123.2 kN)

Variants:
70 shortened version;
Executive Jet 100; 100QC
quick change

Notes: Developed from the Fokker F28, which it superseded in production, the 100 first flew in 1986. The new 70 version was made by simply removing two fuselage plugs. Executive versions of both types can be fitted with long range fuel tanks.

Fokker F28 Fellowship The Netherlands

Type: short-haul airliner   **Accommodation:** two pilots; 65 passengers (1000)

Dimensions:
Length: 97 ft 1 in (29.6 m)
Wingspan: 82 ft 3 in (25.1 m)
Height: 27 ft 9 in (8.5 m)

Weights:
Empty: 38 363 lb (17 546 kg)
Max T/O: 73 000 lb (33 110 kg)
Payload: 23 100 lb (10 478 kg)

Performance:
Cruising speed: 523 mph (843 kmh)
Range: 1710 nm (3169 km)
Power plant: two Rolls Royce RB183-2 Mk555-1P turboprops
Thrust: 19 800 lb (88 kN)

Variants:
1000C cargo; 2000 lengthened; 3000 shortened; 4000 high-density; 5000 short fuselage, long span wing; 6000 longer span wings and longer fuselage

Notes: Fokker's first jet transport, first flown in 1967.

Ilyushin Il-96-300 Russia

Type: long-haul widebody airliner   **Accommodation:** two pilots; flight engineer; 234 passengers

Dimensions:
Length: 181 ft 7 in (55.4 m)
Wingspan: 189 ft 2 in (57.7 m)
Height: 57 ft 7 in (17.6 m)

Weights:
Empty: 257 940 lb (117 000 kg)
Max T/O: 476 200 lb

(216 000 kg)
Payload: 88 185 lb (40 000 kg)

Performance:
Cruising speed: 559 mph (900 kmh)
Range: 5940 nm (11 000 km)
Power plant: four

Aviadvigatel PS-90A turbofans
Thrust: 141 100 lb (627.6 kN)

Variants:
M stretched version;
T freighter

Notes: Very similar in appearance to the Il-86, the 96 can be recognized by its winglets. The Il-96M is the first Russian airliner to be powered by western engines, with four Pratt & Whitney PW2337 turbofans developing 148 000 lb (658.4 kN) of thrust.

Ilyushin Il-86 Camber Russia

Type: medium-haul widebody airliner   **Accommodation:** two pilots; flight engineer; 350 passengers

Dimensions:
Length: 195 ft 8 in (59.4 m)
Wingspan: 157 ft 8 in (48.1 m)
Height: 51 ft 10 in (15.8 m)

Weights:
Empty: n/a
Max T/O: 458 560 lb

(208 000 kg)
Payload: 92 600 lb (42 000 kg)

Performance:
Cruising speed: 590 mph (950 kmh)
Range: 2480 nm (4600 km); 1944 nm (3600 km) with max

payload
Power plant: four KKBM (Kuznetsov) NK-86 turbofans
Thrust: 114 640 lb (510 kN)

Variants:
Maxdome command post (see separate entry)

Notes: First flew in 1976, the Il-86 was only sold to China Northern Airlines and Aeroflot. The 80 Aeroflot aircraft have been divided between its privatised successors.

Ilyushin Il-62M Classic Russia

Type: long-haul airliner   **Accommodation:** two pilots; navigator; radio operator; flight engineer; 178 passengers

Dimensions:
Length: 174 ft 3 in (43.2 m)
Wingspan: 141 ft 9 in (43.2 m)
Height: 40 ft 6 in (12.3 m)

Weights:
Empty: 146 390 lb (66 400 kg)
Max T/O: 357 150 lb

(162 000 kg)
Payload: 50 700 lb (23 000 kg)

Performance:
Cruising speed: 560 mph
(900 kmh)
Range: 4963 nm (9200 km)
Power plant: four Soloviev

D-30KU turbofans
Thrust: 97 000 lb (431.6 kN)

Variants:
Il-62 earlier version; Il-62MK
strengthened version

Notes: First flew in 1963 as Il-62, the 62M was first displayed at the Paris Air Show in 1971, with more powerful engines and increased weight. Very similar to the VC10, but has a longer fuselage.

Ilyushin Il-18V Coot Russia

Type: medium-haul airliner   **Accommodation:** two pilots; navigator; radio operator; flight engineer; 110 passengers

Dimensions:
Length: 117 ft 9 in (35.9 m)
Wingspan: 122 ft 8 in (37.4 m)
Height: 33 ft 4 in (10.2 m)

Weights:
Empty: 77 160 lb (35 000 kg)
Max T/O: 141 100 lb
(64 000 kg)

Payload: 29 750 lb (13 500 kg)

Performance:
Cruising speed: 419 mph
(675 kmh)
Range: 3508 nm (6500 km);
1997 nm (3700 km) with max
payload
Power plant: four Ivchenko

AI-20K turboprops
Thrust: 16 000 ehp
(11 932 kW)

Variants:
Il-18E up-engined version;
Il-18D long-range version

Notes: First flew in 1957 and entered service in 1959. The airframe was used for Il-20/-22 and Il-38 ELINT/reconnaissance, maritime patrol aircraft (see separate entries).

Lockheed L-1011 Tristar USA

Type: long-haul widebody airliner   **Accommodation:** two pilots; flight engineer; 400 passengers

Dimensions:
Length: 177 ft 8 in (54.2 m)
Wingspan: 155 ft 4 in (47.3 m)
Height: 55 ft 4 in (16.8 m)

Weights:
Empty: 249 054 lb
(112 969 kg)

Max T/O: 466 000 lb
(211 375 kg)
Payload: 88 946 lb (40 345 kg)

Performance:
Cruising speed: Mach 0.84
Range: 4533 nm (8400 km)
Power plant: three Rolls-
Royce RB211-22B turbofans
Thrust: 126 000 lb (561 kN)

Variants:
K Mk1 Tanker; 100, 200, 250,
500 extended range versions

Notes: Marshall of Cambridge have converted six Tristars to KC 1/C 2K aerial tankers/transports for the Royal Air Force. They also converted one as a launch vehicle for the Pegasus satellite launcher.

McDonnell Douglas DC-8 Series 20 USA

Type: long-haul airliner

Accommodation: two pilots; flight engineer; 179 passengers

Dimensions:
Length: 150 ft 6 in (45.9 m)
Wingspan: 142 ft 5 in (43.4 m)
Height: 42 ft 4 in (12.9 m)

Weights:
Empty: 127 056 lb (57 632 kg)

Max T/O: 276 00 lb (125 190 kg)
Payload: 34 360 lb (15 585 kg)

Performance:
Max speed: 579 mph (932 kmh)
Range: 4159 nm (7710 km)

Power plant: four Pratt & Whitney JT4A-11 turbojets
Thrust: 70 000 lb (31 780 kN)

Variants:
Series 30 long-range; Series 50 with turbofan engines

Notes: The basic DC-8 first flew in 1955 and has undergone many upgrades and rebuilds since. Series 10 to 50 carried through a programme of re-engining giving a longer range. Series 10 was built for the domestic market and the 40 was powered by Rolls Royce Conway engines.

McDonnell Douglas DC-8 Super 61 USA

Type: long-haul airliner   **Accommodation:** two pilots; flight engineer; 189 passengers

Dimensions:
Length: 187 ft 5 in (57.1 m)
Wingspan: 142 ft 5 in
(43.4 m)
Height: 42 ft 4 in (12.9 m)

Weights:
Empty: 148 897 lb (67 538 kg)
Max T/O: 325 000 lb

(147 415 kg)
Payload: 66 665 lb (30 240 kg)

Performance:
Cruising speed: 600 mph
(965 kmh)
Range: 6209 nm (11 500 km);
3256 nm (6035 km) with max
payload

Power plant: four Pratt &
Whitney JT3D-3B turbofans
Thrust: 76 000 lb (34 472 kg)

Variants:
Super 62 ultra long-range; 63
improved version; freighter

Notes: Super DC-8s shows how designers can stretch an airframe, the longest
version being over 9m longer than the original. The ultra long-range Super 62
has a range of 7381 nm (13 675 km). Series 71, 72 and 73 turbofan-powered

McDonnell Douglas DC-9 USA

Type: short-haul airliner   **Accommodation:** two pilots; 115 passengers

Dimensions:
Length: 119 ft 3 in (36.4 m)
Wingspan: 93 t 5 in (28.5 m)
Height: 27 ft 6 in (8.4 m)

Weights:
Empty: 57 190 lb (25 940 kg)
Max T/O: 121 000 lb

(54 885 kg)
Payload: 31 125 lb (14 118 kg)

Performance:
Cruising speed: 575 mph (926 kmh)
Range: 1670 nm (3095 km)
Power plant: two Pratt &

Whitney JT8D-7 turbofans
Thrust: 28 000 lb (124.6 kN)

Variants:
C-9 military verisons; Series 40 and 50 stretched versions

Notes: The C-9A Nightingale is used by the US Air Force for medical evacuation, the C-9B Skyvan is used by the US Navy for fleet transport duties. A version called VC-9C was ordered for use with the Special Air Missions Wing.

McDonnell Douglas DC-10 USA

Type: long-range widebody airliner   **Accommodation:** two pilots; flight engineer; 380 passengers

Dimensions:
Length: 182 ft 1 in (55.5 m)
Wingspan: 165 ft 4 in (50.4 m)
Height: 58 ft 1 in (17.7 m)

Weights:
Empty: 267 197 lb (121 198 kg)

Max T/O: 580 000 lb (263 085 kg)
Payload: 106 550 lb (48 330 kg)

Performance:
Cruising speed: 610 mph (982 kmh)
Range: 4000 nm (7413 km)

Power plant: three General Electric CF6-50C2B turbofans
Thrust: 162 000 lb (720.6 kN)

Variants:
30ER long-range; 30CF convertible cargo/passenger; 30F freighter; 40 extended range version

Notes: First flew in 1970. The 30CF formed the basis of the KC-10A Extender aerial tanker (see separate entry). The rear cargo bay can house additional fuel tanks.

McDonnell Douglas MD-11 USA

Type: long-haul widebody airliner **Accommodation:** two pilots; 405 passengers

Dimensions:
Length: 200 ft 11 in (61.2 m)
Wingspan: 169 ft 10 in (51.7 m)
Height: 57 ft 9 in (17.6 m)

Weights:
Empty: 288 880 lb (131 035 kg)

Max T/O: 602 500 lb (273 289 kg)
Payload: 112 564 lb (51 058 kg)

Performance:
Cruising speed: 588 mph (945 kmh)
Range: 6787 nm (12 569 km)

Power plant: three Pratt & Whittney PW4460 or General Electric CF6-80C2D1F turbofans
Thrust: P&W 186 000 lb (827.4 kN)

Variants:
11F freighter

Notes: Designed as a follow-on to the DC-10, it can be recognized by its winglets. The MD-11 first flew in 1990, and 108 have been sold to 17 operators by 1995.

McDonnell Douglas MD-80 USA

Type: medium-haul airliner   **Accommodation:** two pilots; 172 passengers

Dimensions:
Length: 147 ft 10 in (45.1 m)
Wingspan: 107 ft 10 in
(32.8 m)
Height: 30 ft 2 in (9.2 m)

Weights:
Empty: 77 888 lb (35 329 kg)
Max T/O: 140 000 lb

(63 503 kg)
Payload: 40 112 lb (18 194 kg)

Performance:
Cruising speed: 575 mph
(925 kmh)
Range: 1564 nm (2897 km)
Power plant: two Pratt &
Whitney JT8D-209 turbofans

Thrust: 37 000 lb (164.6 kN)

Variants:
81 basic version; 82 re-
engined; 83 long-range; 87
short version; 88 advanced
version

Notes: Developed from the DC-9, the MD-80 series is 13.3m longer than the first DC-9s. McDonnell Douglas are working on its successor, the MD-90, which is stretched even further. Executive versions are also available. The MD-81 is also assembled in China.

Tupolev Tu-134 Crusty Russia

Type: short-haul airliner   **Accommodation:** two pilots; navigator; 72 passengers

Dimensions:
Length: 114 ft 10 in (35 m)
Wingspan: 95 ft 1 in (29 m)
Height: 29 ft 7 in (9 m)

Weights:
Empty: 57 100 lb (25 900 kg)
Max T/O: 97 000 lb

(44 000 kg)
Payload: 16 975 lb (7700 kg)

Performance:
Cruising speed: 559 mph
(900 kmh)
Range: 1655 nm (3070 km)
Power plant: Soloviev D-30

turbofans
Thrust: 29 980 lb (13 600 kg)

Variants:
UBL Tu-160 crew trainer; BSh
navigation trainer; Tu-134A
stretched

Notes: Entered service in 1967, initial versions had glazed nose for bombardier. Used in CIS and China. UBL used to train Russian bomber /transport pilots, BSh bomber navigators – both converted from existing airframes.

Tupolev Tu-154 Careless Russia

Type: medium-haul airliner **Accommodation:** two pilots; flight engineer; optional navigator; 167 passengers

Dimensions:
Length: 157 ft 1 in (47.9 m)
Wingspan: 123 ft 2 in (37.5 m)
Height: 37 ft 4 in (11.4 m)

Weights:
Empty: 95 900 lb (43 500 kg)
Max T/O: 198 416 lb

(90 000 kg)
Payload: 44 090 lb (20 000 kg)

Performance:
Cruising speed: Mach 0.9
Range: 2850 nm (5280 km)
Power plant: three Kuznetsov NK-8-2 turbofans

Thrust: 62 850 lb (279.9 kN)

Variants:
154A, 154B developed versions; 154C cargo; 154M reduced size and redesigned tailplane

Notes: First flown in 1968, the Tu-154 was designed to cover the medium stages of Aeroflot's internal routes. To carry out these duties it can operate from low-grade airfields including packed earth and gravel.

Tupolev Tu-204 Russia

Type: medium-haul airliner   **Accommodation:** two pilots; flight engineer; 214 passengers

Dimensions:
Length: 150 ft 11 in (46 m)
Wingspan: 137 ft 9 in (42 m)
Height: 45 ft 7 in (13.9 m)

Weights:
Empty: 128 530 lb (58 300 kg)
Max T/O: 208 550lb (94 600lb)

Payload: 46 269 lb (21 000 kg)

Performance:
Cruising speed: 515 mph
(830 kmh)
Range: 3415 nm (6330 km)
Power plant: two Aviadvigatel
PS-90A turbofans

Thrust: 71 160 lb (3166 kN)

Variants:
100 long-range; C cargo;
120/122 with western
equipment

Notes: The 120 is powered by Rolls-Royce RB211-535 turbofans, the 122 is equipped with Collins avionics. Further versions powered by Rolls-Royce engines and incorporating western avionics are being marketed.

255

Yakovlev Yak-42 Clobber Russia

Type: short-haul airliner   **Accommodation:** two pilots; flight engineer; 120 passengers

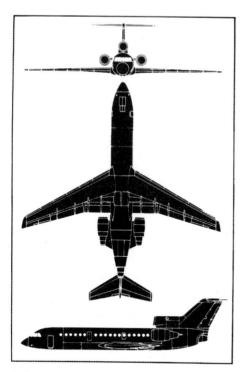

Dimensions:
Length: 119 ft 4 in (36.4 m)
Wingspan: 114 ft 5 in
(34.9 m)
Height: 32 ft 3 in (9.8 m)

Weights:
Empty: 76 092 lb (34 515 kg)

Max T/O: 125 660 lb
(57 000 kg)
Payload: 28 660 lb (13 000 kg)

Performance:
Cruising speed: 503 mph
(810 kmh)
Range: 1080 nm (2000 km)

Power plant: three ZMKB
Progress D-36 turbofans
Thrust: 42 990 lb (191.1 kN)

Variants:
42D long-range; 42T
freighter; 42B with Bendix
avionics

Notes: Designed to replace the Tu-134 Crusty in Aeroflot service, it began
commercial flights in 1980. A Yak-42 is being used for propfan development
testing designated 42E-LL, other versions are used for electro-optical research.

COMMUTER AIRCRAFT

Airtech CN-235 Series 100 Spain/Indonesia

Type: medium-haul commuter   **Accommodation:** two pilots; cabin attendant; 44 passengers

Dimensions:
Length: 70 ft 2 in (21.4 m)
Wingspan: 84 ft 8 in (25.8 m)
Height: 26 ft 10 in (8.2 m)

Weights:
Empty: 21 605 lb (9800 kg)
Max T/O: 33 289 lb

(15 100 kg)
Payload: 8818 lb (4000 kg)

Performance:
Max speed: 276 mph
(445 kmh)
Range: 2110 nm (3908 km);
450 nm (834 km) with

maximum payload
Power plant: two General
Electric CT7-9C turboprops
Thrust: 3500 shp (2610 kW)

Variants:
Series 100 initial version;
Series 200 upgraded version

Notes: Production is carried out equally by CASA in Spain and IPTN in Indonesia. 47 commuters have been delivered, compared to 212 military versions. IPTN is developing its first indigenous aircraft, the N-250-100 based on their experience with the CN-235.

ATR42 France/Italy

Type: medium-haul commuter   **Accommodation:** two pilots; 50 passengers

Dimensions:
Length: 74 ft 7 in (22.7 m)
Wingspan: 80 ft 7 in (24.6 m)
Height: 24 ft 10 in (7.6 m)

Weights:
Empty: 22 685 lb (10 920 kg)

Max T/O: 36 817 lb
(16 700 kg)
Payload: 10 824 lb (4910 kg)

Performance:
Max speed: 310 mph
(498 kmh)

Range: 2420 nm (4482 km)
Power plant: Pratt & Whitney
Canada PW120 turboprops
Thrust: 3600 shp (2684 kW)

Variants:
ATR72 stretched version

Notes: The ATR-72 carries 74 passengers and carries 5000 lb (2268 kg) more payload. A military transport version is also being developed along with a further-stretched ATR-82

BAe Jetstream 41 UK

Type: regional commuter   **Accommodation:** two pilots; cabin attendant; 29 passengers

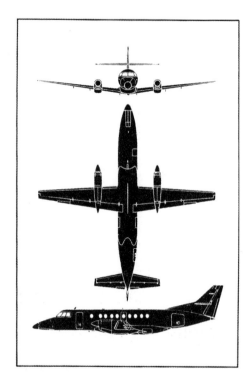

Dimensions:
Length: 63 ft 2 in (19.2 m)
Wingspan: 60 ft (18.3 m)
Height: 18 ft 10 in (5.7 m)

Weights:
Empty: 14 144 lb (6416 kg)

Max T/O: 24 000 lb (10 886 kg)
Payload: 8000 lb (3628 kg)

Performance:
Max speed: 340 mph
(547 kmh)
Range: 774 nm (1433 km)

Power plant: two Garrett
TPE331-14GR/HR turboprops
Thrust: 3210 shp (2460 kW)

Variants:
Combi, passenger/cargo;
Corporate for VIP transport

Notes: Partly built in Switzerland and the USA as well as the UK.

BAe ATP UK

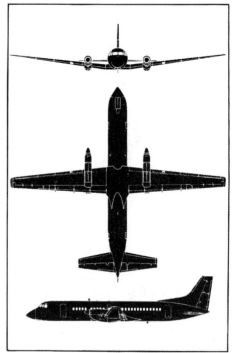

Type: medium-haul commuter   **Accommodation:** two pilots; two cabin attendants; 68 passengers

Dimensions:
Length: 85 ft 4 in (26 m)
Wingspan: 100 ft 6 in (30.6 m)
Height: 24 ft 11 in (7.6 m)

Weights:
Empty: 31 400 lb (14 242 kg)
Max T/O: 52 200 lb (23 678 kg)

Payload: 15 800 lb (7167 kg)

Performance:
Max speed: 312 mph (502 kmh)
Range: 2320 nm (4296 km); 939 nm (1739 km) with max payload
Power plant: two Pratt &

Whitney Canada PW127D turboprops
Thrust: 5500 shp (4102 kW)

Variants:
Jetstream 51 and 61 up-engined versions

Notes: Designed as a successor to the 748 the standard ATP has finished production. Developments are mainly centered on upgrading the engines to PW127Ds.

261

BAe 748 UK

Type: medium-haul commuter   **Accommodation:** two pilots; cabin attendant; 58 passengers

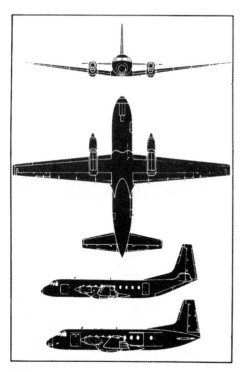

Dimensions:
Length: 67 ft (20.4 m)
Wingspan: 102 ft 5 in (31.2 m)
Height: 24 ft 10 in (7.6 m)

Weights:
Empty: 27 176 lb (12 327 kg)

Max T/O: 46 500 lb (21 092 kg)
Payload: 11 323 lb (5136 kg)

Performance:
Max speed: 281 mph (452 kmh)
Range: 1560 nm (2892 km); 926 nm (1715 km) with max payload

Power plant: two Rolls-Royce Dart RDa.7 Mk552-2 turboprops
Thrust: 4560 ehp (3400 kW)

Variants:
Andover, military version

Notes: Some assembled in India, going to Indian Air Force. Military versions can carry 24 stretchers, has rear-loading ramp and kneeling undercarriage

Beechcraft 1900D USA

Type: regional commuter   **Accommodation:** one or two pilots; 19 passengers

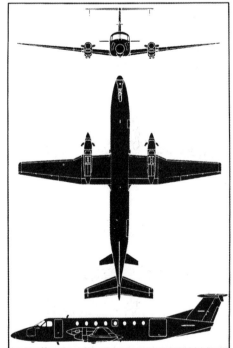

Dimensions:
Length: 57 ft 10 in (17.6 m)
Wingspan: 57 ft 11 in (17.7 m)
Height: 15 ft 6 in (4.7 m)

Weights:
Empty: 10 550 lb (4785 kg)

Max T/O: 16 950 lb (7688 kg)
Payload: 2000 lb (907 kg)

Performance:
Max speed: 331 mph
(533 kmh)
Range: 1500 nm (2778 km)

Power plant: two Pratt &
Whitney Canada PT6A-67D
turboprops
Thrust: 2558 shp (1908 kW)

Variants:
1900C earlier version

Notes: The 1900C is identical from the outside, but has less room inside the passenger compartment, and less powerful engines. The Egyption Air Force operate eight for maritime patrol and Elint work.

263

Beechcraft B99 Airliner USA

Type: short-haul commuter   **Accommodation:** two pilots; 15 passengers

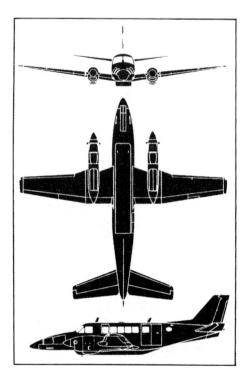

Dimensions:
Length: 44 ft 6 in (13.6 m)
Wingspan: 45 ft 10 in (14 m)
Height: 14 ft 4 in (4.4 m)

Weights:
Empty: 5777 lb (2620 kg)
Max T/O: 10 900 b (4844 kg)

Payload: n\a

Performance:
Max speed: 285 mph (459 kmh)
Range: 1019 nm (1887 km); 723 nm (1339 km) at max power

Power plant: two Pratt & Whitney Canada PT6A-28 turboprops
Thrust: 1360 ehp (1014 kW)

Variants:
B99 executive

Notes: Designed for the air taxi and feeder liner markets, the B99 first flew in 1966. The B99 executive is identical except for the internal cabin layout.

Canadair Challenger Canada

Type: regional airliner   **Accommodation:** two pilots; cabin attendant; 19 passengers

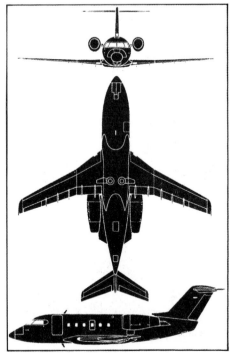

Dimensions:
Length: 68 ft 5 in (20.8 m)
Wingspan: 64 ft 4 in (19.6 m)
Height: 20 ft 8 in (6.3 m)

Weights:
Empty: 20 735 lb (9405 kg)
Max T/O: 45 100 lb (20 457 kg)

Payload: 5240 lb (2377 kg)

Performance:
Max speed: 548 mph (882 kmh)
Range: 3585 nm (6639 km) max
Power plant: two General Electric CF34-3A1 turbofans
Thrust: 18 440 lb (82 kN)

Variants:
CC-144 military version; Challenger 604 re-engined version

Notes: First flown in 1978, 288 aircraft have been built. Later versions of the Challenger had a 'glass' cockpit (601-3A) and extended range (601–3R).

Canadair Regional Jet Canada

Type: regional airliner   **Accommodation:** two pilots; two cabin attendants; 50 passengers

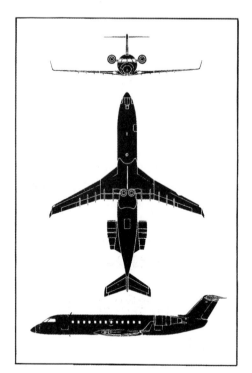

Dimensions:
Length: 87 ft 10 in (26.77 m)
Wingspan: 69 ft 7 in (21.2 m)
Height: 20 ft 5 in (6.2 m)

Weights:
Empty: 29 180 lb (13 236 kg)

Max T/O: 47 450 lb (21 523 kg)
Payload: 8220 lb (3728 kg)

Performance:
Max speed: 286 mph
(621 kmh)
Range: 980 nm (1815 km);

1620 nm (3000 km) 100ER
Power plant: two General
Electric CF34-3A1 turbofans
Thrust: 18 440 lb (82 kN)

Variants:
100ER extended range

Notes: Evolved from the earlier Challenger, the Regional Jet was tailored to carry more passengers over shorter ranges.

Convair 340 Liner USA

Type: regional airliner   **Accommodation:** two pilots; two cabin attendants; 44 passengers

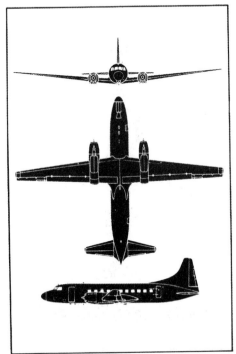

Dimensions:
Length: 79 ft 2 in (24.1 m)
Wingspan: 105 ft 4 in (32.1 m)
Height: 28 ft 2 in (8.6 m)

Weights:
Empty: 29 486 lb (13 382 kg)

Max T/O: 47 000 b (21 338 kg)
Payload: n\a

Performance:
Max speed: 284 mph
(448 kmh)
Range: 1740 nm (3225 km)

Power plant: two Pratt & Whitney R-2800-CB-16 radial engines
Thrust: 3600 hp (5180 kW)

Variants:
600 turboprop upgrade

Notes: The 340 Liner was a larger version of the earlier 240, and first flew 1951. Two Rolls-Royce Dart RDa.10 turboprops with 5500 lb (4102 kW) of thrust are fitted to the turboprop upgrade, it increases the max T/O weight and increases the range.

Convair CV-440 Metropolitan USA

Type: regional airliner   **Accommodation:** two pilots; two cabin attendants; 52 passengers

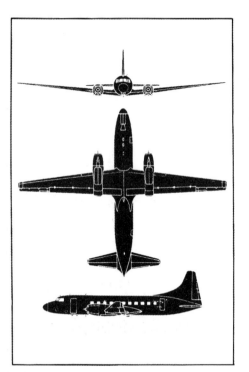

Dimensions:
Length: 79 ft 2 in (24.2 m)
Wingspan: 105 ft 4 in (32 m)
Height: 28 ft 2 in (8.6 m)

Weights:
Empty: 31 305 lb (14 199 kg)

Max T/O: 48 000 lb (21 772 kg)
Payload: n\a

Performance:
Max speed: 310 mph
(499 kmh)
Range: 904 nm (1674 km)

Power plant: two Pratt &
Whitney R-2800-CB-16 radial
engines
Thrust: 4800 hp (3418 kW)

Variants:
CV-640 turboprop upgrade

Notes: The Metropolitan was developed from the earlier 340 Liner incorporating sound proofing for the passenger cabin and higher speed. The 640 has two Rolls-Royce Dart RDa.10 turboprops with 5500 lb (4102 kW) of thrust slightly increasing max T/O weight and increasing range.

de Havilland Canada DHC Dash 8 Canada

Type: medium-haul commuter   **Accommodation:** two pilots; cabin attendant; 37 passengers

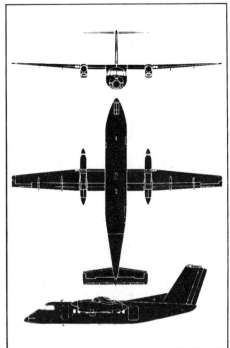

Dimensions:
Length: 73 ft (22.3 m)
Wingspan: 85 ft (25.9 m)
Height: 24 ft 7 in (7.5 m)

Weights:
Empty: 22 886 lb (10 380 kg)

Max T/O: 36 300 lb (16 465 kg)
Payload: 9144 lb (4134 kg)

Performance:
Max speed: 345 mph (556 kmh)
Range: 820 nm (1518 km)

Power plant: two Pratt & Whitney Canada PW120A turboprops
Thrust: 4000 shp (2984 kW)

Variants:
series 300 stretched version

Notes: The series 300 was 11 ft 3 in (3.4 m) longer and could seat 56 passengers. The US Air Force use two modified Dash 8s for missile range control. They have large flat radar panels along the fuselage. Canada uses CC-142 transports and radar-nosed CT-142 navigation trainers.

de Havilland DHC Dash 7 Canada

Type: medium-haul STOL commuter   **Accommodation:** two pilots; two cabin attendants; 50 passengers

Dimensions:
Length: 80 ft 7 in (24.6 m)
Wingspan: 93 ft (28.3 m)
Height: 26 ft 2 in (8 m)

Weights:
Empty: 27 000 lb (12 247 kg)
Max T/O: 44 000 lb (19 958 kg)
Payload: 11 310 lb (5130 kg)

Performance:
Max speed: 266 mph
(428 kmh)
Range: 1170 nm (2168 km);
690 nm (1279 km) with max
payload
Power plant: four Pratt &
Whitney Canada PT6A-50
tuboprops

Thrust: 4880 shp (3340 kW)

Variants:
Series 101 cargo; Series 150
and 151 heavier versions; Dash
7IR ice reconnaissance aircraft
'Grizzly Hunter' classified
drugs interdiction aircraft (US
Army)

Notes: The Dash 7IR can be recognized by its extra dorsal cockpit just behind the flight deck. It is used for patrolling the Labrador coast, checking ice flows and the position of icebergs for the Department of the Environment.

Dornier Do 228 Germany

Type: short-haul commuter   **Accommodation:** one or two pilots; 20 passengers

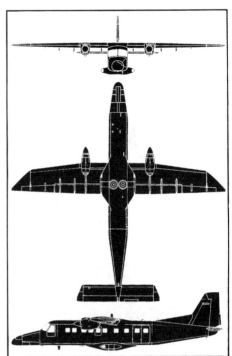

Dimensions:
Length: 49 ft 4 in (15 m)
Wingspan: 55 ft 8 in (17 m)
Height: 15 ft 11 in (4.8 m)

Weights:
Empty: 6507 lb (2980 kg)

Max T/O: 12 566 lb (5700 kg)
Payload: 4689 lb (2127 kg)

Performance:
Max speed: 256 mph
(413 kmh)
Range: 724 nm (1343 km)

Power plant: two Garrett
TPE331-5-252D turboprops
Thrust: 1430 shp (1066 kW)

Variants:
228-200 stretched version;
228-203F freighter

Notes: Military versions are described separately. The Do 228 is also built under licence in India. 228-200s are 5 ft (1.5 m) longer and other models have strengthened floors to take cargo.

Dornier Do 328 Germany

Type: high-speed regional transport

Accommodation: two pilots; two cabin attendants; 33 passengers

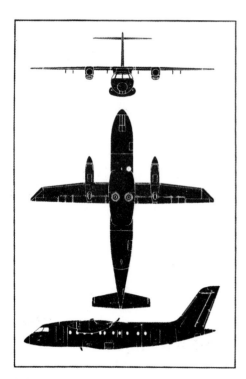

Dimensions:
Length: 69 ft 9 in (21.3 m)
Wingspan: 68 ft 10 in (21 m)
Height: 23 ft 9 in (7.3 m)

Weights:
Empty: 19 422 lb (8810 kg)
Max T/O: 30 071 lb (13 640 kg)

Payload: 7605 lb (3450 kg)

Performance:
Max speed: 388 mph (620 kmh)
Range: 840 nm (1556 km)
Power plant: two Pratt & Whitney Canada PW119B turboprops
Thrust: 4360 shp (3250 kW)

Variants:
328 with improved performance kit

Notes: The improved performance kit aids short field performance, with extra spoilers, drooped ailerons, modified wingtips and larger propellers.

EMBRAER EMB-120 Brasilia Brazil

Type: short-haul commuter   **Accommodation:** two pilots; cabin attendant; 30 passengers

Dimensions:
Length: 65 ft 7 in (20 m)
Wingspan: 64 ft 10 in (19.8 m)
Height: 20 ft 10 in (6.4 m)

Weights:
Empty: 15 741 lb (7140 kg)
Max T/O: 25 353 lb (11 500 kg)

Payload: 6504 lb (2950 kg)

Performance:
Max speed: 313 mph (504 kmh)
Range: 1720 nm (3185 km)
Power plant: two Pratt & Whitney Canada PW118 or

118A turboprops
Thrust: 3600 shp (2684 kW)

Variants:
120 Cargo; 120 Combi; 120QC (quick change); 120-ER advanced version; VC-97 VIP transport

Notes: Cargo versions can carry a payload of 7500 lb (3402 kg). Two retrofits are available, the 120ER advanced Brasilia with increased range and payload, and reduced take-off version (120RT) powered by PW118 engines. The basic 120 has been replaced in production by the 120ER.

EMBRAER EMB-145 Brazil

Type: regional airliner   **Accommodation:** two pilots; flight observer; cabin attendant; 50 passengers

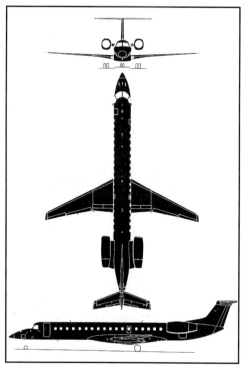

Dimensions:
Length: 98 ft (29.9 m)
Wingspan: 65 ft 9 in (20 m)
Height: 22 ft (6.7 m)

Weights:
Empty: 25 540 lb (11 585 kg)

Max T/O: 43 329 lb (10 200 kg)
Payload: 12 158 lb (5515 kg)

Performance:
Max speed: 472 mph (760 kmh)
Range: 1390 nm (2574 km)

Power plant: two Allison AE 3307A turbofans
Thrust: 14 080 lb (62.64 kN)

Variants:
145ER extended range

Notes: The first EMB-145 was rolled out in August 1995. Some 14 airlines have signed letters of intent to buy 136 aircraft already.

Fairchild Metro USA

Type: short-haul commuter   **Accommodation:** two pilots, 20 passengers

Dimensions:
Length: 59 ft 4 in (18 m)
Wingspan: 57 ft (17.4 m)
Height: 16 ft 8 in (5 m)

Weights:
Empty: 9500 lb (4309 kg)
Max T/O: 16 500 lb (7484 kg)

Payload: 5000 lb (2268 kg)

Performance:
Max speed: 283 mph
(455 kmh)
Range: 1115 nm (2065 km);
533 nm (988 km) with max
payload

Power plant: two Garrett
TPE331-11U-61G turboprops
Thrust: 2000 shp (1492 kW)

Variants:
Expediter cargo version;
Merlin business aircraft

Notes: A special mission version (the MMSA) is being developed to carry AEW, surveillance, ELINT or photo reconnaissance equipment. Called C-26A in US Air Force service, and Tp88 in Swedish service.

Fokker F27 Friendship The Netherlands

Type: regional airliner   **Accommodation:** two pilots; cabin attendant; 60 passengers

Dimensions:
Length: 77 ft 3 in (23.6 m)
Wingspan: 95 ft 1 in (29 m)
Height: 28 ft 2 in (8.6 m)

Weights:
Empty: 24 720 lb (11 213 kg)
Max T/O: 45 900 lb (20 820 kg)

Payload: 13 000 lb (5896 kg)

Performance:
Max speed: 298 mph
(480 kmh)
Range: 935 nm (1741 km)
Power plant: two Rolls-Royce
Dart Mk552 turboprops

Thrust: 4420 shp (3296 kW)

Variants:
Mk440M military version;
Mk500 stretched version;
Mk600 cargo aircraft

Notes: The Fokker F27 first flew in 1955, and ceased production in 1986. A total of 786 were sold to 168 operators in 63 countries.

Fokker 50 The Netherlands

Type: regional airliner   **Accommodation:** two pilots; two cabin attendants; 58 passengers

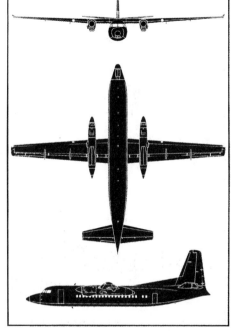

Dimensions:
Length: 82 ft 10 in (25.3 m)
Wingspan: 95 ft 1 in (29 m)
Height: 27 ft 3 in (8.3 m)

Weights:
Empty: 25 916 lb (11 754 kg)
Max T/O: 43 980 lb (19 950 kg)

Payload: 15 093 lb (6846 kg)

Performance:
Max speed: 325 mph
(522 kmh)
Range: 1216 nm (2252 km)
Power plant: two Pratt &
Whitney Canada PW125B

turboprops
Thrust: 5000 shp (3728 kW)

Variants:
50 Utility general purpose
aircraft

Notes: Based on the successful F27 design, an upgraded version is equipped
with PW127B turboprops giving better performance from short runways and
in high temperatures.

Ilyushin Il-114 Russia

Type: regional airliner   **Accommodation:** two pilots; two cabin attendants; 75 passengers

Dimensions:
Length: 88 ft 2 in (26.9 m)
Wingspan: 98 ft 5 in (30 m)
Height: 30 ft 7 in (9.3 m)

Weights:
Empty: 33 070 lb (15 000 kg)
Max T/O: 50 045 lb (22 700 kg)

Payload: 14 330 lb (6500 kg)

Performance:
Max speed: 310 mph (500 kmh)
Range: 2490 nm (4800 km); 540 nm (1000 km) with max payload

Power plant: two Klimov TV7-117 turboprops
Thrust: 4932 shp (3678 kW)

Variants:
re-engined Il-114M

Notes: Designed to replace the An-24, the Il-114 first flew in 1990. Full-scale production has begun, and deliveries began in 1993.

Let L-410 Turbolet Czech Republic

Type: regional airliner   **Accommodation:** two pilots; 19 passengers

Dimensions:
Length: 47 ft 4 in (14.4 m)
Wingspan: 65 ft 6 in (19.9 m)
Height: 19 ft 1 in (5.8 m)

Weights:
Empty: 8785 lb (3985 kg)

Max T/O: 14 110 lb (6400 kg)
Payload: 3560 lb (1615 kg)

Performance:
Max speed: 193 mph (311 kmh)
Range: 744 nm (1380 km)

Power plant: two Motorlet Walter M601 E turboprops
Thrust: 1500 shp (1118 kW)

Variants:
410MU Aeroflot version; 420 advanced version

Notes: Designed in the former Czechoslovakia for Aeroflot's short range routes, the 410 first flew in 1969. The 420 features upgraded engines and western avionics.

279

Let L-610 Czech Republic

Type: regional airliner   **Accommodation:** two pilots; cabin attendant; 40 passengers

Dimensions:
Length: 71 ft 3 in (21.7 m)
Wingspan: 84 ft (25.6 m)
Height: 26 ft 10 in (8.2 m)

Weights:
Empty: 20 326 lb (9220 kg)
Max T/O: 31 967 lb (14 500 kg)

Payload: 9259 lb (4200 kg)

Performance:
Max speed: 272 mph
(437 kmh)
Range: 1280 nm (2370 km);
302 nm (560 km) with max
payload

Power plant: two General
Electric CT7-9D truboprops
Thrust: 3410 shp (2610 kW)

Variants:
610M with Czech engines

Notes: First flown in 1988, 28 have been ordered but none yet delivered. It was originally designed as a replacement for Aeroflot short haul transports, however hard currency problems in Russia are forcing Let to look elsewhere for export orders.

Nippi YS-11A Japan

Type: regional airliner   **Accommodation:** two pilots; two cabin attendants; 60 passengers

Dimensions:
Length: 86 ft 3 in (26.3 m)
Wingspan: 104 ft 11 in (32 m)
Height: 29 ft 5 in (8.9 m)

Weights:
Empty: 33 840 lb (15 350 kg)
Max T/O: 54 010 lb (24 500 kg)

Payload: 16 330 lb (7410 kg)

Performance:
Max speed: 291mph
(469 kmh)
Range: 1137 nm (2110 km);
587nm (1090 km) with max
payload

Power plant: two Rolls-Royce
Dart RDa.10 turboprops
Thrust: 6120 ehp (4563kW)

Variants:
Series 400 freighter; YS-11NT,
YS-11C navigation trainers

Notes: The single YS-11EA is powered by two GE T64-IHI-10J turboprops and was fitted out with the NEX J/ALQ-7 ECM system. It was delivered to the JASDF in December 1991.

Saab 340B Sweden

Type: short-haul commuter　　　**Accommodation:** two pilots; cabin attendant; 37 passengers

Dimensions:
Length: 64 ft 8 in (19.7 m)
Wingspan: 70 ft 4 in (21.4 m)
Height: 22 ft 10 in (6.9 m)

Weights:
Empty: 17 945 lb (8140 kg)
Max T/O: 29 000 lb (13 155 kg)

Payload: 8554 lb (3880 kg)

Performance:
Max speed: 288 mph
(463 kmh)
Range: 935 nm (1732 km)
Power plant: two General
Electric CT7-9B turboprops

Thrust: 3500 shp (2610 kW)

Variants:
340A earlier version;
340AEW&C (see separate
entry)

Notes: The 340B was introduced in 1994 to improve the aircraft's payload/range performance. It featured different engines and increased tailplane span. Over 356 aircraft of all versions have been built, and are in service with 21 airlines.

Saab 2000 Sweden

Type: regional airliner   **Accommodation:** two pilots; one or two cabin attendants; 50 passengers

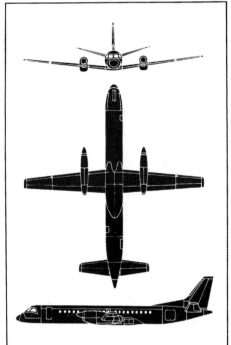

Dimensions:
Length: 88 ft 8 in (27 m)
Wingspan: 81 ft 2 in (24.8 m)
Height: 25 ft 4 in (7.7 m)

Weights:
Empty: 29 762 lb (13 500 kg)

Max T/O: 48 500 lb (22000 kg)
Payload: 13 007 lb (5900 kg)

Performance:
Max speed: 421 mph (678 kmh)
Range: 1425 nm (2639 km)

Power plant: two Allison AE 2100A turboprops
Thrust: 8250 shp (6152 kW)

Variants:
none

Notes: Developed to offer jet speeds with turboprop economy, the first aircraft was delivered to Crossair in August 1994. Major subcontractors include Westland (rear fuselage) and Valmet (tail unit).

Shorts 330 UK

Type: light-haul commuter   **Accommodation:** two pilots; cabin attendant; 30 passengers

Dimensions:
Length: 58 ft (17.7 m)
Wingspan: 74 ft 10 in (22.8 m)
Height: 16 ft 5 in (5 m)

Weights:
Empty: 16 040 lb (7276 kg)
Max T/O: 25 600 lb (11 612 kg)

Payload: 7280 lb (3302 kg)

Performance:
Max Speed: 223 mph (359 kmh)
Range: 1031 nm (1912 km);
446 nm (827 km) with max
payload
Power plant: two Pratt &
Whitney Canada PT6A-45AR
turboprops
Thrust: 2396 shp (1786 kW)

Variants:
C-23A/B US military versions;
330-UTT utility transport;
Sherpa cargo aircraft

Notes: The Sherpa has strengthened wings and undercarriage, new avionics and more powerful engines and can be recognized by the lack of passenger windows. The US Army operates the C-23B, a standard 330 for utility transport; the C-23A, a modified Sherpa, is used by the US Air Force for transporting high priority cargo around Europe.

Shorts 360 Sherpa UK

Type: short-haul commuter   **Accommodation:** two pilots; cabin attendant; 36 passengers

Dimensions:
Length: 70 ft 9 in (21.6 m)
Wingspan: 74 ft 9 in (22.8 m)
Height: 23 ft 10 in (7.3 m)

Weights:
Empty: 17 350 lb (7870 kg)
Max T/O: 27 100 lb
(12 292 kg)

Payload: 8300 lb (3765 kg)

Performance:
Max speed: 249 mph (400 kmh)
Range: 636 nm (1178 km); 402 nm (745 km) with max payload
Power plant: two Pratt &

Whitney Canada PT6A-67R turboprops
Thrust: 2848 shp (2124 kW)

Variants:
360-300F cargo aircraft; 360-300 upgraded version

Notes: More than a stretched version of the 330, the 360 has a redesigned tail unit and more powerful and fuel efficent engines.

Yakovlev Yak-40 Codling Russia

Type: short-haul commuter **Accommodation:** two pilots; cabin attendant; 32 passengers

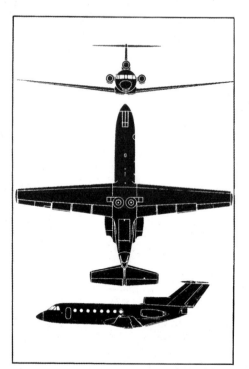

Dimensions:
Length: 66 ft 9 in (20.4 m)
Wingspan: 82 ft (25 m)
Height: 55 ft 9 in (17 m)

Weights:
Empty: 21 715 lb (9850 kg)

Max T/O: 33 070 lb (15 000 kg)
Payload: 3000 lb (1360 kg)

Performance:
Max speed: 373 mph
(600 kmh)
Range: 1080 nm (2000 km)

Power plant: three Ivchenko
AI-25 turbofans
Thrust: 9900 lb (44.1 kN)

Variants:
none

Notes: First flown in 1966, the Yak-40 was the most popular transport in the former Soviet Union. More than 800 aircraft were built, most going to Aeroflot.

EXECUTIVE AIRCRAFT

Aerospatiale SN-601 Corvette France

Type: short-range executive transport   **Accommodation:** one or two pilots; max 14 passengers

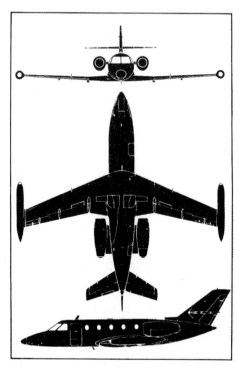

Dimensions:
Length: 45 ft 4 in (13.8 m)
Wingspan: 42 ft 2 in (12.8 m)
Height: 13 ft 10 in (4.2 m)

Weights:
Empty: 7738 lb (3510 kg)
Max T/O: 14 550 lb (6600 kg)

Payload: 2205 lb (1000 kg)

Performance:
Max speed: 472 mph
(760 kmh)
Range: 1380 nm (2555 km);
840 nm (1555 km) with max
payload

Power plant: two Pratt &
Whitney Canada JT15D-4
turbofan
Thrust: 5000 lb (22.2 kN)

Variants:
none

Notes: Very similar to the Hawker 125, its main recognition features are its wing-tip tanks, although they can be removed. Not built in large numbers, the Corvette first flew in 1970.

BAe Jetstream 31 UK

Type: short-range executive transport   **Accommodation:** two pilots; eight to 10 passengers

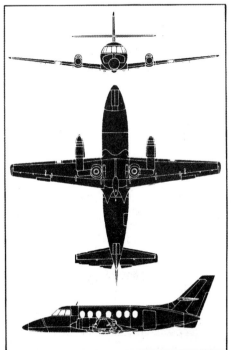

Dimensions:
Length: 47 ft 1 in (14.4 m)
Wingspan: 52 ft (15.8 m)
Height: 17 ft 8 in (5.4 m)

Weights:
Empty: 10 092 lb (4578 kg)

Max T/O: 16 204 lb (7350 kg)
Payload: 3980 lb (1805 kg)

Performance:
Max speed: 304 mph
(489 kmh)
Range: 643 nm (1111 km)

Power plant: two Garrett
TPE331-12UAR turboprops
Thrust: 2040 shp (1520 kW)

Variants:
31 Airliner; 31EZ patrol aircraft; T 3 RN observer trainer

Notes: Flown in 1980, 381 Jetstream 31s have been delivered. The 31 Airliner
has a high-density cabin which seats 19 and is used as an air taxi. Specialist
roles include Saudi Tornado navigator training.

Beechcraft Starship 1 USA

Type: short-range executive transport   **Accommodation:** two pilots; eight passengers

Dimensions:
Length: 46 ft 1 in (14 m)
Wingspan: 54 ft 4 in (16.6 m)
Height: 12 ft 11 in (3.9 m)

Weights:
Empty: 10 120 lb (4590 km)

Max T/O: 14 900 lb (6758 kg)
Payload: 2480 lb (1125 kg)

Performance:
Max speed: 384 mph (619 kmh)
Range: 1576 nm (2919 km)

Power plant: two Pratt &
Whitney PT6A-67A turboprops
Thrust: 2400 shp (1790 kW)

Variants:
2000A improved version

Notes: An unmistakable design, the Starship first flew in 1989, and fewer than 30 are in service. The 2000A carries only six passengers but has more space for fuel and baggage.

Beechcraft 400A Beechjet USA

Type: medium-range executive transport   **Accommodation:** two pilots; eight passengers

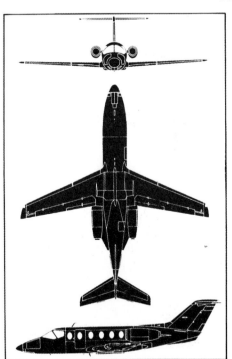

Dimensions:
Length: 48 ft 5 in (14.7 m)
Wingspan: 43 ft 6 in (13.3 m)
Height: 13 ft 11 in (4.2 m)

Weights:
Empty: 10 125 lb (4593 kg)
Max T/O: 16 100 lb (7303 kg)

Payload: 3100 lb (1406 kg)

Performance:
Max speed: 539 mph (867 kmh)
Range: 1900 nm (3519 km)
Power plant: two Pratt & Whitney Canada JT15D-5

turbofans
Thrust: 5800 lb (25.8 kN)

Variants:
T-1A Jayhawk trainer; T-400 JASDF version

Notes: Beech aquired the rights to the Mitsubishi Diamond II, improved it and called it the Beechjet 400. The T-1A Jayhawk is used for training US Air Force KC-10, KC-135, C-5 and C-17 crews.

Beechcraft Super King Air 200 USA

Type: medium-range executive transport   **Accommodation:** one or two pilots; eight executive passengers; 13 high density

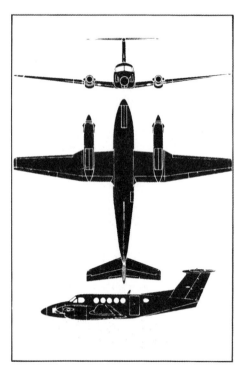

Dimensions:
Length: 43 ft 9 in (13.3 m)
Wingspan: 54 ft 6 in (16.6 m)
Height: 15 ft (4.6 m)

Weights:
Empty: 8102 lb (3675 kg)
Max T/O: 12 500 lb (5670 kg)

Payload: 1500 lb (680.4 kg)

Performance:
Max speed: 339 mph (545 kmh)
Range: 1974 nm (3656 km)
Power plant: two Pratt & Whitney Canada PT6A-42

turboprops
Thrust: 1700 shp (1268 kW)

Variants:
200C cargo version; 200T with tip tanks; 300 advanced version; 1300 Commuter

Notes: Military versions include the RC-12H Guardrail common sensor (described separately), and C-12/Tp101 light transports for the US and Swedish air forces. The 300 was built for the European market and has winglets and six passenger windows.

Beechcraft Queen Air USA

Type: short-range executive transport   **Accommodation:** one or two pilots; four passengers

Dimensions:
Length: 35 ft 6 in (10.8 m)
Wingspan: 50 ft 3 in (15.3 m)
Height: 14 ft 2 in (4.3 m)

Weights:
Empty: 5277 lb (2393 kg)
Max T/O: 8800 lb (3992 kg)

Payload: n\a

Performance:
Max speed: 248 mph (400 kmh)
Range: 1076 nm (1994 km)
Power plant: two Lycoming IGSO-540-A1D piston engines

Thrust: 760 hp (566 kW)

Variants:
Queen Airliner; Model 65 Queen Air; Queen Air 80, more powerful engines

Notes: Very similar to the King Air, it can be recognized by its square passenger windows and piston engines. The Airliner version has seating for seven passengers.

Beechcraft King Air USA

Type: short-range business transport   **Accommodation:** two pilots; four passengers

Dimensions:
Length: 35 ft 6 in (10.8 m)
Wingspan: 50 ft 3 in (15.3 m)
Height: 14 ft 2 in (4.3 m)

Weights:
Empty: 6052lb (2745 kg)
Max T/O: 10 100 lb (4581 kg)

Payload: n\a

Performance:
Max speed: 287 mph (462 kmh)
Range: 1125 nm (2084 km)
Power plant: two Pratt & Whitney Canada PT6A-28

turboprops
Thrust: 1360 shp (1014 kW)

Variants:
T-44A trainer; C90B advanced version

Notes: The T-44A is the US Navy's advanced pilot trainer and has more powerful engines. The C90B has more powerful engines, improved soundproofing, vibration damping and redesigned interior.

Cessna 650 Citation III USA

Type: long-range executive transport   **Accommodation:** two pilots; nine passengers

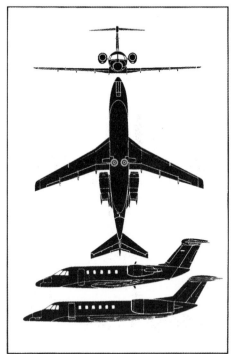

Dimensions:
Length: 55 ft 5 in (16.9 m)
Wingspan: 53 ft 6 in (16.3 m)
Height: 16 ft 9 in (5.1 m)

Weights:
Empty: 11 811 lb (5357 kg)

Max T/O: 22 000 lb (9979 kg)
Payload: 3489 lb (1583 kg)

Performance:
Max speed: 543 mph
(874 kmh)
Range: 2346 nm (4348 km)

Power plant: two Garrett
TFE731-3B-100S turbofans
Thrust: 7300 lb (32.5 kN)

Variants:
VI low cost version; VII
advanced version

Notes: First flew in 1979, deliveries began in 1983, over 180 aircraft have
been sold. The Citation VI has lower cost avionics suite and looks identical.
The VII has two Garrett TFE731-4R-2S engines giving a higher top speed.

Cessna 550 Citation II USA

Type: medium-range executive transport **Accommodation:** two pilots; six to 10 passengers

Dimensions:
Length: 47 ft 2 in (14.4 m)
Wingspan: 52 ft 2 in (15.9 m)
Height: 15 ft (4.6 m)

Weights:
Empty: 7725 lb (3504 kg)

Max T/O: 14 100 lb (6396 kg)
Payload: 3100 lb (1406 kg)

Performance:
Max speed: 443 mph
(713 kmh)
Range: 1760 nm (3260 km)

Power plant: two Pratt &
Whitney Canada JT15D-4B
turbofans
Thrust: 5000 lb (22.2 kN)

Variants:
Citation I earlier version

Notes: Stretched development of original Citation I with new wing aerofoil and engines flew in 1977. Production ended in 1984 in favour of Citation S/II, but brought back into production in 1985. Over 670 examples built.

Cessna 560 Citation V USA

Type: medium-range executive transport   Accommodation: two pilots; six to 10 passengers;

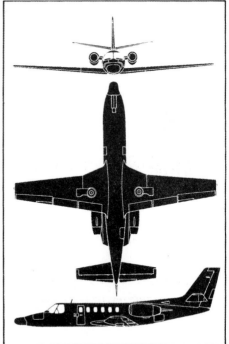

Dimensions:
Length: 48 ft 10 in (14.9 m)
Wingspan: 53 ft 2 in (15.9 m)
Height: 15 ft (4.6 m)

Weights:
Empty: 8828 lb (4004 kg)

Max T/O: 15 900 lb (7212 kg)
Payload: 4700 lb (2132 kg)

Performance:
Max speed: 492 mph (791 kmh)
Range: 1920 nm (3558 km)

Power plant: two Pratt & Whitney Canada JT15D-5A turbofans
Thrust: 5800 lb (25.8 kN)

Variants:
Citation S/II earlier verison

Notes: The S/II was a stretched Citation II that was also configured for air ambulance work. The Citation V received another fuselage extension along with new engines and advanced avionics.

Cessna 525 Citationjet USA

Type: short-range executive transport   **Accommodation:** two pilots; six passengers

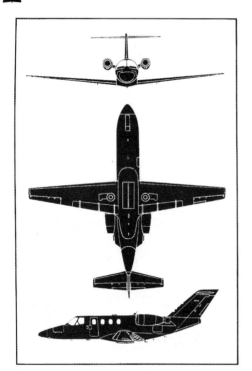

Dimensions:
Length: 42 ft 7 in (12.9 m)
Wingspan: 46 ft 9 in (14.3 m)
Height: 13 ft 8 in (4.2 m)

Weights:
Empty: 6275 lb (2846 kg)

Max T/O: 10 400 lb (4717 kg)
Payload: 721 lb (327 kg)

Performance:
Max speed: 438 mph (704 kmh)
Range: 1485 nm (2750 km)

Power plant: two Williams-Rolls FJ44 turbofans
Thrust: 3800 lb (16.9 kN)

Variants:
none

Notes: The smallest in the Citation range, the Citationjet can be recognized by its deeper fuselage, shorter fuselage and T tail.

Dassault-Mystère Falcon 100 France

Type: short-range executive transport   **Accommodation:** two pilots; eight passengers

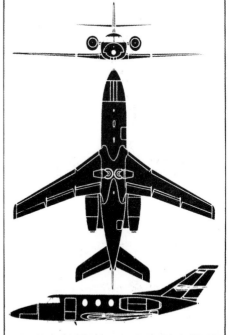

Dimensions:
Length: 45 ft 5 in (13.8 m)
Wingspan: 42 ft 11 in (13.1 m)
Height: 15 ft 1 in (4.6 m)

Weights:
Empty: 11 145 lb (5055 kg)

Max T/O: 19 300 lb (8755 kg)
Payload: 2875 lb (1305 kg)

Performance:
Max speed: 566 mph (912 kmh)
Range: 1595 nm (2900 km)
Power plant: two Garrett

TFE731-2 turbofans
Thrust: 6460 lb (28.8 kN)

Variants:
Falcon 10 earlier version; 10MER trainer

Notes: The 10MER is used by the French Navy for training pilots to use the Agave radar on the Super Etendard.

Dassault-Mystère Falcon 200 France

Type: medium-range executive transport   **Accommodation:** two pilots; nine executive passengers; 12 high-density

Dimensions:
Length: 56 ft 3 in (17.2 m)
Wingspan: 53 ft 6 in (16.3 m)
Height: 17 ft 5 in (5.3 m)

Weights:
Empty: 18 190 lb (8250 kg)
Max T/O: 32 000 lb (14 515 kg)
Payload: 2790 lb (1265 kg)

Performance:
Max speed: 541 mph (870 kmh)
Range: 2510 nm (4650 km)
Power plant: two Garrett ATF 3-6A-4C turbofans
Thrust: 10 400 lb (46.3 kN)

Variants:
Falcon 20 early version; cargo aircraft; HU-25 Guardian US Coast Guard version; HU-25B with SLAR and HU-25C with AN/APG-66; Falcon 20H Guardian Aeronavale aircraft; Falcon 20SNA trainer for Mirage aircrew; Norwegian Elint/EW aircraft

Dassault-Mystère Falcon 50 France

Type: long-range executive transport   **Accommodation:** two pilots; nine passengers

Dimensions:
Length: 60 ft 9 in (18.5 m)
Wingspan: 61 ft 10 in (18.9 m)
Height: 22 ft 10 in (6.9 m)

Weights:
Empty: 20 170 lb (9150 kg)

Max T/O: 40 780 lb (18 500 kg)
Payload: 4784 lb (2170 kg)

Performance:
Max speed: 546 mph (880 kmh)
Range: 3500 nm (6482 km)
Power plant: three Garrett
TFE731-3 turbofans
Thrust: 11 100 lb (49.5 kN)

Variants:
air ambulance; T.16 in Spanish service

Notes: The three-engined layout allows long-distance flights over deserts and oceans within public transport regulations. adopted for VIP transport by several countries.

Dassault-Mystère Falcon 900 France

Type: long-range executive transport   **Accomodation:** two pilots; 19 passengers

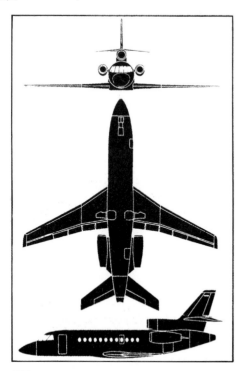

Dimensions:
Length: 66 ft 3 in (20.2 m)
Wingspan: 63 ft 5 in (19.3 m)
Height: 24 ft 9 in (7.5 m)

Weights:
Empty: 22 575 lb (10 240 kg)

Max T/O: 45 500 lb (20 640 kg)
Payload: 3053 lb (1385 kg)

Performance:
Max speed: 575 mph (927 kmh)
Range: 3900 nm (7229 km)

Power plant: three Garrett TFE731-5AR-1C turbofans
Thrust: 13 500 lb (60 kN)

Variants:
maritime patrol; 900B re-engined version

Notes: The 900B is powered by three TFE731-5BR turbofans and modified to comply with noise regulations, older 900s can be retrofitted to bring them up to 900B standard. The Japanese Maritime Self Defence Force uses two for maritime patrol. They can be recognized by their large search windows and hatch for marker flares and sonobuoys.

Gulfstream III USA

Type: long-range executive transport   **Accommodation:** two pilots; optional cabin attendant; 19 passengers

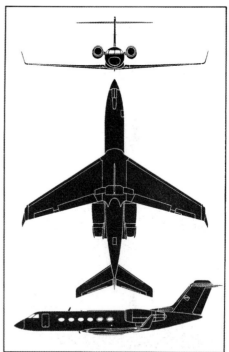

Dimensions:
Length: 83 ft 1 in (25.3 m)
Wingspan: 77 ft 10 in
(23.7 m)
Height: 24 ft 4 in (7.4 m)

Weights:
Empty: 38 000 lb (17 236 kg)
Max T/O: 69 700 lb (31 615 kg)

Payload: 1600 lb (726 kg)

Performance:
Max speed: 576 mph
(928 kmh)
Range: 4100 nm (7598 km)
Power plant: two Rolls-Royce
Spey Mk511-8 turbofans
Thrust: 22 800 lb (101.4 kN)

Variants:
II earlier version; IV advanced
version; SRA-4 special missons
version; C-20 VIP transport;
SMA-3 fisheries protection
and SAR aircraft

Notes: C-20 used by US armed services and Swedish Air Force (Tp 102). SRA-4s can be fitted with ventral canoe housing ECM, ESM, comms intercept or SLAR. Gulfstream IIs have no winglets, although many refitted with III wing.

Gulfstream I/I-C USA

Type: long-range executive transport   Accommodation: two pilots; 10 to 14 passengers

Dimensions:
Length: 63 ft 9 in (19.4 m)
Wingspan: 78 ft 6 in (23.9 m)
Height: 22 ft 9 in (6.9 m)

Weights:
Empty: 21 900 lb (9933 kg)

Max T/O: 35 100 lb (15 920 kg)
Payload: 4270 lb (1937 kg)

Performance:
Max speed: 348 mph
(560 kmh)
Range: 2203 nm (4088 km)

Power plant: two Rolls-Royce
Dart RDa 7/1 Mk529-8E
turboprops
Thrust: 4420 shp (3296 kW)

Variants:
TC-4C trainer

Notes: First flew in 1958, it was originally built by Grumman. The US Navy uses the TC-4C to train A-6 Intruder navigators, and it can be recognised by the large nose radome.

Raytheon Hawker 125 Series 600 UK

Type: medium-range executive transport   **Accommodation:** two pilots; eight executive passengers; 14 high density

Dimensions:
Length: 50 ft 6 in (15.4 m)
Wingspan: 47 ft (14.3 m)
Height: 17 ft 3 in (5.3 m)

Weights:
Empty: 12 530 lb (5683 kg)

Max T/O: 25 000 lb (11 340 kg)
Payload: 2000 lb (907 kg)

Performance:
Max speed: 368 mph (592 kmh)
Range: 1650 nm (3057 km)

Power plant: two Rolls-Royce Bristol Viper 601-22 turbojets
Thrust: 7500 lb (33.4 kN)

Variants:
CC.2 RAF designation;
Dominie navigation trainer;

Notes: Raytheon bought BAe Corporate Jets in 1993 and the 125 is marketed under the Raytheon Hawker name. The BAe 125 went through five series of upgrades, each tailored for a different country and customer specification.

305

Raytheon Hawker 125 Series 800 UK

Type: long-range executive transport

Accommodation: two pilots; up to 14 passengers

Dimensions:
Length: 51 ft 2 in (15.6 m)
Wingspan: 51 ft 4 in (15.7 m)
Height: 17 ft 7 in (5.4 m)

Weights:
Empty: 15 600 lb (7076 kg)
Max T/O: 27 400 lb (12 428 kg)

Payload: 2000 lb (907 kg)

Performance:
Max speed: 525 mph (845 kmh)
Range: 2825 nm (5232 km)
Power plant: two Garrett TFE731-5R turbofans

Thrust: 8600 lb (38.3 kN)

Variants:
800FI calibration aircraft; 700 similar but with original wing and avionics

Notes: Development of the last series of 125, the 800 has a refined wing, extra fuel capacity and Garrett engines. It can be recognised by its rounded windscreen and larger engine pods.

Raytheon Hawker 1000 UK

Type: long-range executive transport

Accommodation: two pilots; eight executive passengers; 15 high-density

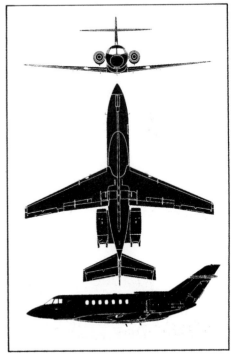

Dimensions:
Length: 53 ft 10 in (16.4 m)
Wingspan: 51 ft 4 in (15.7 m)
Height: 17 ft 1 in (5.2 m)

Weights:
Empty: 17 220 lb (7811 kg)

Max T/O: 31 000 lb (14 060 kg)
Payload: 2300 lb (1043 kg)

Performance:
Max speed: 539 mph
(867 kmh)
Range: 3350 nm (6204 km)

Power plant: two Pratt &
Whitney Canada PW305B
turbofans
Thrust: 10 400 lb (42.3 kN)

Variants:

IAI 1125 Astra Israel

Type: long-range executive transport   **Accommodation:** two pilots; six passengers

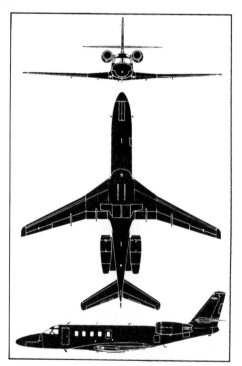

Dimensions:
Length: 55 ft 7 in (16.9 m)
Wingspan: 52 ft 8 in (16 m)
Height: 18 ft 2 in (5.5 m)

Weights:
Empty: 13 225 lb (5999 kg)

Max T/O: 23 500 lb (10 659 kg)
Payload: 2775 lb (1259 kg)

Performance:
Max speed: 533 mph (858 kmh)
Range: 2814 nm (5211 km)

Power plant: two Garrett
TFE731-3A-200G turbofans
Thrust: 7400 lb (32.9 kN)

Variants:
Astra SP upgraded version
Astra Galaxy advanced version

Notes: A development of the straight-winged IAI Westwind, the Astra SP features upgraded avionics and redesigned interior. The Galaxy is a complete redesign and was designed for non-stop trans-Atlantic flights.

IAI 1123 Westwind Israel

Type: medium-range executive transport   **Accommodation:** two pilots; 10 passengers

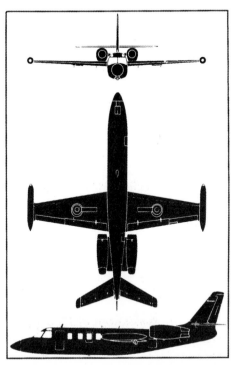

Dimensions:
Length: 52 ft 3 in (15.9 m)
Wingspan: 44 ft 9 in (13.6 m)
Height: 15 ft 9 in (4.8 m)

Weights:
Empty: 12 300 lb (5578 kg)

Max T/O: 22 850 lb (10 364 kg)
Payload: 3300 lb (1496 kg)

Performance:
Max speed: 542 mph (872 kmh)
Range: 2420 nm (4490 km)

Power plant: two Garrett AiResearch TFE731-3-1G turbofans
Thrust: 7400 lb (32.9 kN)

Variants:
124N coastal patrol aircraft

Notes: Israel Aircraft Industries bought the rights to the Rockwell Jet Commander, IAI stretched it and added wingtip tanks and called it the Westwind. It is used by the Israeli Navy as the SeaScan for electronic reconnaissance and tactical support.

Learjet 24 USA

Type: short-range executive transport   **Accommodation:** two pilots; six passengers

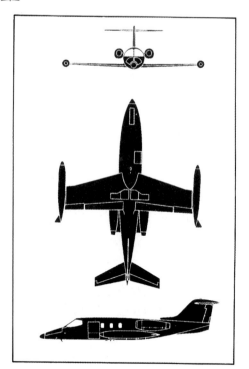

Dimensions:
Length: 43 ft 3 in (13.2 m)
Wingspan: 35 ft 7 in (10.8 m)
Height: 12 ft 3 in (3.7 m)

Weights:
Empty: 7130 lb (3234 kg)

Max T/O: 13 500 lb (6123 kg)
Payload: 3870 lb (1755 kg)

Performance:
Max speed: 545 mph
(877 kmh)
Range: 1472 nm (2728 km)

Power plant: two General
Electric CJ610-8A turbojets
Thrust: 6200 lb (27.6 kN)

Variants:
23 early version; 25 stretched
version; 28 with winglets

Notes: More than 1700 Learjets of all types have been sold since the first one flew in 1963. Some aircraft have been fitted with a large ventral camera installation.

Learjet 35/36 USA

Type: medium-range executive transport   **Accommodation:** two pilots; eight passengers

Dimensions:
Length: 48 ft 8 in (14.8 m)
Wingspan: 39 ft 6 in (12 m)
Height: 12 ft 3 in (3.7 m)

Weights:
Empty: 10 119 lb (4590 kg)
Max T/O: 18 300 lb (8300 kg)

Payload: 3381 lb (1534 kg)

Performance:
Max speed: 542 mph
(872 kmh)
Range: 2196 nm (4067 km)
Power plant: two Garrett
TFE731-2-2B turbofans

Thrust: 7000 lb (31. kN)

Variants:
U-36A, C-21A military
transport; EC-35A, RC-35A
special missions aircraft

Notes: A larger, longer-ranged version of the original Learjet, the 35 was launched in 1973. C-21s are used for priority transport, EC-35As for EW training, RC-35As for photographic reconnaissance, U-35As for target towing and utility roles.

Learjet 60 USA

Type: medium-range executive transport   **Accommodation:** two pilots; nine passengers

Dimensions:
Length: 58 ft 8 in (17.9 m)
Wingspan: 43 ft 9 in (13.3 m)
Height: 14 ft 8 in (4.5 m)

Weights:
Empty: 13 480 lb (6278 kg)

Max T/O: 23 100 lb (10 478 kg)
Payload: n\a

Performance:
Max speed: 533 mph
(858 kmh)
Range: 2398 nm (4441 km)

Power plant: two Pratt &
Whitney Canada PW305
turbofans
Thrust: 9200 lb (40.9 kN)

Variants:
55 early version

Notes: A widebody development, the 60 replaced the 55 in 1992. By combining the wings of a 55 with the fuselage and engines of a 35, Learjet have produced the 31 with a higher speed and digital avionics.

Lockheed Jetstar II USA

Type: long-range executive transport

Accommodation: two pilots; 10 passengers

Dimensions:
Length: 60 ft 5 in (18.4 m)
Wingspan: 54 ft 5 in (16.6 m)
Height: 20 ft 5 in (6.2 m)

Weights:
Empty: 24 178 lb (10 967 kg)

Max T/O: 43 750 lb (19 844 kg)
Payload: 2822 lb (1280 kg)

Performance:
Max speed: 547 mph (880 kmh)
Range: 2770 nm (5132 km)

Power plant: four AiResearch TFE731-3 turbofans
Thrust: 14 800 lb (66 kN)

Variants:
Jetstar early version; C-140 utility military transport

Notes: The Jetstar was put back into production in 1975 and features modern engines with increased range and lower noise levels. It is also available as an upgrade package for earlier Jetstar Is. First flew in 1957.

MBB HFB 320 Hansa Germany

Type: short-range executive transport   **Accommodation:** two pilots; 7 to 11 passengers

Dimensions:
Length: 54 ft 6 in (16.6 m)
Wingspan: 47 ft 6 in (14.5 m)
Height: 16 ft 2 in (4.9 m)

Weights:
Empty: 12 125 lb (5500 kg)

Max T/O: 20 280 lb (9200 kg)
Payload: 3520 lb (1600 kg)

Performance:
Max speed: 513 mph
(825 kmh)
Range: 1304 nm (2420 km)

Power plant: two General
Electric CJ610-5 turbojets
Thrust: 5900 lb (2670kg)

Variants:
none

Notes: An unconventional forward swept-wing design, the Hansa was built in small numbers. A high-density feederliner version was available, seating 15.

Piaggio P.180 Avanti Italy

Type: short-range executive transport   **Accommodation:** one or two pilots; nine passengers

Dimensions:
Length: 47 ft 3 in (14.4 m)
Wingspan: 46 ft (14 m)
Height: 12 ft 11 in (3.9 m)

Weights:
Empty: 7500 lb (3402 kg)

Max T/O: 11 550 lb (5239 kg)
Payload: 2000 lb (907 kg)

Performance:
Max speed: 455 mph
(732 kmh)
Range: 1400 nm (2594 km)

Power plant: Pratt & Whitney
Canada PT6A-66 turboprops
Thrust: 2970 shp (2214 kW)

Variants:
none

Notes: An unmistakable design, the position of the wing set far-back allows for a unobstructed cabin, with no wing roots or carry through. The foreplane also provides lift.

Piper PA-31-350 Chieftain USA

Type: short-range executive transport

Accommodation: two pilots; six passengers

Dimensions:
Length: 34 ft 7 in (10.5 m)
Wingspan: 40 ft 8 in (12.4 m)
Height: 13 ft (3.9 m)

Weights:
Empty: 4219 lb (1914 kg)

Max T/O: 7000 lb (3175 kg)
Payload: 350 lb (159 kg)

Performance:
Max speed: 270 mph (435 kmh)
Range: 885 nm (1640 km)

Power plant: two Lycoming TIO-540-J2BD piston engines
Thrust: 700 hp (522 kW)

Variants:
high-density commuter version; PA-31P pressurised

Notes: Developed from the Navajo, the Chieftain has a longer fuselage. The high-density version carries 10 passengers. The fuselage floor is strengthened to allow carriage of light cargo pallets.

Rockwell Sabreliner 75 USA

Type: medium-range executive transport   **Accommodation:** two pilots; 10 passengers

Dimensions:
Length: 47 ft 2 in (14.4 m)
Wingspan: 44 ft 8 in (13.6 m)
Height: 17 ft 3 in (5.3 m)

Weights:
Empty: 13 200 lb (5987 kg)
Max T/O: 21 380 lb (9698 kg)

Payload: 5500 lb (2494 kg)

Performance:
Max speed: Mach 0.80
Range: 1712 nm (3173 km)
Power plant: two General Electric CF700-2D-2 turbofans
Thrust: 9000 lb (40 kN)

Variants:
T-39 trainer; CT-39 transport; 60, 65 earlier versions; Sabreliner 80 with CF700 engines; Tp 86 Swedish military Sabreliner 40

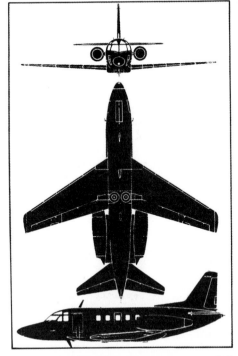

Notes: The original Sabreliner first flew in 1958 and was designed as a radar intercept officer training aircraft, and utility transport for the US Air Force and US Navy.

Swearingen SJ30 USA

Type: medium-range executive transport   **Accommodation:** one or two pilots; seven passengers

Dimensions:
Length: 42 ft 7 in (12.9 m)
Wingspan: 36 ft 4 in (11.1 m)
Height: 13 ft 11 in (4.2 m)

Weights:
Empty: 6210 lb (2817 kg)

Max T/O: 10 400 lb (4717 kg)
Payload: 2800 lb (1270 kg)

Performance:
Max speed: 541 mph
(871 kmh)
Range: 1730 nm (3204 km)

Power plant: two Williams-
Rolls FJ44 turbofans
Thrust: 3800 lb (16.9 kN)

Variants:
none

Notes: The SJ30 has reported orders for 66, to be delivered in 1997. FAA
certification has yet to be awarded.

UTILITY AIRCRAFT

ASTA Nomad Australia

Type: STOL utility aircraft   **Accommodation:** two pilots; 12 passengers

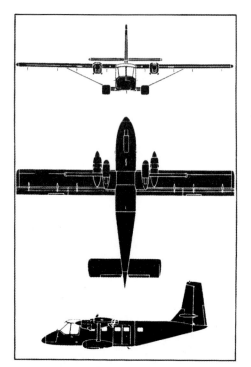

Dimensions:
Length: 41 ft 3 in (12.6 m)
Wingspan: 54 ft 2 in (16.5 m)
Height: 18 ft 2 in (5.5 m)

Weights:
Empty: 5002 lb (2269 kg)
Max T/O: 8500 lb (3855 kg)

Payload: 1728 lb (784 kg)

Performance:
Cruising speed: 193 mph
(311 kmh)
Range: 730 nm (1352 km)
Power plant: two Allison
250-B17C turboprops

Thrust: 840 shp (626 kW)

Variants:
Missionmaster military
version; Searchmaster coastal
patrol; N24 stretched fuselage

Notes: Capable of operating from unprepared runways 730 ft (223 m) in length. Nomads can be configured for commuter transport, cargo or flying doctor roles, and can be fitted with floats.

Antonov An-14 Clod Ukraine

Type: STOL utility aircraft   **Accommodation:** one pilot; seven passengers

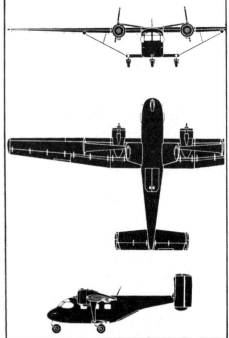

Dimensions:
Length: 37 ft 1 in (11.3 m)
Wingspan: 72 ft 2 in (21.9 m)
Height: 15 ft 2 in (4.6 m)

Weights:
Empty: n\a
Max T/O: 7935 lb (3600 kg)

Payload: 1590 lb (720 kg)

Performance:
Max speed: 190 mph (118 kmh)
Range: 366 nm (680 km); 253 nm (470 km) with max payload

Power plant: two Ivchenko AI-14RF radial engines
Thrust: 600 hp (447 kW)

Variants:
Chinese version Capital No1

Notes: Called Pchelka (Little Bee) in Russian service, the An-14 started production in 1965. Military versions have been built and also an executive version.

Antonov An-2 Colt Ukraine

Type: utility biplane

Accommodation: one or two pilots; 10 passengers

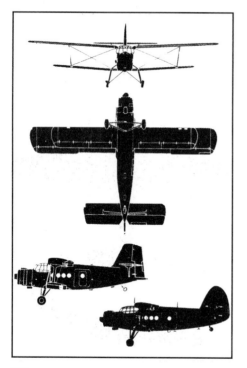

Dimensions:
Length: 42 ft 6 in (12.9 m)
Wingspan: 59 ft 8 in (18.2 m)
Height: 13 ft 9 in (4.2 m)

Weights:
Empty: 7605 lb (3450 kg)
Max T/O: 12 125 lb (5500 kg)

Payload: 3300 lb (1500 kg)

Performance:
Max speed: 157 mph
(253 kmh)
Range: 488 nm (905 km)
Power plant: one Shvetsov
ASh-62 IR radial engine

Thrust: 1000 hp (745.7 kW)

Variants:
An-3 turboprop; Harbin Y-5
Chinese version; Delaero T-101
Gratch monoplane version

Notes: Many versions of the basic An-2 have been developed including agricultural sprayer, military transport, air ambulance, water bomber, meteorological research and floatplane. No longer built in the Ukraine, but production continues in Poland. First flew in 1947.

Beriev Be-32 Cuff Russia

Type: utility transport   **Accommodation:** two pilots; 17 passengers

Dimensions:
Length: 51 ft 6 in (15.7 m)
Wingspan: 55 ft 9 in (17 m)
Height: 18 ft 1 in (5.5 m)

Weights:
Empty: 10 495 lb (4760 kg)

Max T/O: 16 090 lb (7300 kg)
Payload: 4190 lb (1900 kg)

Performance:
Max speed: 304 mph
(490 kmh)
Range: 944 nm (1750 km)

Power plant: two Mars TVD-10B turboprops
Thrust: 2022 shp (1508 kW)

Variants:
Be-30 earlier version

Notes: Development from the Be-30 began in 1967, but the programme was terminated as delveries of Let-410 began from Czechoslovakia. Due to shortages in hard currency development was restarted as deliveries of Lets dried up.

Canadair CL-415 Canada

Type: amphibious utility aircraft   **Accommodation:** two pilots; 30 passengers

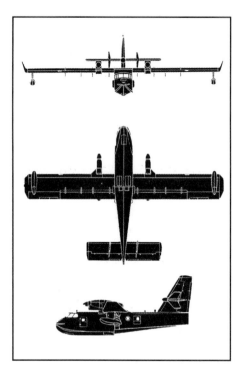

Dimensions:
Length: 65 ft (19.8 m)
Wingspan: 93ft 11in (28.6m)
Height: 29 ft 5 in (8.9 m)

Weights:
Empty: 27 783 lb (12 602 kg)
Max T/O: 43 850 lb (19 890 kg)

Payload: 13 500 lb (6123 kg)
Performance:
Cruising speed: 234 mph
(376 kmh)
Range: 1310 nm (2426 km)
Power plant: two Pratt &
Whittney Canada PW123AF
turboprops

Thrust: 4760 shp (3550 kW)

Variants:
CL-215 piston engined
version; firefighter; CL-215T
designation given to re-
engined CL-215s; CL-415 new-
build turboprop

Notes: Developed from piston-engined CL-215, the -415 can be configured
for SAR and maritime patrol. When firefighting it can carry 6130 litres of
water and has an onboard foam mixer.

Cessna 208 Caravan 1 USA

Type: utility transport   **Accommodation:** one pilot; seven passengers

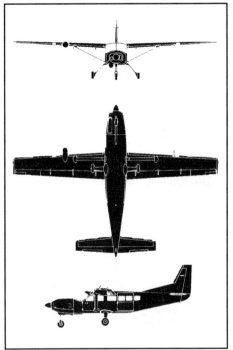

Dimensions:
Length: 37 ft 7 in (11.5 m)
Wingspan: 52 ft 1 in (15.8 m)
Height: 11 ft 8 in (3.6 m)

Weights:
Empty: 3862 lb (1752 kg)
Max T/O: 8000 lb (3629 kg)

Payload: 3500 lb (1587 kg)

Performance:
Cruising speed: 212 mph (341 kmh)
Range: 1085 nm (2009 km)
Power plant: one Pratt & Whitney Canada PT6A-114

turboprop
Thrust: 600 shp (447 kW)

Variants:
208B stretched version; Grand Caravan passenger version; U-27A military designation

Notes: First flown in 1982, over 600 have been delivered. The U-27A has a 84 cu ft (2.8m2) cargo pannier under the fuselage. The Grand Caravan can carry 14 passengers. A floatplane version is also available.

de Havilland Canada DHC-6 Twin Otter Canada

Type: STOL utility transport **Accommodation:** two pilots; 20 passengers

Dimensions:
Length: 51 ft 9 in (15.8 m)
Wingspan: 65 ft (19.8 m)
Height: 19 ft 6 in (5.9 m)

Weights:
Empty: 7415 lb (3363 kg)
Max T/O: 12 500 lb (5670 kW)
Payload: 4280 lb (1941 kg)

Performance:
Cruising speed: 210 mph (338 kmh)
Range: 920 nm (1704 km)
Power plant: two Pratt & Whitney Canada PT6A-27 turboprops
Thrust: 1240 shp (924 kW)

Variants:
DHC-6-200 lengthened nose, increased baggage capacity; DHC-6-300M military transport; DHC-300M (COIN) provision for armour., cabin machine gun and hardpoints; DHC-6-300MR maritime version with search radar and underwing searchlight

Dornier Do 28P Skyservant Germany

Type: STOL utility transport   **Accommodation:** one or two pilots; 13 passengers

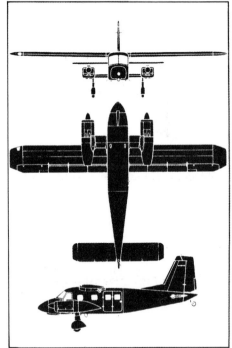

Dimensions:
Length: 37 ft 5 in (11.4 m)
Wingspan: 51 ft (15.6 m)
Height: 12 ft 9 in (3.9 m)

Weights:
Empty: 5132 lb (2328 kg)
Max T/O: 8470 lb (3842 kg)

Payload: 2806 lb (1273 kg)

Performance:
Max speed: 202 mph
(325 kmh)
Range: 566 nm (1050 km)
Power plant: two Lycoming
ISGO-540-A1E piston engines

Thrust: 760 hp (566 kW)

Variants:
Do128-6 turboprop
development; Do 28D-1
increased span

Notes: First flown in 1966, over 260 have been delivered to 25 countries. The Do 128-6 is powered by two Pratt & Whitney Canada PT6A-110 turboprops.

Dornier Do 28B Germany

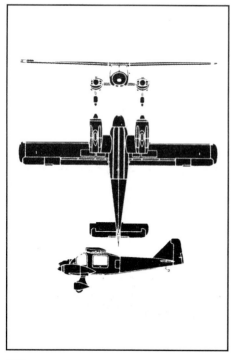

Type: STOL utility aircraft   **Accommodation:** one pilot; seven passengers

Dimensions:
Length: 29 ft 6 in (9 m)
Wingspan: 45 ft 3 in (13.8 m)
Height: 9 ft 2 in (2.8 m)

Weights:
Empty: 3660 lb (1660 kg)
Max T/O: 5400 lb (2450 kg)

Payload: n\a

Performance:
Max speed: 174 mph
(280 kmh)
Range: 1100 nm (1680 km);
715 nm (1150 km) with max
payload

Power plant: two Lycoming
IO-540A piston engines
Thrust: 580 hp (432 kW)

Variants:
A-I-S floatplane; B-1 up-
engined version

Notes: First flown in 1959. The Do 28B is a twin-engined version of the
earlier Do 27, and formed the basis of the Skyservant.

Dornier Seastar Germany/Malaysia

Type: STOL utility amphibian   **Accommodation:** two pilots; 12 passengers

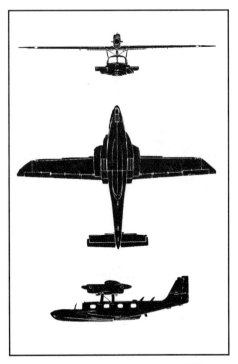

Dimensions:
Length: 41 ft 8 in (12.7 m)
Wingspan: 58 ft 2 in (17.7 m)
Height: 15 ft 10 in (4.8 m)

Weights:
Empty: 6173 lb (2800 kg)
Max T/O: 10 141 lb (4600 kg)

Payload: 2460 lb (1116 kg)

Performance:
Crusing speed: 207 mph (333 kmh)
Endurance: seven hours 45min; nine hours 30min on one engine

Power plant: two Pratt & Whittney Canada PT6A-135A turboprops
Thrust: 1300 shp (970 kW)

Variants:
Ambulance; VIP; cargo; maritime patrol; SAR

Notes: Originally designed by German company Dornier Seastar, the aircraft is produced in Malaysia under a joint venture group. Indonesian Air Transport was the launch customer and orders for 25 more have been received.

HAMC Y-12 (II) China

Type: STOL utility transport **Accommodation:** two pilots; 17 passengers

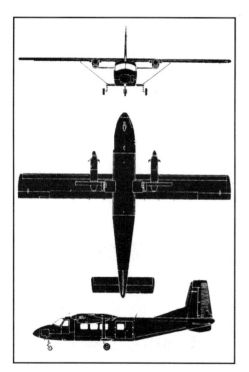

Dimensions:
Length: 48 ft 9 in (14.9 m)
Wingspan: 56 ft 6 in (17.2 m)
Height: 18 ft 7 in (5.7 m)

Weights:
Empty: 7055 lb (3200 kg)
Max T/O: 11 684 lb (5300 kg)

Payload: 3748 lb (1700 kg)

Performance:
Max speed: 204 mph
(328 kmh)
Range: 723 nm (1340 km)
Power plant: two Pratt &
Whitney Canada PT6A-27

turboprops
Thrust: 1240 shp (924 kW)

Variants:
Y12(I) earlier version; Y-12(III)
advanced version; Y-11 earlier,
smaller, aircraft with reduced
fuselage cross-section

Notes: First flown in 1984, over 80 have been delivered. Future plans under development include a stretched version and a pressurised cabin.

Lake LA-250 Renegade USA

Type: light STOL utility amphibian   **Accommodation:** one pilot; five passengers

Dimensions:
Length: 28 ft 4 in (8.6 m)
Wingspan: 38 ft 4 in (11.7 m)
Height: 10 ft (3.1 m)

Weights:
Empty: 1850 lb (839 kg)
Max T/O: 3050 lb (1383 kg)

Payload: 200 lb (90 kg)

Performance:
Max speed: 160 mph
(258 kmh)
Range: 900 nm (1668 km)
Power plant: one Textron
Lycoming IO-540-C4B5 piston

engine
Thrust: 250 hp (186 kW)

Variants:
270 Turbo Renegade; LA4
Buccaneer earlier version

Notes: The turbocharged 270 set a world altitude record for light amphibians in 1988 by reaching 24 500 ft (7465 m).

McKinnon G-21G Turbo-Goose USA

Type: utility amphibian   **Accommodation:** one pilot; 11 passengers

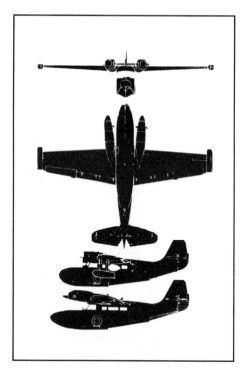

Dimensions:
Length: 39 ft 7 in (12.1 m)
Wingspan: 50 ft 10 in (15.5 m)
Height: n\a

Weights:
Empty: 6700 lb (3039 kg)

Max T/O: 12 500 lb (5670 kg)
Payload: n\a

Performance:
Max speed: 243 mph (391 kmh)
Range: 1390 nm (2575 km)

Power plant: two Pratt & Whittney Canada PT6A-27 turboprops
Thrust: 1360 shp (1014 kW)

Variants:
G-21 Goose earlier version

Notes: The original G-21 was flown in 1937 and turboprop conversions began in 1966. The G-21G has a stretched nose to house a radar and retractable wingtip floats.

Mitsubishi Mu-2 Japan

Type: STOL utility transport   **Accommodation:** two pilots; six passengers

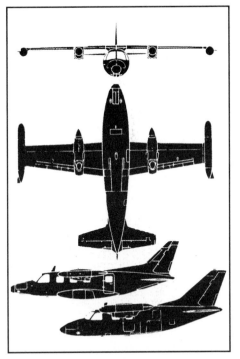

Dimensions:
Length: 38 ft 10 in (11.8 m)
Wingspan: 39 ft 5 n (12 m)
Height: 13 ft 8 in (4.2 m)

Weights:
Empty: 5920 lb (2685 kg)
Max T/O: 10 800 lb (4900 kg)

Payload: 374 lb (170 kg)

Performance:
Cruising speed: 345 mph
(555 kmh)
Range: 1460 nm (2700 km)
Power plant: two AiResearch
TPE 331-6-251M turboprops

Thrust: 1448 ehp (1080 kW)

Variants:
2J, 2N, 2K and 2P up-engined
versions; 2L and 2M heavier
versions

Notes: First flown in 1963, production ceased in 1986 after 755 had been
delivered. Used in Japan for search and rescue and transport.

333

Pilatus PC-6B Turbo Porter Switzerland

Type: STOL utility transport   **Accommodation:** two pilots; nine passengers

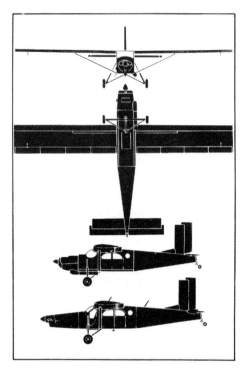

Dimensions:
Length: 36 ft 1 in (11 m)
Wingspan: 52 ft (15.9 m)
Height: 10 ft 6 in (3.2 m)

Weights:
Empty: 2800 lb (1270 kg)
Max T/O: 6173 lb (2800 kg)
Payload: 2491 lb (1130 kg)

Performance:
Max speed: 174 mph (280 kmh)
Range: 870 nm (1612 km); 394 nm (730 km) with max payload
Power plant: one Pratt & Whitney Canada PT6A-27 turboprop

Thrust: 680 hp (507 kW)

Variants:
PC-6 original piston-enginerd Porter; AU-23A Peacemaker, armed Fairchild-built version

Notes: Over 500 Turbo Porters produced in Switzerland and by Fairchild in the USA. PC-6s have also been flown with Astazou and Garrett engines.

Pilatus Britten-Norman Islander UK

Type: utility transport   **Accommodation:** one pilot; nine passengers

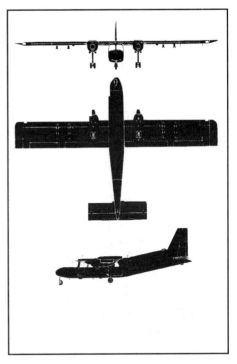

Dimensions:
Length: 35 ft 7 in (10.8 m)
Wingspan: 49 ft (14.9 m)
Height: 13 ft 8 in (4.2 m)

Weights:
Empty: 4114 lb (1866 kg)
Max T/O: 6600 lb (2993 kg)

Payload: 1526 lb (692 kg)

Performance:
Max speed: 170 mph
(274 kmh)
Range: 1216 nm (2252 km)
Power plant: two Textron
Lycoming IO-540 piston

engines
Thrust: 520 hp (388 km/h)

Variants:
BN-2A/B; BN2T Turbine
Islander

Notes: The BN-2T is powered by Allison 250-B17C turboprops. The basic
version is also produced in Romania and the Philippines.

Pilatus Britten-Norman Trislander UK

Type: utility transport   **Accommodation:** one pilot; 17 passengers

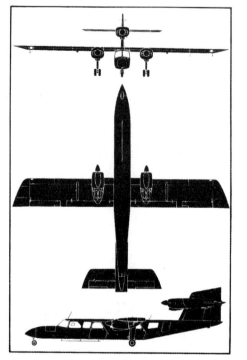

Dimensions:
Length: 49 ft 3 in (15 m)
Wingspan: 53 ft (16.2 m)
Height: 14 ft 2 in (4.3 m)

Weights:
Empty: 5843 lb (2650 kg)

Max T/O: 10 000 lb (4536 kg)
Payload: n\a

Performance:
Max speed: 180 mph
(290 kmh)
Range: 868 nm (1610 km)

Power plant: three Lycoming
O-540-E4C5 piston engines
Thrust: 780 hp (582 kW)

Variants:
none

Notes: Developed from the standard twin-engined version, the Trislander first flew in 1970. The two aircraft are 75 per cent similar in components, the only difference being the redesigned rear fuselage and the stretched main cabin.

SATIC A300-600T Super Transporter (Beluga) France/Germany

Type: outsized cargo aircraft   **Accommodation:** two pilots; two flight engineers

Dimensions:
Length: 184 ft 10 in (56.2 m)
Wingspan: 147 ft (44.8 m)
Height: 57 ft 3 in (17.3 m)

Weights:
Empty: 186 290 lb (84 501 kg)
Max T/O: 330 675 lb

(150 000 kg)
Payload: 100 310 lb
(45 500 kg)

Performance:
Max speed: 484 mph
(780 kmh)
Range: 900 nm (1666 km)

Power plant: two General
Electric GE CF6-80C2A8
turbofans
Thrust: 118 000 lb (524.8 kN)

Variants:
none

Notes: Designed to replace the ageing Super Guppy transports for carrying Airbus components. The Super Transporter has a 123ft 8in (37.7m) long unpressurised cargo cabin, with a volume of 49 440 cu ft (140 m). SATIC believes there is a potential market for 20 more, including military versions.

Shorts Skyvan UK

Type: STOL utility transport   **Accommodation:** pilot; loadmaster; 22 troops; 19 passengers

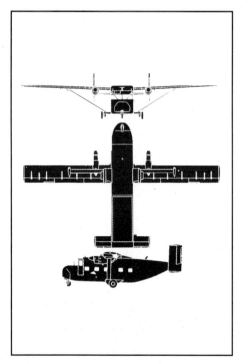

Dimensions:
Length: 40 ft 1 in (12.2 m)
Wingspan: 64 ft 11 in (19.8 m)
Height: 15 ft 1 in (4.6 m)

Weights:
Empty: 7344 lb (3331 kg)

Max T/O: 12 500 lb (5670 kg)
Payload: 4600 lb (2086 kg)

Performance:
Max speed: 250 mph
(402 kmh)
Range: 600 nm (1115 km)

Power plant: two Garrett
TPE331-2-201A turboprops
Thrust: 1430 shp (1066 kW)

Variants:
3M military version

Notes: A very rugged design, the Skyvan first flew in 1963. Production ceased in 1987 after 150 had been built.

LIGHT AIRCRAFT

Aero Boero 115 Argentina

Type: light utility aircraft   **Accommodation:** pilot, two passengers

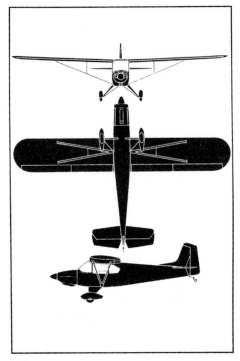

Dimensions:
Length: 23 ft 2 in (7.1 m)
Wingspan: 35 ft 4 in (10.8 m)
Height: 6 ft 8 in (2.1 m)

Weights:
Empty: 1226 lb (556 kg)

Max T/O: 1768 lb (802 kg)

Performance:
Max speed: 136 mph
(220 kmh)
Range: 664 nm (1230 km)
Power Plant: Textron

Lycoming O-235-C2A piston
engine
Thrust: 115 hp (86 kW)

Variants:
95 earlier version; 180 Glider
Tug; agricultural version

Notes: The original AB95 first flew in 1957, and has undergone a number of refinements, engine changes and upgrades.

Atlas C4M Kudu South Africa

Type: light transport   **Accommodation:** two pilots, four passengers

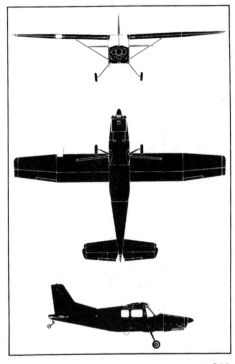

Dimensions:
Length: 30 ft 6 in (9.3 m)
Wingspan: 42 ft 10 in (13.7 m)
Height: 12 ft (3.6 m)

Weights:
Empty: 2711 lb (1230 kg)

Max T/O: 4497 lb (2040 kg)
Payload: 1235 lb (560 kg)

Performance:
Max speed: 161 mph (259kmh)
Range: 700 nm (1297 km)
Power plant: one Piaggio-

Lycoming GSO-480-B1B3 piston engine
Thrust: 340 hp (254 kW)

Variants:
AL.60 export version

Beechcraft B58 Baron USA

Type: light transport   **Accommodation:** two pilots, four passengers

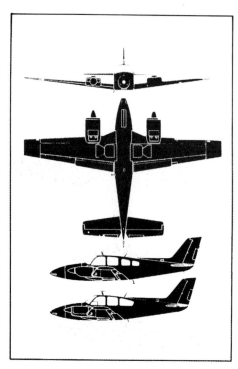

Dimensions:
Length: 29 ft 10 in (9.1 m)
Wingspan: 37 ft 10 in
(11.5 m)
Height: 9 ft 9 in (3 m)

Weights:
Empty: 3570 lb (1619 kg)

Max T/O: 5500 lb (2495 kg)
Payload: 700 lb (317 kg)

Performance:
Max speed: 239 mph
(386 kmh)
Range: 1575 nm (2917 km)
Power plant: two Teledyne

Continental IO-550-C piston
engines
Thrust: 600 hp (448 kW)

Variants:
B55 earlier version; T-42A
Cochise trainer

Notes: First flown in 1960, the Baron is widely used as a training aircraft by airlines.

Beechcraft B60 Duke USA

Type: light transport   **Accommodation:** two pilots, four passengers

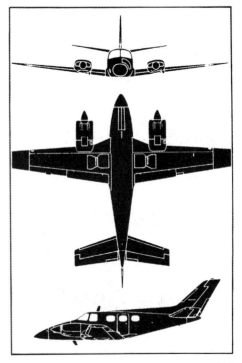

Dimensions:
Length: 33 ft 10 in (10.3 m)
Wingspan: 39 ft 3 in (11.9 m)
Height: 12 ft 4 in (3.8 m)

Weights:
Empty: 4380 lb (1987 kg)

Max T/O: 6775 lb (3073 kg)
Payload: n\a

Performance:
Max speed: 283 mph
(455 kmh)
Range: 1112 nm (2079 km)

Power plant: two Lycoming
TIO-541-E1C4 turbocharged
piston engines
Thrust: 760 hp (566 kg)

Variants:
none

Notes: First flown in 1966. The Duke features a pressurised cabin and
turbocharged engines to enable it to operate up to 30 000 ft (9145 m).

Beechcraft B76 Duchess USA

Type: light transport   **Accommodation:** two pilots, two passengers

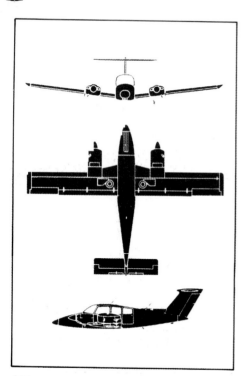

Dimensions:
Length: 29 ft (8.9 m)
Wingspan: 38 ft (11.6 m)
Height: 9 ft 6 in (2.9 m)

Weights:
Empty: 2466 lb (1119 kg)

Max T/O: 3900 lb (1769 kg)
Payload: 200 lb (90 kg)

Performance:
Max speed: 197 mph
(317 kmh)
Range: 843 nm (1563 km)

Power plant: two Avco
Lycoming 360–A1G6D piston
engines
Thrust: 360 hp (286 kW)

Variants:
none

Notes: First flown in 1977, the Duchess was designed for personal light transport and trainer markets. Some 429 were built.

Beech 18 USA

Type: light transport   **Accommodation:** two pilots, nine passengers

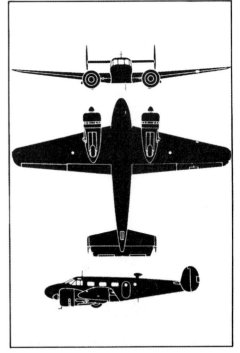

Dimensions:
Length: 35 ft 2 in (10.7 m)
Wingspan: 48 ft 8 in (15.1 m)
Height: 9 ft 4 in (2.8 m)

Weights:
Empty: 5845 lb (2651 kg)
Max T/O: 9900 lb (4490 kg)

Payload: 300 lb (136 kg)

Performance:
Max speed: 236 mph (380 kmh)
Range: 1326 nm (2460 km)
Power plant: two Pratt & Whitney R-985AN-14B radial engines
Thrust: 900 hp (671 kW)

Variants:
Super 18 advanced version; Westwind turboprop conversion

Notes: First flown in 1937, examples of the Beech 18 are still flying in regular service.

Beechcraft Bonanza V35B USA

Type: light sports aircraft   **Accommodation:** one pilot, four passengers

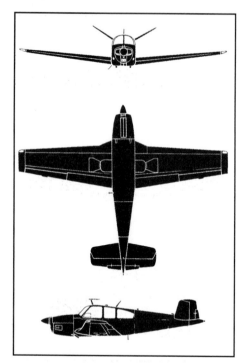

Dimensions:
Length: 26 ft 5 in (8.1 m)
Wingspan: 33 ft 6 in (10.2 m)
Height: 7 ft 7 in (2.3 m)

Weights:
Empty: 2106 lb (955 kg)

Max T/O: 3400 lb (1542 kg)
Payload: 270 lb (123 kg)

Performance:
Max speed: 209 mph
(338 kmh)
Range: 889 nm (1648 km)

Power plant: one Continental
IO-520-BB piston engine
Thrust: 285 hp (212 kW)

Variants:
many engine modifications

Notes: First flown in 1945, production ended in 1985 after 10 390 had been built.

Beechcraft Bonanza Model F33A USA

Type: light sports aircraft   **Accommodation:** one pilot, four passengers

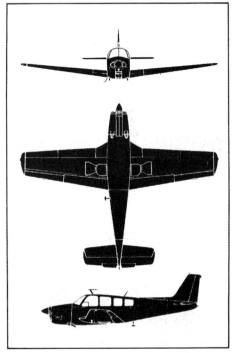

Dimensions:
Length: 26 ft 8 in (8.1 m)
Wingspan: 33 ft 6 in (10.2 m)
Height: 8 ft 3 in (2.5 m)

Weights:
Empty: 2242 lb (1017 kg)
Max T/O: 3400 lb (1542 kg)

Payload: 270 lb (123 kg)

Performance:
Max speed: 209 mph (338 kmh)
Range: 889 nm (1648 km)
Power plant: one Teledyne Continental IO-520-BB piston engine
Thrust: 285 hp (212 kW)

Variants:
F33C aerobatic version; B36TC turbocharged version; A36 utility version

Notes: First flown in 1959, the F33A was developed from the original Bonanza. Main differences between the two are the conventional tail unit on the F33A as opposed to the butterfly tail on the V35B.

Beechcraft Sierra 200 USA

Type: light sports aircraft   **Accommodation:** one pilot, three passengers

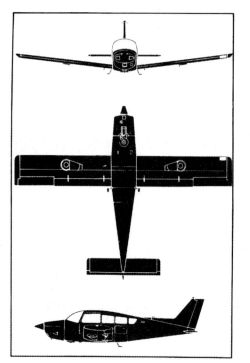

Dimensions:
Length: 25 ft 9 in (7.8 m)
Wingspan: 32 ft 9 in (9.9 m)
Height: 8 ft 1 in (2.5 m)

Weights:
Empty: 1494 lb (678 kg)

Max T/O: 2030 lb (920 kg)
Payload: 270 lb (122 kg)

Performance:
Max speed: 167 mph
(269 kmh)
Range: 686 nm (1271 km)

Power plant: one Avco
Lycoming O-360-A4K piston
engine
Thrust: 180 hp (134 kW)

Variants:
Sundowner 180 basic version

Notes: First flown as the Musketeer Super R in 1969, the Sierra was renamed when deliveries began in 1974. The Sundowner has a lower powered engine and non-retractable undercarriage.

Beechcraft Skipper USA

Type: light training aircraft   **Accommodation:** two pilots, one passenger

Dimensions:
Length: 23 ft 10 in (7.3 m)
Wingspan: 30 ft (9.1 m)
Height: 7 ft 6 in (2.3 m)

Weights:
Empty: 1103 lb (500 kg)

Max T/O: 1650 lb (748 kg)
Payload: n\a

Performance:
Max speed: 120 mph (196 kmh)
Range: 413 nm (764 km)
Power plant: one O-235

piston engine
Thrust: 115 hp (85 kw)

Variants:
none

Notes: Built in small numbers, the Skipper is mainly used for training purposes.

Bellanca Viking USA

Type: light sports aircraft   **Accommodation:** two pilots, two passengers

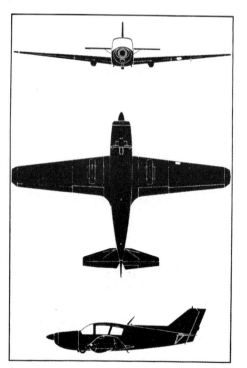

Dimensions:
Length: 26 ft 4 in (8 m)
Wingspan: 34 ft 2 in (10.4 m)
Height: 7 ft 4 in (2.2 m)

Weights:
Empty: 2247 lb (1019 kg)

Max T/O: 3325 lb (1508 kg)
Payload: 186 lb (84 kg)

Performance:
Max speed: 208 mph (335 kmh)
Range: 929 nm (1722 km)

Power plant: one Continental IO-520-K
Thrust: 300 hp (224 kW)

Variants:
Turbo Viking turbocharged version

Notes: Developed from the earlier 260C, the Viking has three different engine fits. Over 1500 were built before production ceased in 1980.

Bellanca **Skyrocket** USA

Type: light sports aircraft   **Accommodation:** one pilot, five passengers

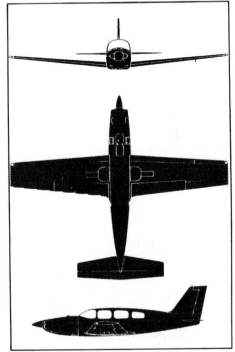

Dimensions:
Length: 28 ft 11 in (8.8 m)
Wingspan: 35 ft (10.7 m)
Height: n\a

Weights:
Empty: 2420 lb (1098 kg)

Max T/O: 4200 lb (1905 kg)
Payload: 200 lb (91 kg)

Performance:
Max speed: 326 mph (525 kmh)
Range: 1586 nm (2937 km)

Power plant: one Continental GTSIO-520-F piston engine
Thrust: 435 hp (324 kW)

Variants:
none

Notes: Design began in 1963 to make a highly efficent airframe using adanced materials. The Skyrocket holds a number of speed records for its class.

Cessna 310 USA

Type: light transport aircraft   **Accommodation:** two pilots, three passengers

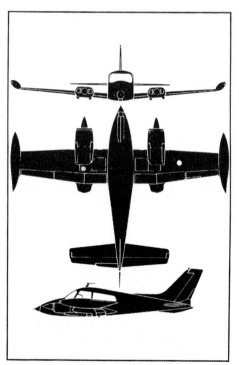

Dimensions:
Length: 13 ft 11 in (9.7 m)
Wingspan: 36 ft 11 in (11.2 m)
Height: 10 ft 8 in (3.3 m)

Weights:
Empty: 3347 lb (1518 kg)

Max T/O: 5500 lb (2495 kg)
Payload: 950 lb (430 kg)

Performance:
Max speed: 238 mph (383 kmh)
Range: 1440 nm (2668 km)
Power plant: two Continental

IO-520-M piston engines
Thrust: 570 hp (424 kW)

Variants:
U-3 US Air Force designation; Turbo System Turbocharged version; 320 Skynight turbosupercharged version

Notes: First flown in 1953, turbocharged versions were introduced in 1968. Over 5000 were built, earlier models having an unswept fin.

Cessna 340A USA

Type: light transport aircraft   **Accommodation:** one or two pilots, four passengers

Dimensions:
Length: 34 ft 4 in (10.5 m)
Wingspan: 38 ft 1 m (11.6 m)
Height: 12 ft 7 in (3.8 m)

Weights:
Empty: 3878 lb (1759 kg)

Max T/O: 5990 lb (2717 kg)
Payload: 930 lb (422 kg)

Performance:
Max speed: 281 mph (452 kmh)
Range: 1377 nm (2552 km)

Power plant: two Continental TSIO-520-N piston engines
Thrust: 620 hp (462 kW)

Variants:
340A II

Notes: Developed from the 310, the 340 has a pressurised cabin and more internal space.

353

Cessna T303 Crusader USA

Type: light transport   **Accommodation:** one pilot, five passengers

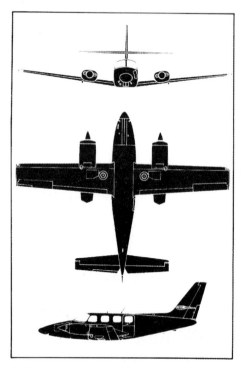

Dimensions:
Length: 30 ft 5 in (9.3 m)
Wingspan: 39 ft (11.9 m)
Height: 13 ft 4 in (4.1 m)

Weights:
Empty: 3364 lb (1526 kg)

Max T/O: 5150 lb (2336 kg)
Payload: 590 lb (267 kg)

Performance:
Max speed: 249 mph
(400 kmh)
Range:

Power plant: two Continental
LSIO/LTSIO-520-AE piston
engines
Thrust: 500 hp (372 kW)

Variants:
none

Notes: First flown in 1978, production was halted in 1987 after only 297 had
been built.

Cessna Titan USA

Type: light transport aircraft   **Accommodation:** two pilots, six passengers

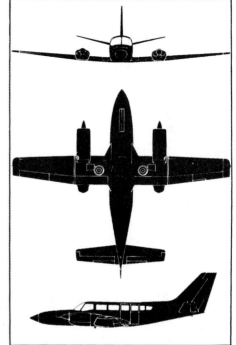

Dimensions:
Length: 39 ft 6 in (12 m)
Wingspan: 46 ft 4 in (14.1 m)
Height: 13 ft 3 in (4 m)

Weights:
Empty: 4804 lb (2179 kg)
Max T/O: 8400 lb (3810 kg)

Payload: 1500 lb (680 kg)

Performance:
Max speed: 267 mph (430 kmh)
Range: 1809 nm (3350 km)
Power plant: two Continental GTSIO-520-M piston engines

Thrust: 750 hp (560 kW)

Variants:
402C long-span wing and tip tanks; 404 Titan larger tail and stretched fuselage derivative of 402

Notes: First flown in 1975, it was originally called the Model 404. Capable of operating from small strips, it is often used as a feederliner.

Cessna 421 Golden Eagle USA

Type: light transport aircraft   **Accommodation:** two pilots, eight passengers

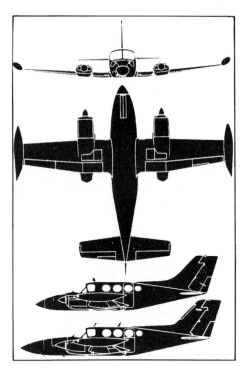

Dimensions:
Length: 36 ft 4 in (11.1 m)
Wingspan: 41 ft 1 in (12.5 m)
Height: 11 ft 5 in (3.5 m)

Weights:
Empty: 4579 lb (2077 kg)
Max T/O: 7450 lb (3379 kg)

Payload: 1500 lb (680 kg)

Performance:
Max speed: 297 mph (478 kmh)
Range: 1487 nm (2755 km)
Power plant: two Continental GTSIO-520-L piston engines

Thrust: 750 hp (560 kW)

Variants:
421 pressurised version of 411; 421B/C longer span wings, longer nose; strengthened undercarriage

Notes: First flown in 1965, over 1900 examples were delivered. Earlier versions were equipped with wingtip fuel tanks.

Cessna 401/402 USA

Type: light transport   **Accommodation:** two pilots, four passengers

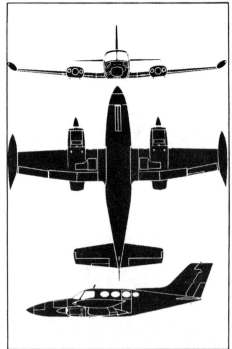

Dimensions:
Length: 36 ft 1 in (11 m)
Wingspan: 39 ft 10 in (12.1 m)
Height: 11 ft 8 in (3.6 m)

Weights:
Empty: 4002 lb (1815 kg)

Max T/O: 6300 lb (2858 kg)
Payload: 1340 lb (606 kg)

Performance:
Max speed: 264 mph (424 kmh)
Range: 1231 nm (2280 km)
Power plant: two Continental

TSIO-520E piston engines
Thrust: 600 hp (224 kW)

Variants:
Ambassador all-passenger version; Courier utility version; Utililiner; Businessliner

Notes: The Utililiner can be quickly configured for cargo or passenger duties while the Businessliner is a dedicated business transport.

Cessna 414A Chancellor USA

Type: light transport   **Accommodation:** two pilots, five passengers

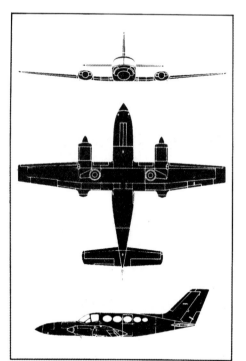

Dimensions:
Length: 33 ft 9 in (10.3 m)
Wingspan: 39 ft 11 in
(12.2 m)
Height: 11 ft 8 in (3.6 m)

Weights:
Empty: 4373 lb (1984 kg)

Max T/O: 6350 lb (2880 kg)
Payload: 1090 lb (494 kg)

Performance:
Max speed: 275 mph
(443 kmh)
Range: 1300 nm (2409 km)
Power plant: two Continental

TSIO-520-N piston engines
Thrust: 310 hp (231 kW)

Variants:
414 II advanced version

Notes: Introduced in 1969 as a replacement for earlier non-pressurized aircraft, over 1000 were built. Pressurized version of 401B.

Cessna Model 180 Skywagon USA

Type: light sports aircraft   **Accommodation:** one pilot, max five passengers

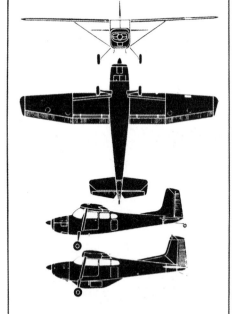

Dimensions:
Length: 25 ft 7 in (7.8 m)
Wingspan: 35 ft 10 in
(10.9 m)
Height: 7 ft 9 in (2.4 m)

Weights:
Empty: 1650 lb (749 kg)
Max T/O: 2800 lb (1270 kg)

Payload: 400 lb (181 kg)

Performance:
Max speed: 170 mph
(274 kmh)
Range: 1010 nm (1872 km)
Power plant: one Continental
O-470-U piston engine
Thrust: 230 hp (171 kW)

Variants:
Model 185 cargo version;
Floatplane; Skiplane;
Amphibian; 182 advanced
version; U-17B military
version of 185; U-17C military
version of 180

Notes: 1700+ built before production ceased in 1981. 185 recognised by ventral cargo bay. Model 182 features fixed tricycle undercarriage and swept fin.

Cessna Model 172 Skyhawk USA

Type: light sports aircraft   **Accommodation:** two pilots, two passengers

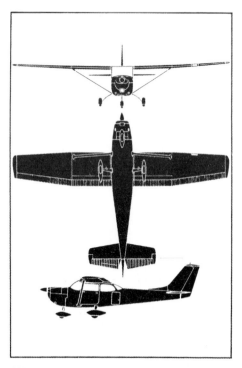

Dimensions:
Length: 26 ft 11 in (8.2 m)
Wingspan: 35 ft 10 in (10.9 m)
Height: 8 ft 9 in (2.7 m)

Weights:
Empty: 1433 lb (650 kg)

Max T/O: 2400 lb (1089 kg)
Payload: 120 lb (54 kg)

Performance:
Max speed: 141 mph (228 kmh)
Range: 875 nm (1620 km)
Power plant: one Avco Lycoming O-320-D2J piston engine
Thrust: 160 hp (119 kW)

Variants:
T-41 Mescalero; floatplane; FR 172K armed version

Notes: One of the most popular light aircraft ever, some 35 545 examples have been built, including the Reims F172 built in France.

Cessna Model 152 Aerobat USA

Type: light sports aircraft   **Accommodation:** two pilots

Dimensions:
Length: 24 ft 1 in (7.3 m)
Wingspan: 32 ft 8 in (9.9 m)
Height: 8 ft 6 in (2.6 m)

Weights:
Empty: 1104 lb (501 kg)

Max T/O: 1670 lb (757 kg)
Payload: 120 lb (54 kg)

Performance:
Max speed: 125 mph (202 kmh)
Range: 625 nm (1158 km)

Power plant: one Avco Lycoming O-235-N2C piston engine
Thrust: 108 hp (80 kW)

Variants:
150 early version

Notes: Very similar to its larger stablemate the 172 Skyhawk, the Aerobat was based on early tail sitting versions of the Model 120/140. Production ended in 1977 after 24 000 had been built, many of them in France by Reims

Cessna Cardinal RG II USA

Type: light sports aircraft   **Accommodation:** two pilots, two passengers

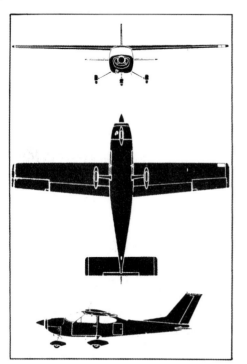

Dimensions:
Length: 27 ft 3 in (8.3 m)
Wingspan: 35 ft 6 in (10.8 m)
Height: 8 ft 7 in (2.6 m)

Weights:
Empty: 1765 lb (801 kg)

Max T/O: 2800 lb (1270 kg)
Payload: 120 lb (54 kg)

Performance:
Max speed: 180 mph
(290 kmh)
Range: 895 nm (1657 km)

Power plant: one Lycoming
IO-360-A1B6D piston engine
Thrust: 200 hp (149 kW)

Variants:
Cardinal with fixed
undercarriage

Notes: The main differences between the Cardinal and other high-winged
Cessnas is its lack of wing bracing struts and undercarriage.

Cessna Stationair 6 USA

Type: light transport   **Accommodation:** two pilots, four to eight passengers

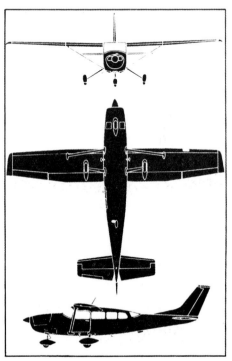

Dimensions:
Length: 28 ft 3 in (8.6 m)
Wingspan: 35 ft 10 in
(10.9 m)
Height: 9 ft 3 in (2.8 m)

Weights:
Empty: 1946 lb (883 kg)

Max T/O: 3600 lb (1633 kg)
Payload: n\a

Performance:
Max speed: 179 mph
(289 kmh)
Range: 900 nm (1666 km)
Power plant: one Continental

IO-520-F piston engine
Thrust: 300 hp (224 kW)

Variants:
Turbo Stationair 6; Stationair
7 and 8 stretched versions

Notes: Designed for the easy loading of small pallets and cargo, the Stationairs can be configured for all-cargo (with one pilot) or all passenger. The 7 and 8 designations refer to the number of passengers they can each carry.

Cessna Model 210 Centurion USA

Type: light sports aircraft   **Accommodation:** two pilots, four passengers

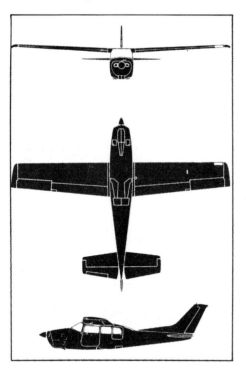

Dimensions:
Length: 28 ft 2 in (8.6 m)
Wingspan: 38 ft 10 in
(12.4 m)
Height: 9 ft 8 in (2.9 m)

Weights:
Empty: 2220 lb (1007 kg)

Max T/O: 3850 lb (1746 kg)
Payload: 240 lb (109 kg)

Performance:
Max speed: 202 mph
(324 kmh)
Range: 1010 nm (1872 km)
Power plant: one Continental

IO-520-L piston engine
Thrust: 300 hp (224 kW)

Variants:
T210 Turbo Centurion;
Pressurized Centurion

Notes: First flown in 1957, the Centurion was Cessna's first light aircraft to feature retractable undercarriage. The pressurised version can be recognised by its four smaller, rounder windows.

Cessna Model 337 Skymaster (O-2A) USA

Type: light transport aircraft   **Accommodation:** two pilots, two passengers

Dimensions:
Length: 29 ft 9 in (9.1 m)
Wingspan: 38 ft 2 in (11.6 m)
Height: 9 ft 2 in (2.7 m)

Weights:
Empty: 2800 lb (1270 kg)
Max T/O: 4630 lb (2100 kg)

Payload: 300 lb (136 kg)

Performance:
Max speed: 198 mph
(319 kmh)
Range: 1235 nm (2288 km)
Power plant: two Continental
IO-360-GB piston engines

Thrust: 420 hp (312 kW)

Variants:
O-2A observation aircraft;
Turbo-Skymaster; P337
Pressurized Skymaster

Notes: The most distinctive of Cessna's light aircraft, all O-2As have been
withdrawn from US Air Force service.

EAPL Eagle X-TS Australia/Malaysia

Type: light sports aircraft   **Accommodation:** two pilots

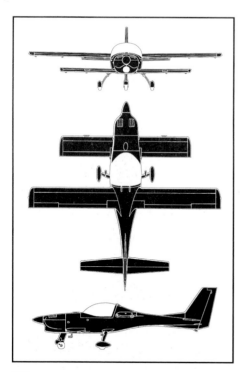

Dimensions:
Length: 21 ft 5 in (6.5 m)
Wingspan: 23 ft 6 in (7.2 m)
Height: 7 ft 5 in (2.3 m)

Weights:
Empty: 930 lb (422 kg)

Max T/O: 1433 lb (650 kg)
Payload: n\a

Performance:
Max speed: 144 mph
(231 kmh)
Range: 520 nm (963 km)

Power plant: one Teledyne
Continental IO-240-A piston
engine
Thrust: 125 hp (92 kW)

Variants:
none

Notes: A very unusual design, the Eagle is the first all-composite aircraft built
in Australia. Production now moved to Malaysia.

EMBRAER EMB-110 Bandeirante Brazil

Type: short-haul commuter   **Accommodation:** two pilots, 21 passengers

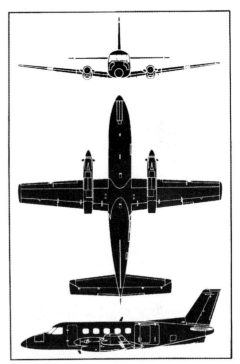

Dimensions:
Length: 47 ft 10 in (14.6 m)
Wingspan: 50 ft 3 in (15.3 m)
Height: 16 ft 1 in (4.9 m)

Weights:
Empty: 7751 lb (3516 kg)
Max T/O: 12 500 lb (5670 kg)

Payload: 3774 lb (1712 kg)

Performance:
Max speed: 286 mph (460 kmh)
Range: 1080 nm (2001 km)
Power plant: two Pratt & Whitney Canada PT6A-34

turboprops
Thrust: 1500 hp (1118 kW)

Variants:
110P1 stretched version; 110P1K SAR version; for military versions see separate entry

Notes: Sold to 80 operators in 36 countries, 500 EMB-110s were delivered before production ceased in 1990.

EMBRAER EMB-121 Xingu Brazil

Type: executive transport   **Accommodation:** two pilots, nine passengers

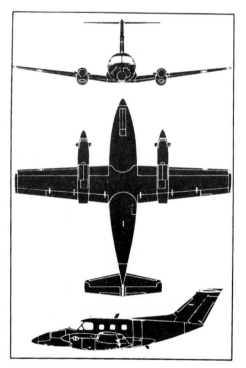

Dimensions:
Length: 40 ft 2 in (12.2 m)
Wingspan: 46 ft 1 in (14.1 m)
Height: 15 ft 10 in (4.8 m)

Weights:
Empty: 7984 lb (3620 kg)

Max T/O: 12 500 lb (5670 kg)
Payload: 1896 lb (860 kg) max

Performance:
Max speed: 280 mph
(450 kmh)
Range: 1270 nm (2352 km)

Power plant: two Pratt &
Whitney Canada PT6A-28
turboprops
Thrust: 1200 hp (1014 kW)

Variants:
re-engined EMB-121A1 Xingu II

Notes: First flown in 1976, the Xingu is certified for single pilot operation. The Xingu II is powered by two PT6A-135 turboprops.

EXTRA 300 Germany

Type: aerobatic competition aircraft   **Accommodation:** one pilot

Dimensions:
Length: 23 ft 4 in (7.1 m)
Wingspan: 26 ft 3 in (8 m)
Height: 8 ft 7 in (2.6 m)

Weights:
Empty: 1389 lb (630 kg)
Max T/O: 1808 lb (820 kg)

Payload: none

Performance:
Max speed: 213 mph
(407 kmh)
Range: 526 nm (974 km)
Power plant: one Textron
Lycoming AEIO-540-L1B5

piston engine
Thrust: 300 hp (224 kW)

Variants:
300S shorter version; EXTRA
230 wooden wings

Notes: Design work began in 1987 and first aircraft flew 1988. 60+ delivered.

Fairchild Merlin 300 USA

Type: medium-haul executive transport

Accommodation: two pilots, ten passengers

Dimensions:
Length: 42 ft 2 in (12.8 m)
Wingspan: 47 ft 10 in (16.6 m)
Height: 16 ft 10 in (5.1 m)

Weights:
Empty: 8450 lb (3833 kg)

Max T/O: 13 230 lb (6001 kg)
Payload: 900 lb (408 kg)

Performance:
Max speed: 340 mph
(548 kmh)
Range: 2312 nm (4284 km)

Power plant: two Garrett
TPE331-10U-503G turboprops
Thrust: 1800 hp (1342 kW)

Variants:
Merlin III earlier version

Notes: Production of the Merlin III ended in 1982, and was superseded by the Merlin 300. The main difference between the two is the addition of winglets in the later aircraft.

Fournier/Sportavia RF6-180 Sportsman France/Germany

Type: light sports aircraft   **Accommodation:** two pilots, two passengers

Dimensions:
Length: 23 ft 5 in (7.2 m)
Wingspan: 34 ft 5 in (10.5 m)
Height: 8 ft 4 in (2.6 m)

Weights:
Empty: 1311 lb (595 kg)

Max T/O: 2425 lb (1100 kg)
Payload: n\a

Performance:
Max speed: 180 mph (290 kmh)
Range: 815 nm (1510 km)

Power plant: one Lycoming O-360-A1F6D piston engine
Thrust: 180 hp (134 kW)

Variants:
RF-6B Club twin seat aerobatic version

Notes: First flown in 1973, the Sportsman is built in Germany, to a French design. The RF-6B Club is broadly similar with the removal of the rear seats and a smaller canopy.

371

Fuji FA-200 Aero Subaru Japan

Type: light sports aircraft   **Accommodation:** two pilots, two passengers

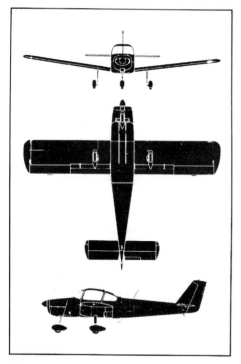

Dimensions:
Length: 26 ft 9 in (8.2 m)
Wingspan: 30 ft 11 in (9.4 m)
Height: 8 ft 6 in (2.6 m)

Weights:
Empty: 1366 lb (620 kg)

Max T/O: 2335 lb (1060 kg)
Payload: 220 lb (100 kg)

Performance:
Max speed: 138 mph (222 kmh)
Range: 655 nm (1215 km)

Power plant: one Lycoming O-320-D2A piston engine
Thrust: 160 hp (119 kW)

Variants:
re-engined 180 and 180AO versions

Notes: First flown in 1965, the 160 and 180 designation refers to the engine power.

FFA AS202 Bravo Switzerland

Type: light sports aircraft   **Accommodation:** two pilots

Dimensions:
Length: 23 ft 5 in (7.2 m)
Wingspan: 31 ft 11 in (9.7 m)
Height: 9 ft 2 in (2.8 m)

Weights:
Empty: 1565 lb (710 kg)

Max T/O: 2160 lb (980 kg)
Payload: 220 lb (100 kg)

Performance:
Max speed: 150 mph
(241 kmh)
Range: 615 nm (1140 km)

Power plant: one Textron
Lycoming AEIO-360-B1F
piston engine
Thrust: 180 hp (134 kW)

Variants:
Wren trainer; Turbine Bravo

Notes: First flown in 1969, it was developed in conjunction with SIAI-Marchetti of Italy. The Wren is used by the BAe Flying College for elementary training. The Turbine Bravo is fitted with an Allison 250-B17C turboprop.

FLS Optica UK

Type: light observation aircraft   **Accommodation:** two pilots, one passenger

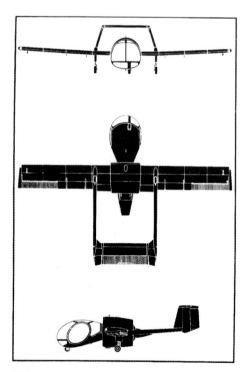

Dimensions:
Length: 26 ft 9 in (8.2 m)
Wingspan: 39 ft 4 in (12 m)
Height: 6 ft 6 in (1.9 m)

Weights:
Empty: 2090 lb (948 kg)
Max T/O: 2899 lb (1315 kg)

Payload: 510 lb (231 kg)

Performance:
Max speed: 132 mph (213 kmh)
Range: 570 nm (1056 km)
Power plant: one ducted Textron Lycoming IO-540-4A5D piston engine
Thrust: 260 hp (194 kW)

Variants:
FLS Scoutmaster proposed surveillance version with radar and FLIR

FLS Club Sprint UK

Type: light sports aircraft   **Accommodation:** two pilots

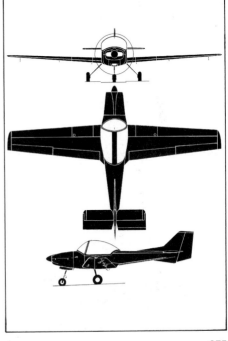

Dimensions:
Length: 21 ft 10 in (6.7 m)
Wingspan: 30 ft 8 in (9.4 m)
Height: 7 ft 7 in (2.3 m)

Weights:
Empty: 1100 lb (499 kg)
Max T/O: 1650 lb (748 kg)

Payload: 100 lb (45 kg)

Performance:
Max speed: 140 mph
(226 kmh)
Range: 620 nm (1149 km)
Power plant: one Textron
Lycoming O-235–L2A piston
engine
Thrust: 118 hp (88 kW)

Variants:
re-engined Super 160; Sprint
Aerobatic version

Notes: First flown in 1993, now being marketed as a basic trainer for aircraft clubs.

General Avia Pinguino Italy

Type: light trainer   Accommodation: two pilots

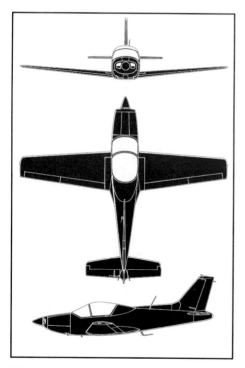

Dimensions:
Length: 24 ft 3 in (7.4 m)
Wingspan: 27 ft 10 in (8.5 m)
Height: 9 ft 3 in (2.8 m)

Weights:
Empty: 1124 lb (510 kg)

Max T/O: 1653 lb (750 kg)
Payload: none

Performance:
Max speed: 166 mph
(269 kmh)
Range: 730 nm (1352 km)

Power plant: one Textron
Lycoming O-235-D2A piston
engine
Thrust: 116 hp (86 kW)

Variants:
retractable undercarriage

Notes: First flown in 1989, deliveries began in 1993. Mainly used at club level for basic training.

Grob G 115 Germany

Type: light sports aircraft   **Accommodation:** two pilots

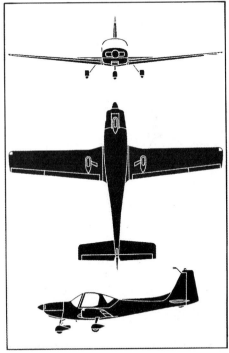

Dimensions:
Length: 24 ft 5 in (7.4 m)
Wingspan: 32 ft 9 in (10 m)
Height: 9 ft (2.7 m)

Weights:
Empty: 1433 lb (650 kg)
Max T/O: 2028 lb (920 kg)

Payload: n/a

Performance:
Max speed: 168 mph
(270 kmh)
Range: 650 nm (1204 km)
Power plant: one Textron
Lycoming O-320-D1A piston

engine
Thrust: 160 hp (119 kW)

Variants:
115 Bavarian; 115D1 Aerobatic
version

Notes: First flown in 1985, production ceased during the early 1990s but has restarted at a rate of 10 a month. The Bavarian was developed for the US market, with fuel in the wings and revised instrument layout.

Grob G 115T Acro Germany

Type: basic trainer   **Accommodation:** two pilots

Dimensions:
Length: 28 ft (8.8 m)
Wingspan: 32 ft 9 in (10 m)
Height: 8 ft 5 in (2.6 m)

Weights:
Empty: 1962 lb (890 kg)

Max T/O: 2976 lb (1350 kg)
Payload: 992 lb (450 kg)

Performance:
Max speed: 183 mph
(295 kmh)
Range: 870 nm (1612 km)

Power plant: one Textron Lycoming AEIO-540-D4A5
piston engine
Thrust: 260 hp (194 kW)

Variants:
none

Notes: Aimed at the US Air Force Enhanced Flight Screener competition, Grob is now marketing it for the civil training market.

Grob GF 200 Germany

Type: touring aircraft   **Accommodation:** one pilot, three passengers

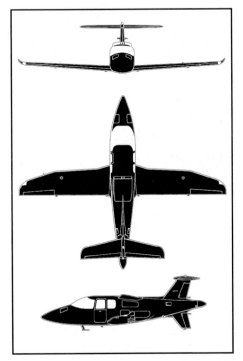

Dimensions:
Length: 28 ft 6 in (8.7 m)
Wingspan: 36 ft (11 m)
Height: 10 ft 10 in (3.3 m)

Weights:
Empty: n\a
Max T/O: 3527 lb (1600 kg)

Payload: 1278 lb (580 kg)

Performance:
Max speed: 229 mph
(370 kmh)
Range: 977 nm (1810 km)
Power plant: Textron
Lycoming TIO-540

turbocharged piston engine
Thrust: 270 hp (201 kW)

Variants:
Unpressurised and pressurised

Notes: First flown in 1991, a turboprop-powered version is under development.

Gulfstream GA-7 Cougar USA

Type: light transport   **Accommodation:** two pilots, two passengers

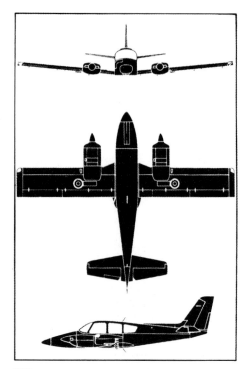

Dimensions:
Length: 29 ft 10 in (9.1 m)
Wingspan: 36 ft 10 in (11.2 m)
Height: 10 ft 4 in (3.2 m)

Weights:
Empty: 2588 lb (1174 kg)

Max T/O: 3800 lb (1724 kg)
Payload: n\a

Performance:
Max speed: 200 mph
(322 kmh)
Range: 1098 nm (2035 km)

Power plant: two Lycoming
0-320-D1D piston engine
Thrust: 320 hp (239 kW)

Variants:
none

Notes: Originally a Grumman design, the Cougar first flew in 1974, and is used mainly in the training role.

Gulfstream AA-5A Cheetah USA

Type: light sports aircraft   **Accommodation:** one pilot, three passengers

Dimensions:
Length: 22 ft (6.7 m)
Wingspan: 31 ft 6 in (9.6 m)
Height: 8 ft (2.4 m)

Weights:
Empty: 1303 lb (591 kg)

Max T/O: 2200 lb (998 kg)
Payload: 120 lb (54 kg)

Performance:
Max speed: 157 mph
(253 kmh)
Range: 814 nm (1509 km)

Power plant: one Lycoming
O-320-E2G piston engine
Thrust: 150 hp (112 kW)

Variants:
re-engined AA-5B Tiger

Notes: First flown in 1970, the Cheetah was originally a Grumman design. The Tiger has a greater fuel load and a 180 hp (134 kW) engine.

Gulfstream AA-1C USA

Type: light sports aircraft   **Accommodation:** one pilot, one passenger

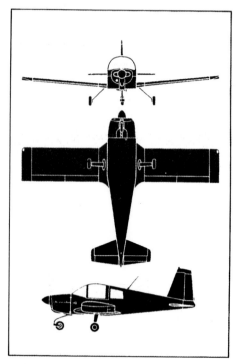

Dimensions:
Length: 19 ft 3 in (5.9 m)
Wingspan: 24 ft 5 in (7.5 m)
Height: 7 ft 6 in (2.3 m)

Weights:
Empty: 1002 lb (454 kg)

Max T/O: 1600 lb (726 kg)
Payload: 100 lb (45 kg)

Performance:
Max speed: 145 mph (234 kmh)
Range: 384 nm (711 km)

Power plant: one Lycoming O-235-L2C piston engine
Thrust: 115 hp (85.7 kW)

Variants:
T-Cat dual control; Lynx deluxe version

Notes: First flown in 1970, the AA-1C was originally designed as a training aircraft.

Helio Super Courier USA

Type: STOL light transport   **Accommodation:** two pilots, four passengers

Dimensions:
Length: 31 ft (9.4 m)
Wingspan: 39 ft (11.9 m)
Height: 8 ft 10 in (2.7 m)

Weights:
Empty: 2080 lb (943 kg)
Max T/O: 3400 lb (1542 kg)

Payload: 1000 lb (454 kg)

Performance:
Max speed: 167 mph (269 kmh)
Range: 1198 nm (2220 km) with external fuel
Power plant: one Lycoming

GO-480-G1D6 piston engine
Thrust: 295 hp (220 kW)

Variants:
U-10 US Air Force designation; Trigear

Notes: First flown in 1958, the US Air Force used Couriers for COIN duties. The Trigear can be recognised by its tricycle undercarriage.

Helio AU-24A Stallion USA

Type: STOL light transport   **Accommodation:** two pilots, eight passengers

Dimensions:
Length: 39 ft 6 in (12.1 m)
Wingspan: 41 ft (12.5 m)
Height: 9 ft 3 in (2.8 m)

Weights:
Empty: 2726 lb (1236 kg)

Max T/O: 5100 lb (2313 kg)
Payload: 1420 lb (644 kg)

Performance:
Max speed: 210 mph
(338 kmh)
Range: 1090 nm (1755 km)

Power plant: Pratt & Whitney
Canada PT6A-27 turboprop
Thrust: 620 hp (462 kW)

Variants:
none

Notes: First flown in 1964, the Stallion has been developed in civil and
military versions. Most US Air Force aircraft were handed over to the Khmer
Air Force.

Jarbiru LSA Australia

Type: light sports aircraft   **Accommodation:** two pilots

Dimensions:
Length: 16 ft 5 in (5 m)
Wingspan: 26 ft 4 in (8 m)
Height: 6 ft 7 in (2.1 m)

Weights:
Empty: 518 lb (235 kg)

Max T/O: 948 lb (430 kg)
Payload: n\a

Performance:
Max speed: 114 mph
(182 kmh)
Range: 360 nm (667 km)

Power plant: one Jarbiru 1600
piston engine
Thrust: 60 hp (44 kW)

Variants:
none

Notes: First flown in 1989, the LSA (Light Sports Aircraft) is one of a series of
very light aircraft to have come out of Australia.

385

Laverda Falco F8 Italy

Type: light sports aircraft   **Accommodation:** two pilots

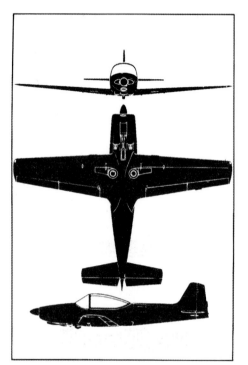

Dimensions:
Length: 21 ft 4 in (6.5 m)
Wingspan: 26 ft 3 in (8 m)
Height: 7 ft 6 in (2.3 m)

Weights:
Empty: 1212 lb (550 kg)

Max T/O: 1808 lb (820 kg)
Payload: 90 lb (40 kg)

Performance:
Max speed: 202 mph
(325 kmh)
Range: 755 nm (1400 km)

Power plant: one Lycoming
O-320-B3B piston engine
Thrust: 160 hp (119 kW)

Variants:
F8L America US version; re-
engined Super Falcon

Notes: First flown in 1955. The Falco is fully aerobatic and was a popular
basic trainer, however it is becoming a rare sight today.

LA-250 Renegade USA

Type: light amphibian   **Accommodation:** pilot, five passengers

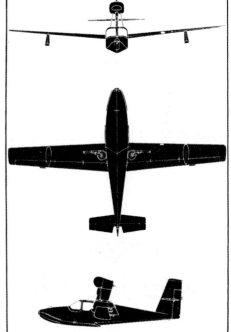

Dimensions:
Length: 28 ft 4 in (8.6 m)
Wingspan: 38 ft 4 in (11.7 m)
Height: 10 ft (3.1 m)

Weights:
Empty: 1850 lb (839 kg)
Max T/O: 3050 lb (1383 kg)

Payload: n\a

Performance:
Max speed: 160 mph (258 kmh)
Range: 900 nm (1668 km)
Power plant: one Textron Lycoming IO-540-C4B5 piston engine
Thrust: 250 hp (186 kW)

Variants:
Lake LA4 Buccaneer early version; Turbo Renegade

Notes: The latest development of the 1948 C-1 Skimmer, over 1300 have been built. The Turbo Renegade has a turbocharged engine, which enabled it to set a world altitude record for light amphibians.

Let L-200 Morava Czech Republic

Type: light transport aircraft   **Accommodation:** two pilots, three passengers

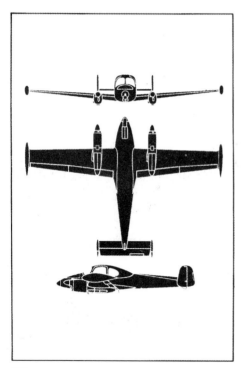

Dimensions:
Length: 28 ft 3 in (8.6 m)
Wingspan: 40 ft 4 in (12.3 m)
Height: 7 ft 4 in (2.3 m)

Weights:
Empty: 2932 lb (1330 kg)

Max T/O: 4300 lb (1950 kg)
Payload: 297 lb (135 kg)

Performance:
Max speed: 180 mph
(290 kmh)
Range: 921 nm (1710 km)

Power plant: two M337
piston engines
Thrust: 420 hp (313 kW)

Variants:
re-engined 200A and 200D

Notes: First flown in 1957, the Morava is a very distinctive aircraft. It can be converted to carry stretchers.

Mooney Ranger USA

Type: light sports aircraft   **Accommodation:** two pilots, two passengers

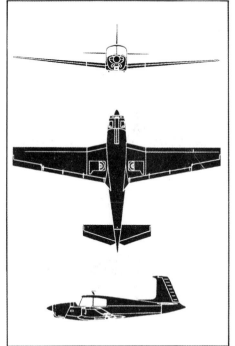

Dimensions:
Length: 24 ft 8 in (7.5 m)
Wingspan: 36 ft 1 in (11 m)
Height: 8 ft 4 in (2.5 m)

Weights:
Empty: 1784 lb (809 kg)

Max T/O: 2740 lb (1243 kg)
Payload: 120 lb (54 kg)

Performance:
Max speed: 202 mph
(325 kmh)
Range: 1059 nm (1961 km)

Power plant: Textron
Lycoming IO-360-A3B6D
piston engine
Thrust: 200 hp (149 kW)

Variants:
201ATS trainer; M20R tourer

Notes: Mooney have developed a range of aircraft with the Ranger's distinctive straight tail fin. The original Ranger first flew in 1961 and versions are still in production.

Mudry CAP 10B France

Type: light sports aerobatic aircraft   **Accommodation:** two pilots

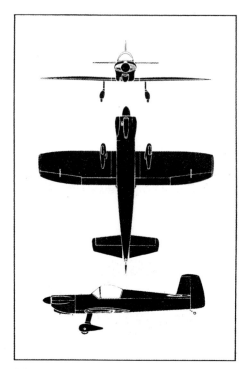

Dimensions:
Length: 23 ft 6 in (7.2 m)
Wingspan: 26 ft 5 in (8.1 m)
Height: 8 ft 4 in (2.6 m)

Weights:
Empty: 1213 lb (550 kg)
Max T/O: 1675 lb (760 kg)

Payload: 44 lb (20 kg)

Performance:
Max speed: 168 mph
(270 kmh)
Range: 539 nm (1000 km)
Power plant: one Textron
Lycoming AEIO-360-B2F

piston engine
Thrust: 180 hp (134 kW)

Variants:
CAP 231, 232 competition
aircraft

Notes: First flown in 1968, the CAP 10B has been superseded in production by the 231 and the latest 232.

Patenavia P68 Victor Italy

Type: light transport   **Accommodation:** one or two pilots, five passengers

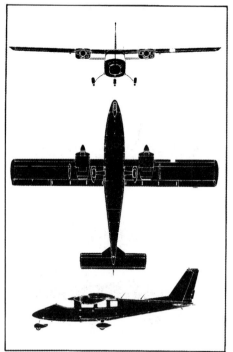

Dimensions:
Length: 31 ft 4 in (9.5 m)
Wingspan: 39 ft 4 in (12 m)
Height: 11 ft 1 in (3.4 m)

Weights:
Empty: 2866 lb (1300 kg)

Max T/O: 4387 lb (1990 kg)
Payload: 399 lb (181 kg)

Performance:
Max speed: 200 mph
(322 kmh)
Range: 1210 nm (2241 km)

Power plant: two Textron
Lycoming IO-360-A1B6 piston
engine
Thrust: 400 hp (298 kW)

Variants:
68 Observer 2; 68R Pulsar

Notes: Production began in 1978 and was restarted in 1993. The Observer has an all glass nose for better visibility, and the Pulsar has retractable undercarriage.

Pilatus PC-12 Switzerland

Type: medium-haul executive transport   **Accommodation:** one or two pilots, nine passengers

Dimensions:
Length: 47 ft 2 in (14.4 m)
Wingspan: 52 ft 9 in (19.1 m)
Height: 13 ft 11 in (4.3 m)

Weights:
Empty: 5260 lb (2386 kg)
Max T/O: 8818 lb (4000 kg)

Payload: 2639 lb (1197 kg)

Performance:
Max speed: 276 mph
(444 kmh)
Range: 1600 nm (2963 km)
Power plant: one Pratt &
Whitney Canada PT6A-67B

turboprop
Thrust: 1605 hp (1197 kW)

Variants:
PC-12F freighter; Combi;
Military version

Notes: An unusual design in having only one engine and a pressurised cabin, the PC-12 first flew in 1991.

Piper PA-31 Navajo USA

Type: light sports aircraft   **Accommodation:** two pilots, four passengers

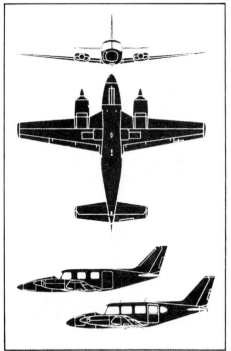

Dimensions:
Length: 32 ft 7 in (9.9 m)
Wingspan: 40 ft 8 in (12.4 m)
Height: 13 ft (3.9 m)

Weights:
Empty: 3991 lb (1810 kg)
Max T/O: 6500 lb (2948 kg)

Payload: 350 lb (159 kg)

Performance:
Max speed: 261 mph
(420 kmh)
Range: 1065 nm (1973 km)
Power plant: two Lycoming
TIO-540-A2C piston engines

Thrust: 620 hp (231 kW)

Variants:
Navajo C/R; Pressurized
Navajo; Navajo Chieftain
stretched version

Notes: First flown in 1964, the Navajo has gone through a number of modifications, the Navajo Chieftain being the most recognizable.

Piper PA-23 Aztec USA

Type: light transport aircraft   **Accommodation:** two pilots, four passengers

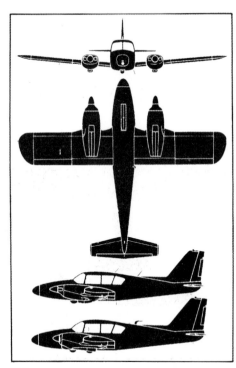

Dimensions:
Length: 31 ft 2 in (9.5 m)
Wingspan: 37 ft 2 in (11.3 m)
Height: 10 ft 4 in (3.2 m)

Weights:
Empty: 3221 lb (1461 kg)

Max T/O: 5200 lb (2360 kg)
Payload: cargo only 1600 lb (725 kg)

Performance:
Max speed: 215 mph (346 kmh)

Range: 1320 nm (2445 km)
Power plant: two Lycoming IO-540-C4B5 piston engine
Thrust: 500 hp (373 kW)

Variants:
see notes

Notes: First flown in 1958, the Aztec has been modified with uprated engines and avionics on a regular basis.

Piper PA-30 Twin Commanche USA

Type: light transport aircraft   **Accommodation:** two pilots, four or six passengers

Dimensions:
Length: 25 ft 2 in (7.7 m)
Wingspan: 35 ft 11 in (10.9 m)
Height: 8 ft 2 in (2.5 m)

Weights:
Empty: 2210 lb (1002 kg)

Max T/O: 3725 lb (1690 kg)
Payload 250 lb (113 kg)

Performance:
Max speed: 272 mph (330 kmh)
Range: 1180 nm (2190 km)

Power plant: two Lycoming IO-320-B piston engines
Thrust: 320 hp (239 kW)

Variants:
Turbo Commanche

Notes: First flown in 1962, it was developed from the earlier single engined Commanche. Turbo Commanche features turbocharged engines, and the tip tanks can be removed. Similar to the Aztec, the Commanche can be recognised by its more pointed nose.

Piper PA-34 Seneca USA

Type: light transport aircraft   **Accommodation:** two pilots, four passengers

Dimensions:
Length: 28 ft 7 in (8.7 m)
Wingspan: 38 ft 10 in (11.8 m)
Height: 9 ft 10 in (3 m)

Weights:
Empty: 2823 lb (1280 kg)

Max T/O: 4570 lb (2073 kg)
Payload: 200 lb (90 kg)

Performance:
Max speed: 225 mph
(361 kmh)
Range: 882 nm (1635 km)

Power plant: two Continental
TSIO-360-E piston engines
Thrust: 400 hp (298 kW)

Variants:
PZL-112 M-20 Mewa Polish
version

Notes: First flown in 1971, the Seneca is very similar to the earlier Twin
Commanche. It can be recognised through the number of windows (four)
along each side.

Piper PA-60 Aerostar USA

Type: light transport aircraft   **Accommodation:** two pilots, four passengers

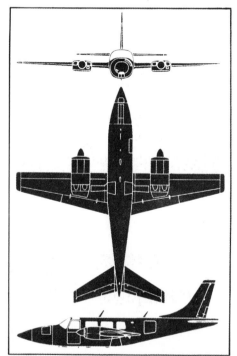

Dimensions:
Length: 34 ft 9 in (10.6 m)
Wingspan: 34 ft 2 in (10.4 m)
Height: 12 ft 1 in (3.7 m)

Weights:
Empty: 3737 lb (1695 kg)

Max T/O: 5500 lb (2495 kg)
Payload: 240 lb (109 kg)

Performance:
Cruising speed: 253 mph (408 kmh)
Range: 1201 nm (2225 km)

Power plant: two Avco Lycoming IO-540-AA1A5 piston engines
Thrust: 580 hp (432 kW)

Variants:
602P pressurised

Notes: First flown in 1967, the Aerostar was taken out of production in 1982 after 1000 had been built. It is very different from other Piper designs with a deeper fuselage and mid-mounted wing.

Piper PA-31T Cheyenne II USA

Type: light transport aircraft   **Accommodation:** two pilots, six passengers

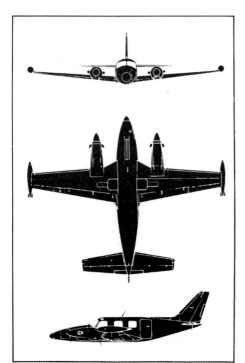

Dimensions:
Length: 34 ft 8 in (10.6 m)
Wingspan: 42 ft 8 in (13 m)
Height: 12 ft 9 in (3.9 m)

Weights:
Empty: 5018 lb (2276 kg)

Max T/O: 9000 lb (4082 kg)
Payload: 500 lb (227 kg)

Performance:
Max speed: 325 mph
(524 kmh)
Range: 1510 nm (2796 km)

Power plant: two Pratt &
Whitney Canada PT6A-28
turboprops
Thrust: 1240 hp (924 kW)

Variants:
executive; T-1040

Notes: First flown in 1969, the Cheyenne was Piper's first turboprop design. The T-1040 commuter has the forward fuselage of the Chieftain with the nose tail and wings of the Cheyenne.

Piper PA-42 Cheyenne III USA

Type: light transport aircraft   **Accommodation:** two pilots, nine passengers

Dimensions:
Length: 43 ft 4 in (13.2 m)
Wingspan: 47 ft 8 in (14.5 m)
Height: 14 ft 9 in (4.5 m)

Weights:
Empty: 6837 lb (3101 kg)

Max T/O: 11 200 lb (5080 kg)
Payload: n\a

Performance:
Max speed: 351 mph (565 kmh)
Range: 2270 nm (4204 km)

Power plant: two Pratt & Whitney Canada PT6A-61 turboprops
Thrust: 1440 hp (1074 kW)

Variants:
re-engined Cheyenne 400

Notes: Developed from the original Cheyenne, the III features a T-tail and a longer fuselage. The 400 is fitted with two Garrett TPE331-14A/14B turboprops.

Piper PA-44 Seminole USA

Type: light transport aircraft   **Accommodation:** two pilots, two passengers

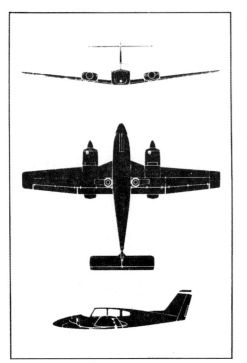

Dimensions:
Length: 27 ft 7 in (8.4 m)
Wingspan: 38 ft 7 in (11.7 m)
Height: 8 ft 6 in (2.6 m)

Weights:
Empty: 2354 lb (1068 kg)

Max T/O: 3800 lb (1723 kg)
Payload: 200 lb (91 kg)

Performance:
Max speed: 193 mph
(311 kmh)
Range: 915 nm (1695 km)

Power plant: two Textron
Lycoming O-360-A1H6 piston
engine
Thrust: 360 hp (268 kW)

Variants:
Turbo-Seminole

Notes: First flown in 1976, the Seminole is very similar to the Beechcraft
Duchess. The Seminole can be recognised by its engines protruding over the
trailing edge of the wing.

Piper PA-46-310P Malibu Mirage USA

Type: light transport aircraft   **Accommodation:** one pilot, five passengers

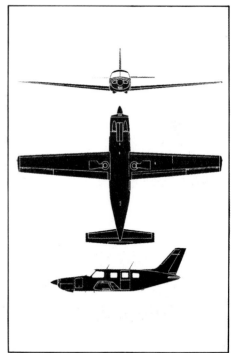

Dimensions:
Length: 28 ft 7 in (8.7 m)
Wingspan: 43 ft (13.1 m)
Height: 11 ft 6 in (3.5 m)

Weights:
Empty: 2626 lb (1191 kg)

Max T/O: 4300 lb (1950 kg)
Payload: 100 lb (45 kg)

Performance:
Max speed: 273 mph (439 kmh)
Range: 1260 nm (2335 km)

Power plant: one Textron Lycoming TIO-540-AE2A piston engine
Thrust: 350 hp (261 kW)

Variants:
none

Notes: When deliveries began in 1983 Piper claimed the Malibu was the only single-engined pressurised light aircraft. Over 520 have been delivered.

Piper Arrow III USA

Type: light sports aircraft   **Accommodation:** two pilots, two passengers

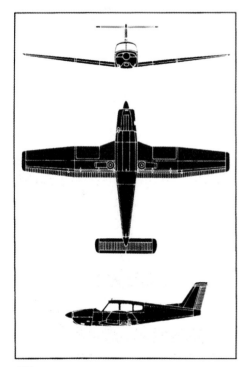

Dimensions:
Length: 24 ft 8 in (7.5 m)
Wingspan: 35 ft 5 in (10.8 m)
Height: 7 ft 10 in (2.4 m)

Weights:
Empty: 1667 lb (756 kg)
Max T/O: 1900 lb (1315 kg)

Payload: 200 lb (90 kg)

Performance:
Max speed: 175 mph (281 kmh)
Range: 875 nm (1621 km)
Power plant: one Textron Lycoming IO-360-C1C6 piston engine
Thrust: 200 hp (149 kW)

Variants:
Turbo Arrow III; Archer earlier model

Notes: A development of the basic Cherokee line, the Arrow is structurally very similar, with the exception of the retractable undercarriage. The Archer is very similar but has fixed undercarriage. Earlier Arrows lacked the T-tail.

Piper Lance USA

Type: light sports aircraft   **Accommodation:** two pilots, four passengers

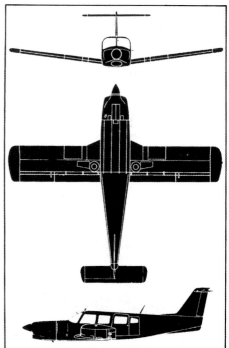

Dimensions:
Length: 27 ft 7 in (8.4 m)
Wingspan: 32 ft 9 in (10 m)
Height: 9 ft (2.7 m)

Weights:
Empty: 1973 lb (895 kg)

Max T/O: 3600 lb (1633 kg)
Payload: 200 lb (90 kg)

Performance:
Max speed: 190 mph
(306 kmh)
Range: 864 nm (1601 km)

Power plant: one Lycoming
IO-540-K1G5 piston engine
Thrust: 300 hp (224 kW)

Variants:
Lance II; Turbo Lance III

Notes: The Lance is a combination of the Cherokee SIX fuselage and wings, Arrow II/III nose and Seneca II landing gear and fuel tanks. Later models featured the Arrow IV's T-tail.

Piper PA-28/PA-32 Cherokee USA

Type: light sports aircraft   **Accommodation:** two pilots, two passengers

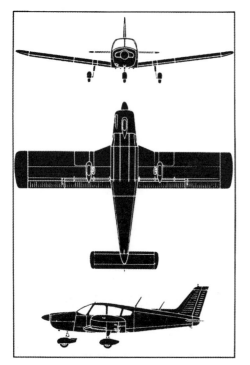

Dimensions:
Length: 23 ft 9 in (7.2 m)
Wingspan: 35 ft (10.7 m)
Height: 7 ft 3 in (2.2 m)

Weights:
Empty: 1416 lb (642 kg)

Max T/O: 2550 lb (1156 kg)
Payload: 200 lb (90 kg)

Performance:
Max speed: 147 mph
(237 kmh)
Range: 630 nm (1168 km)

Power plant: one Lycoming
0-320 piston engine
Thrust: 150 hp (112 kw)

Variants:
Cherokee Warrior II; Cherokee
SIX; re-engined Dakota

Notes: The basis for a number of single-engined Piper designs, the Cherokee was announced in 1964. The Warrior has a longer more tapered wing, the SIX has a longer fuselage with four passengers.

Piper PA-32-301 Saratoga USA

Type: light sports aircraft   **Accommodation:** two pilots, four passengers

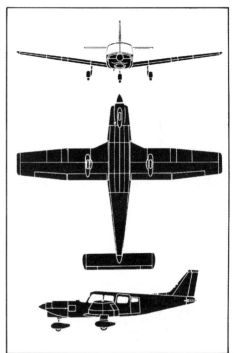

Dimensions:
Length: 27 ft 8 in (8.4 m)
Wingspan: 36 ft 2 in (11 m)
Height: 8 ft 2 in (2.5 m)

Weights:
Empty: 1935 lb (878 kg)

Max T/O: 3600 lb (1633 kg)
Payload 200 lb (90 kg)

Performance:
Max speed: 175 mph (282 kmh)
Range: 960 nm (1778 km)

Power plant: one Textron Lycoming IO-540-K1G5 piston engine
Thrust: 300 hp (224 kW)

Variants:
Saratoga SP; Turbo Saratoga

Notes: The largest of the Cherokee-based aircraft, over 800 Saratogas have been delivered.

Piper PA-18 Super Cub USA

Type: light utility aircraft   **Accommodation:** two pilots in tandem

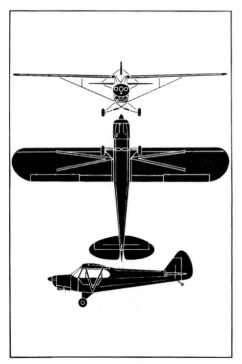

Dimensions:
Length: 22 ft 6 in (6.8 m)
Wingspan: 35 ft 3 in (10.8 m)
Height: 6 ft 8 in (2.1 m)

Weights:
Empty: 1062 lb (482 kg)

Max T/O: 1750 lb (794 kg)
Payload: 50 lb (22 kg)

Performance:
Max speed: 130 mph (210 kmh)
Range: 400 nm (741 km)

Power plant: one Textron Lycoming O-20 piston engine
Thrust: 150 hp (112 kW)

Variants:
see notes

Notes: Many versions of the basic Cub have been developed since production began in 1949. More than 40 000 examples have been built.

PZL-Warszawa PZL-104 Wilga Poland

Type: light utility aircraft   **Accommodation:** one pilot, three passengers

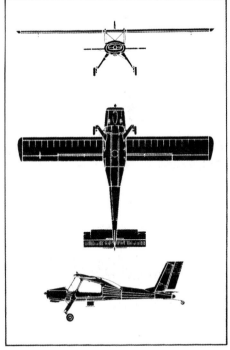

Dimensions:
Length: 26 ft 6 in (8.1 m)
Wingspan: 36 ft 5 in (11.1 m)
Height: 9 ft 8 in (2.9 m)

Weights:
Empty: 1919 lb (870 kg)

Max T/O: 2866 lb (1300 kg)
Payload: 77 lb (35 kg)

Performance:
Max speed: 120 mph (194 kmh)
Range: 275 nm (510 km)

Power plant: PZL AI-14RA-KAF piston engine
Thrust: 260 hp (194 kW)

Variants:
Wilga 35M extended range

Notes: The Wilga is also used as a Glider tug, and in this role can tow up to three gliders with a maximum weight of 2480 lb (1125 kg).

PZL-Warszawa PZL-105L Flaming Poland

Type: light utility aircraft   **Accommodation:** one pilot, five passengers

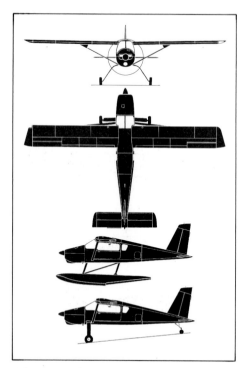

Dimensions:
Length: 28 ft 5 in (8.6 m)
Wingspan: 42 ft 6 in (12.9 m)
Height: 9 ft 5 in (2.8 m)

Weights:
Empty: 2535 lb (1150 kg)

Max T/O: 4078 lb (1850 kg)
Payload: 992 lb (450 kg)

Performance:
Max speed: 162 mph
(260 kmh)
Range: 529 nm (981 km)

Power plant: one Textron
Lycoming IO-720-A1B piston
engine
Thrust: 400 hp (298 kW)

Variants:
105M with VMKB engine

Notes: First flown in 1989, the Flaming (Flamingo) has a STOL capability.

Robin ATL Club France

Type: light sports aircraft   **Accommodation:** two pilots

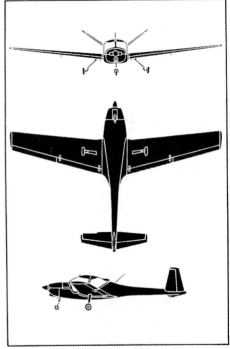

Dimensions:
Length: 22 ft (6.7 m)
Wingspan: 33 ft 7 in (10.2 m)
Height: 6 ft 6 in (2 m)

Weights:
Empty: 794 lb (360 kg)

Max T/O: 1278 lb (580 kg)
Payload: n\a

Performance:
Max speed: 124 mph
(200 kmh)
Range: 539 nm (1000 km)

Power plant: one JPX 4T 60A
piston engine
Thrust: 65 hp (48 kW)

Variants:
Model 88 improved version;
re-engined Model 89

Notes: First flown in 1983, the ATL Club is powered by a converted
Volkswagen car engine.

Robin HR100 France

Type: light sports aircraft   **Accommodation:** two pilots, three passengers

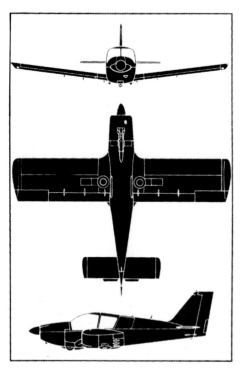

Dimensions:
Length: 24 ft 10 in (7.6 m)
Wingspan: 29 ft 9 in (9.1 m)
Height: 8 ft 10 in (2.7 m)

Weights:
Empty: 1852 lb (840 kg)

Max T/O: 3086 lb (1400 kg)
Payload: n\a

Performance:
Max speed: 196 mph
(315 kmh)
Range: 1149 nm (2130 km)

Power plant: one Lycoming
O-360 piston engine
Thrust: 180 hp (134 kW)

Variants:
100/210 Safari II; 100/250TR;
100/285 Tiara; 100 4+2

Notes: The first Robin HR100 flew in 1971, the 100/250TR has a fuel-injected engine of 250 hp (186 kW), the Tiara has retractable undercarriage. The 4+2 has an enlarged cockpit for six people.

Robin 200 France

Type: light trainer   **Accommodation:** two pilots

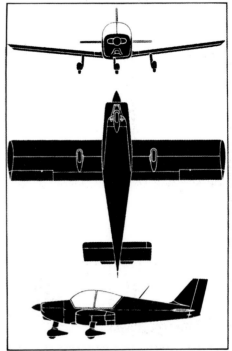

Dimensions:
Length: 21 ft 9 in (6.6 m)
Wingspan: 27 ft 4 in (8.3 m)
Height: 6 ft 4 in (1.9 m)

Weights:
Empty: 1157 lb (525 kg)

Max T/O: 1719 lb (780 kg)
Payload: n\a

Performance:
Cruising speed: 140 mph
(225 kmh)
Range: 566 nm (1050 km)

Power plant: one Textron
Lycoming O-235-L2A piston
engine
Thrust: 118 hp (88 kW)

Variants:
HR200 earlier version

Notes: The Robin HR200 first flew in 1971 and was taken out of production
in 1976. A new production version was launched in 1992.

Robin DR400 France

Type: light sports aircraft   **Accommodation:** two pilots, two or three passengers

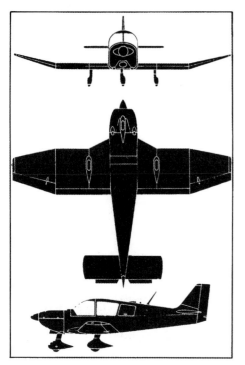

Dimensions:
Length: 22 ft 10 in (6.9 m)
Wingspan: 28 ft 7 in (8.7 m)
Height: 7 ft 3 in (2.2 m)

Weights:
Empty: 1179 lb (535 kg)

Max T/O: 1984 lb (900 kg)
Payload: 121 lb (55 kg)

Performance:
Max speed: 150 mph (241 kmh)
Range: 464 nm (860 km)
Power plant: one Textron

Lycoming O-235-L2A piston
engine
Thrust: 112 hp (84 kW)

Variants:
400 Cadet trainer; 400/160
Major; 400 Remo glider tug

Notes: First flown in 1972, and has been through a process of constant development. The first versions seated two adults and two children, the later versions up to five adults. Remos can be recognised by their double silencers under the fuselage.

Robin R3000 France

Type: light sports aircraft   **Accommodation:** two pilots, two passengers

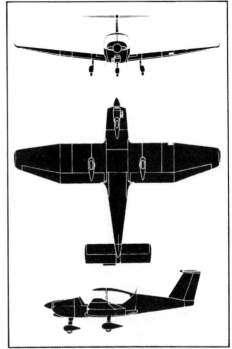

Dimensions:
Length: 24 ft 7 in (7.5 m)
Wingspan: 32 ft 2 in (9.8 m)
Height: 8 ft 8 in (2.7 m)

Weights:
Empty: 1433 lb (650 kg)

Max T/O: 2315 lb (1050 kg)
Payload: 88 lb (40 kg)

Performance:
Max speed: 168 mph
(270 kmh)
Range: 799 nm (1480 km)

Power plant: one Textron
Lycoming O-320-D2A piston
engine
Thrust: 160 hp (119 kW)

Variants:
3000/140 and 3000/160

Notes: First flown in 1980, the R3000 comes with two engine fits, a 160 or 180 hp engine.

Rockwell Commander USA

Type: light sports aircraft   **Accommodation:** one pilot, three passengers

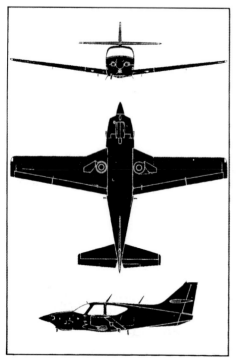

Dimensions:
Length: 25 ft (7.6 m)
Wingspan: 35 ft 7 in (10.8 m)
Height: 8 ft 5 in (2.6 m)

Weights:
Empty: 1773 lb (804 kg)

Max T/O: 2800 lb (1270 kg)
Payload: n\a

Performance:
Max speed: 173 mph
(278 kmh)
Range: 846 nm (1569 km)

Power plant: one Lycoming
IO-360-C1D6 piston engine
Thrust: 200 hp (149 kW)

Variants:
re-engined 112TCA; 114
upgraded version

Notes: First flown in 1970, the Commander 114 has a more powerful engine
and internal equipment changes.

Socata TB 9 Tampico France

Type: light sports aircraft **Accommodation:** two pilots, three passengers

Dimensions:
Length: 25 ft (7.6 m)
Wingspan: 32 ft (9.8 m)
Height: 10 ft 6 in (3.2 m)

Weights:
Empty: 1444 lb (655 kg)

Max T/O: 2332 lb (1058 kg)
Payload: 100 lb (45 kg)

Performance:
Max speed: 140 mph
(226 kmh)
Range: 653 nm (1210 km)

Power plant: one Textron
Lycoming O-320-D2A piston
engine
Thrust: 160 hp (119 kW)

Variants:
TB-10 Tobago; TB 20 Trinidad

Notes: First flown in 1977, the Tobago has a more powerful engine and is used for pilot training. The Trinidad has retractable undercarriage.

Socata Rallye France

Type: light sports aircraft   **Accommodation:** two pilots, two passengers

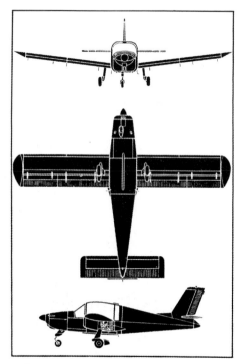

Dimensions:
Length: 23 ft 10 in (7.3 m)
Wingspan: 31 ft 11 in (9.7m)
Height: 9 ft 2 in (2.8 m)

Weights:
Empty: 1530 lb (694 kg)
Max T/O: 2580 lb (1170 kg)

Payload: 242 lb (110 kg)

Performance:
Max speed: 171 mph
(275 kmh)
Range: 675 nm (1250 km)
Power plant: one Lycoming
piston engine

Thrust: between 125 and 235
hp (93 to 175 kW)

Variants:
re-engined 125, 150, 180, 220,
235 versions; 235G Guerrier
military version

Notes: The Rallye has been re-engined on a regular basis, the type number corresponding to the horsepower. Full details are given for the most powerful.

Sukhoi Su-26 Russia

Type: aerobatic competition aircraft   **Accommodation:** one pilot

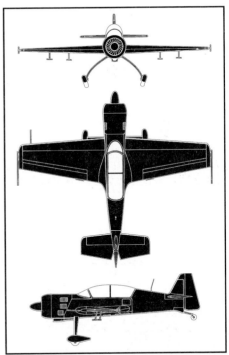

Dimensions:
Length: 22 ft 5 in (6.8 m)
Wingspan: 25 ft 7 in (7.8 m)
Height: 9 ft 1 in (2.8 m)

Weights:
Empty: 1554 lb (705 kg)

Max T/O: 2205 lb (1000 kg)
Payload: none

Performance:
Max speed: 192 mph
(310 kmh)
Range: 432 nm (800 km)

Power plant: VMKB M-14PF
radial engine
Thrust: 394 hp (294 kW)

Variants:
Su-29 advanced version; Su-38 agricultural version

Notes: The Su-29 is very similar but has greater wingspan and length for increased manoeuvrability. There is a two-seat version of the Su-29 for training. The pilot's seat is inclined at 45 deg to counter the effects of g forces.

Thurston TSC-1 Teal USA

Type: light amphibian   **Accommodation:** two pilots

Dimensions:
Length: 23 ft 10 in (7.3 m)
Wingspan: 36 ft (10.9 m)
Height: 9 ft 2 in (2.7 m)

Weights:
Empty: 1500 lb (680 kg)

Max T/O: 2300 lb (1043 kg)
Payload: 250 lb (113 kg)

Performance:
Max speed: 116 mph
(187 kmh)
Range: 434 nm (804 km)

Power plant: one Textron
Lycoming 0-360-A1F6D piston
engine
Thrust: 180 hp (134 kW)

Variants:
TA16 Seafire larger version

Notes: First flown in 1968, the larger Seafire was orignally known as the Teal III. It has a more powerful engine and can seat four people.

Zlin 142 Czech Republic

Type: light sports aircraft   **Accommodation:** two pilots

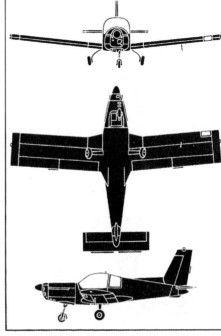

Dimensions:
Length: 23 ft 1 in (7.1 m)
Wingspan: 29 ft 10 in (9.1 m)
Height: 8 ft 10 in (2.7 m)

Weights:
Empty: 1422 lb (645 kg)
Max T/O: 2138 lb (970 kg)

Payload: 100 lb (45 kg)

Performance:
Max speed: 140 mph (226 kmh)
Range: 286 nm (530km)
Power plant: one Avia M337A piston engine

Thrust: 210 hp (156 kW)

Variants:
43 larger version; 42 early version; 242 westernized version

Notes: The 43 can seat four people, the 42 has non-retractable undercarriage and the 242 has a Lycoming engine and a straight wing.

Zlin Z 50L/Z Czech Republic

Type: aerobatic competition aircraft   **Accommodation:** one pilot

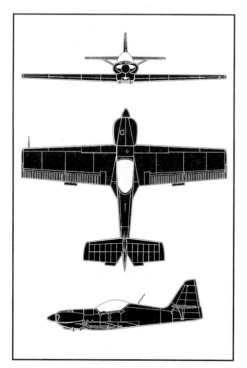

Dimensions:
Length: 21 ft 8 in (6.6 m)
Wingspan: 28 ft 1 in (8.6 m)
Height: 6 ft 6 in (2 m)

Weights:
Empty: 1256 lb (570 kg)

Max T/O: 1587 lb (720 kg)
Payload: none

Performance:
Max speed: 182 mph
(293 kmh)
Range: 345 nm (640 km)

Power plant: one Lycoming
AEIO-540-D4B5 piston engine
Thrust: 260 hp (194 kW)

Variants:
re-engined 50LS

Notes: First flown in 1975, the L50 is stressed to g limits of +9g to -6g. The 50LS is powered by a 300 hp (224 kW).

HELICOPTERS

Aerospatiale SA 315B Alouette II France

Type: light helicopter   **Accommodation:** one pilot; four passengers

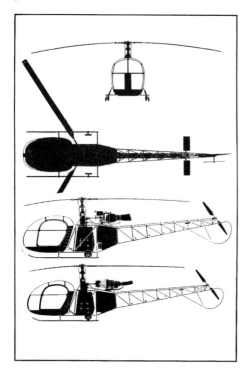

Dimensions:
Length: 33 ft 8 in (10.3 m)
Rotor Diameter: 36 ft 1 in (11 m)
Height: 10 ft 1 in (3.1 m)

Weights:
Empty: 2251 lb (1021 kg)

Max T/O: 5070 lb (2300 kg)
Payload: 2500 lb (1135 kg)

Performance:
Max speed: 130 mph (210 kmh)
Range: 278 nm (515 km)
Power plant: one Turbomeca

Artouste IIIB turboshaft
Power: 870 shp (649 kW)

Variants:
SA 315B Cheetah Indian built;
SA 318C Astazou

Notes: The SA 315B was developed from earlier Alouettes specifically for the Indian armed forces. It incorporated the airframe of the Alouette II with the power plant and rotor system of the Alouette III. Production is still underway in India, where it has set a number of helicopter altitude records.

Aerospatiale SA 319B Astazou
Alouette III France

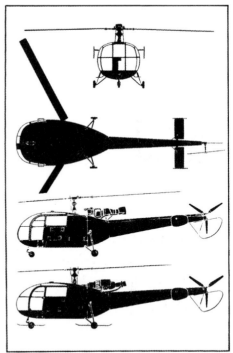

Type: light helicopter   **Accommodation:** two pilots, five passengers

Dimensions:
Length: 33 ft 4 in (10.2 m)
Rotor diameter: 36 ft 1 in (11 m)
Height: 9 ft 9 in (2.9 m)

Weights:
Empty: 2436 lb (1105 kg)
Max T/O: 4630 lb (2100 kg)
Payload: 1650 lb (750 kg)

Performance:
Max speed: 136 mph (220 kmh)
Range: 325 nm (605 km)
Power plant: one Astazou XIV turboshaft
Power: 600 shp (447 kW)

Armament:
AS.12 guided missiles; ASW torpedoes; machine guns; rocket pods

Variants:
ASW helicopter; Chetak Indian built; IAR 316B Romanian-built; IAR 317 Skyfox Romanian gunship

Aerospatiale (Eurocopter) SA 341 Gazelle France

Type: light helicopter   **Accommodation:** one pilot, four passengers

Dimensions:
Length: 39 ft 3 in (11.9 m)
Rotor diameter: 34 ft 5 in (10.5 m)
Height: 10 ft 2 in (3.2 m)

Weights:
Empty: 2022 lb (917 kg)
Max T/O: 3970 lb (1800 kg)
Payload: 1540 lb (700 kg)

Performance:
Max speed: 193 mph (310 kmh)
Range: 361 nm (670 km); 193 nm (360 km) with max payload
Power plant: one Turbomeca Astazou IIIA turboshaft
Power: 590 shp (440 kW)

Armament:
AS.11, AS.12, HOT AT guided missiles; machine guns; rockets

Variants:
G/J commercial versions; C/D training versions; K Kuwaiti version; M French army version

Notes: The first helicopter to feature a fenestron tail rotor, it was also built under licence in the UK (Westland), and Yugoslavia (Soko). Yugoslav versions can carry the SA-7 Grail infra-red seeking missile and AT-3 Sagger guided missiles.

Aerospatiale (Eurocopter)
SA 360 Dauphin France

Type: light helicopter   **Accommodation:** two pilots, eight passengers

Dimensions:
Length: 36 ft (10.9 m)
Rotor diameter: 37 ft 8 in
(11.5 m)
Height: 11 ft 6 in (3.5 m)

Weights:
Empty: 3439 lb (1560 kg)
Max T/O: 6613 lb (3000 lb)

Performance:
Max speed: 196 mph
(315 kmh)

Range: 367 nm (680 km)
Power plant: one Turbomeca
Astazou XVIIA turboshaft
Power: 1050 shp (783 kW)

Variants:
SA 361H up-engined version

Notes: A follw-on design from the Alouette III, the Dauphin first flew in
1972. The Dauphin has broken three speed records for its class. The SA 361H
is powered by a more powerful Astazou XX turboshaft.

425

Aerospatiale (Eurocopter) SA 365
Dauphin 2 France

Type: light helicopter   **Accommodation:** two pilots, 11 passengers

Dimensions:
Length: 38 ft 1 in (11.6 m)
Rotor diameter: 39 ft 2 in (11.9 m)
Height: 13 ft (3.9 m)

Weights:
Empty: 4974 lb (2256 kg)
Max T/O: 9370 lb (4250 kg)

Payload: n\a

Performance:
Max speed: 184 mph (296 kmh)
Range: 484 nm (897 km)
Power plant: two Turbomeca Arriel IC2 turboshafts
Power: 1478 shp (1102 kW)

Armament:
SA.365F only, AS.15TT ASMs

Variants:
SA.365F naval version; HH-65A Dolphin SAR; air ambulance

Notes: Also built under licence in China (Harbin) and Brazil (Helibras). The US Coast Guard operates 101 HH-65As for search and rescue. Police and Coast Guard versions can be recognized by their longer nose radomes, the SA.365F has a 350 deg radar under the nose.

Aerospatiale (Eurocopter) AS 565 Panther France

Type: light helicopter   **Accommodation:** two pilots, 10 troops

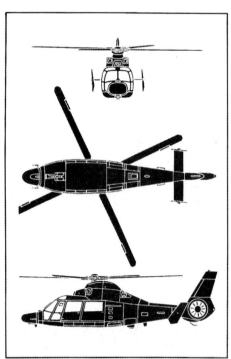

Dimensions:
Length: 38 ft 1 in (11.6 m)
Rotor diameter: 39 ft 2 in (11.9 m)
Height: 13 ft (3.9 m)

Weights:
Empty: 4971 lb (2255 kg)
Max T/O: 9369 lb (4250 kg)
Payload: 3527 lb (1600 kg)

Performance:
Max speed: 184 mph (296 kmh)
Range: 472 nm (875 km)
Power plant: two Turbomeca Arriel IMI turboshafts
Power: 1566 shp (1168 kW)

Armament:
Giat M621 20 mm cannon

pods; Matra Mistral AAMs; HOT AT missiles; 68 mm, 70 mm rockets; AS.15TT ASMs; ASW torpedoes

Variants:
UA utility version; AA/CA armed versions; MA/SA naval versions

Notes: Military version of Dauphin 2. The CA is armed with HOT anti-tank missiles, AA with forward firing cannon and rockets. Only SA can carry the AS-15TT missile and torpedoes. Also built in Brazil as the BH 565/HM-1.

Aerospatiale (Eurocopter)
AS 350 Ecureuil France

Type: light helicopter   **Accommodation:** two pilots, four passengers

Dimensions:
Length: 35 ft 10 in (10.9 m)
Rotor diameter: 35 ft (10.7 m)
Height: 10 ft 11 in (3.3 m)

Weights:
Empty: 2526 lb (1146 kg)
Max T/O: 4630 lb (2100 kg)
Payload: n\a

Performance:
Max speed: 178 mph
(287 kmh)
Range: 394 nm (730 km)
Power plant: one Turbomeca
Arriel 1B turboshaft
Power: 641 shp (478 kmh)

Armament:
Giat M621 20 mm cannon
pod; 7.62 mm machine gun
pod; 68 mm/70 mm rockets;
TOW AT missile

Variants:
B2 re-engined; firefighter;
Fennec military version;
355/555 twin-engined

Notes: A very popular design especially with police forces, over 1700 have
been delivered since it first flew in 1974. The 355 is powered by two TM 319
1A Arrius turboshafts. Both versions are built under licence in Brazil.

Aerospatiale (Eurocopter) AS 330 Puma France

Type: medium lift helicopter   **Accommodation:** two pilots, loadmaster, 20 troops

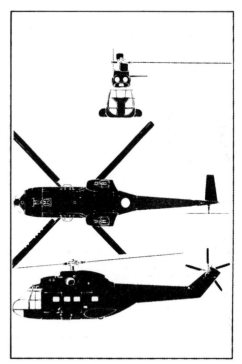

Dimensions:
Length: 46 ft 1 in (14.1 m)
Rotor diameter: 49 ft 2 in (15 m)
Height: 16 ft 10 in (5.1 m)

Weights:
Empty: 8303 lb (3766 kg)
Max T/O: 16 315 lb (7400 kg)
Payload: 7055 lb (3200 kg)

Performance:
Max speed: 168 mph (271 kmh)
Range: 309 nm (572 km)
Power plant: two Turbomeca Turmo IVC turboshafts
Power: 3150 shp (2350 kW)

Armament:
machine guns; South African versions have been fitted with rocket launched guided weapons and cannon.

Variants:
J civil version; L military versions; HC.1 RAF designation; Oryx South African upgrade

Notes: Also built by Westland in the UK and IAR in Romania. Upgrades from Atlas of South Africa can allow a wide range of new weapons and avionics.

Aerospatiale (Eurocopter)
AS 332 Super Puma France

Type: medium lift helicopter   **Accommodation:** two pilots, loadmaster, 25 passengers

Dimensions:
Length: 50 ft 11 in (15.5 m)
Rotor diameter: 51 ft 2 in (15.6 m)
Height: 16 ft 1 in (4.9)

Weights:
Empty: 9546 lb (4330 kg)
Max T/O: 19 841 lb (9000 kg)
Payload: 9920 lb (4500 kg)

Performance:
Max speed: 172 mph (278 kmh)
Range: 672 nm (1245 km)
Power plant: two Turbomeca Makila IA1 free turbines
Power: 3754 shp (2800 kW)

Armament:
20 mm or 7.62 mm guns; 68 mm or 70 mm rockets; naval versions can carry the AM 39 Exocet ASM.

Variants:
VIP transport; military AS 532 Cougar for ASW and utility roles; Horizon battlefield surveillance platform

Notes: An advanced version of the Puma. A stretched version, the MkII was designed primarily for the offshore oil industry and VIP transport. Horizon carries the Orphée radar under the fuselage and was used by French forces in the 1991 Gulf War.

Aerospatiale SA 321 Super Frelon France

Type: heavy lift helicopter   **Accommodation:** two pilots, up to 37 passengers

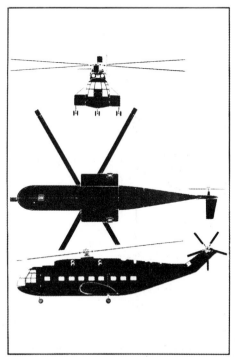

Dimensions:
Length: 63 ft 7 in (19.4 m)
Rotor diameter: 62 ft
(18.9 m)
Height: 16 ft 2 in (4.9 m)

Weights:
Empty: 15 130lb (6863 kg)
Max T/O: 28 660 lb (13 000 kg)
Payload: 11 023 lb (5000 kg)

Performance:
Max speed: 171 mph
(275 kmh)
Range: 549 nm (1020 km)
Power plant: three Turbomeca
Turmo IIIC turboshafts
Power: 4710 shp (3510 kW)

Armament:
ASW torpedoes; depth
charges; machine guns

Variants:
F airliner; G ASW version; H/Ja
utility versions; K non-
amphibious for Israel; L non-
amphibious for South Africa;
M SAR variant for Libya

Notes: Only 100 built. Most versions fully amphibious, however the H model
has no stabilising floats. A Chinese version is also built by CAF, called the Z-8.

Agusta A 109 Italy

Type: light helicopter   **Accommodation:** two pilots, six passengers

Dimensions:
Length: 37 ft 6 in (11.4 m)
Rotor diameter: 36 ft 1 in (11 m)
Height: 11 ft 5 in (3.5 m)

Weights:
Empty: 3503 lb (1590 kg)
Max T/O: 5997 lb (2720 kg)
Payload: 2000 lb (907 kg)

Performance:
Max speed: 193 mph (311 kmh)
Range: 420 nm (778 km)
Power plant: two Allison 250-C20R/1 turboshafts
Power: 900 shp (670 kW)

Armament:
TOW anti-tank missiles; Stinger AAMs; 7.62 mm or 12.7 mm gun pods 70/80 mm rocket launchers

Variants:
109CM; 109EOA anti-tank version; 109KN naval version; 109Max air ambulance

Agusta A 129 Mangusta Italy

Type: attack helicopter   **Accommodation:** two pilots in tandem

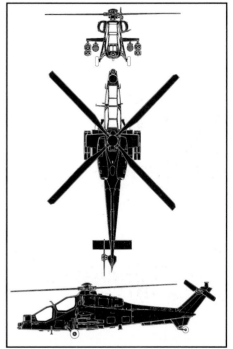

Dimensions:
Length: 40 ft 3 in (12.3 m)
Rotor diameter: 39 ft (11.9 m)
Height: 11 ft (3.3 m)

Weights:
Empty: 5575 lb (2529 kg)
Max T/O: 9039 lb (4100 kg)
Warload: 2645 lb (1200 kg)

Performance:
Max speed: 183 mph (294 kmh)
Endurance: 3 hours 5 minutes
Power plant: two Rolls-Royce 1004 turboshafts
Power: 1650 shp (1230 kW)

Armament:

four hardpoints; TOW 2 or 2A AT missiles; Hellfire; AIM-9L Sidewinder, Matra Mistral AAMs; machine gun pods; rockets

Variants:
anti-ship version; export version

Notes: In service with the Italian army only. The export model is powered by T800 engines, and has an optional 12.7 mm cannon under the nose. A version has also been flown with a five-bladed rotor

Agusta-Bell AB 212 ASW Italy

Type: shipborne anti-submarine helicopter

Accommodation: two pilots, sonar operator, radar operator, or seven passengers

Dimensions:
Length: 42 ft 4 in (12.9 m)
Rotor diameter: 48 ft 2 in (14.7 m)
Height: 14 ft 10 in (4.5 m)

Weights:
Empty: 7450 lb (4320 kg)
Max T/O: 11 176 lb (5070 kg)
Payload: 5000 lb (2270 kg)

Performance:
Max speed: 122 mph (196 kmh)
Range: 360 nm (667 km)
Power plant: one Pratt & Whitney PT6T-6 turbo twin pac
Power: 1875 shp (1398 kW)

Armament:
Marte Mk2, Sea Skua ASMs; ASW torpedoes; depth charges

Variants:
AB 212ECM with RHAWS and ESM used by Greece and Turkey

Notes: Multi-role shipborne design, the 212 ASW can carry out anti-shipping strike or anti-submarine patrol, and can also give mid-course guidance to Ottomat ASMs. Over 100 are in service, and production continues.

Agusta-Sikorsky AS-61 Italy/USA

Type: medium-lift naval helicopter

Accommodation: two pilots, (SH-3H) two sonar operators, 28 passengers

Dimensions:
Length: 54 ft 9 in (16.7 m)
Rotor diameter: 62 ft (18.9 m)
Height: 15 ft 6 in (4.7 m)

Weights:
Empty: 11 865 lb (5382 kg)
Max T/O: 21 000 lb (9525 kg)
Payload: 8000 lb (3630 kg)

Performance:
Max speed: 165 mph (267 kmh)
Range: 630 nm (1166 km)
Power plant: two General Electric T58-GE-100 turboshafts
Power: 3000 shp (2236 kW)

Armament:
(SH-3H) ASW torpedoes; depth charges; AS.12, Marte Mk2 or Exocet or Harpoon ASMs

Variants:
SH-3H shipborne ASW version; 61N1 Silver offshore transport; 61R SAR version

Notes: Agusta began licence building the Sikorsky S-61 in 1967. Agusta has produced several other variants including VIP transports and utility versions.

435

Atlas CSH-2 Rooivalk South Africa

Type: attack helicopter   **Accommodation:** pilot (rear), co-pilot/gunner (front)

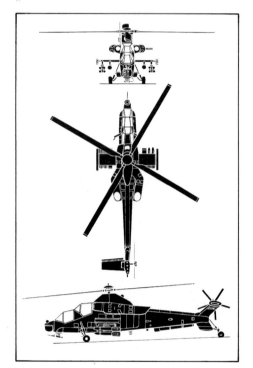

Dimensions:
Length: 53 ft 9 in (16.4 m)
Rotor diameter: 51 ft 1 in (15.6 m)
Height: 15 ft (4.6 m)

Weights:
Empty: 13 029 lb (5910 kg)
Max T/O: 19 290 lb (8750 kg)
Warload: 3022 lb (1371 kg)

Performance:
Max speed: 192 mph (309 kmh)
Range: 507 nm (940 km); 720 nm (133 5km) with external fuel
Power plant: two Topaz turboshafts
Power: 4000 shp (2982 kW)

Armament:
one 20 mm GA-1 Rattler cannon; ZT-3 Swift or ZT-35 AT missiles; V3C Darter AAMs; 68 mm rockets

Variants:
none

Notes: First flown in 1990, the Rooivalk is South Africa's first indigenous helicopter design. Developed from licence-built AS 330 Puma transport helicopter, with similar engines and rotor system.

Bell Model 47 USA

Type: light helicopter   **Accommodation:** two pilots, one passenger

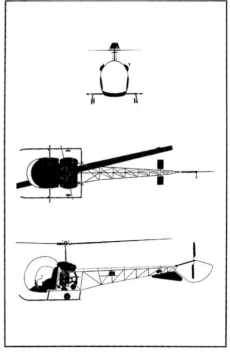

Dimensions:
Length: 31 ft 7 in (9.6 m)
Rotor diameter: 37 ft 1 in (11.3 m)
Height: 9 ft 3 in (2.8 m)

Weights:
Empty: 1848 lb (838 kg)

Max T/O: 2850 lb (1293 kg)
Payload: 1000 lb (455 kg)

Performance:
Max speed: 105 mph (169 kmh)
Range: 324 nm (520 km)
Power plant: one Lycoming

VO-540-B1B piston engine
Power: 280 hp (208.9 kW)

Variants:
air ambulance; agricultural sprayer

Notes: First flew in 1945, the Model 47 was produced in Italy and the UK as well as the USA. In the air ambulance role two stretchers can be carried above the skids, outside the cabin.

Bell Model 205 UH-1 Iroquois (Huey) USA

Type: medium lift helicopter   **Accommodation:** two pilots, 12 passengers, six stretchers

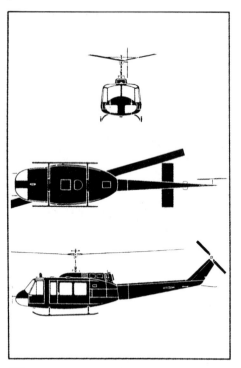

Dimensions:
Length: 41 ft 9 in (17.6 m)
Rotor diameter: 48 ft (14.6 m)
Height: 14 ft 5 in (4.4 m)

Weights:
Empty: 5210 lb (2363 kg)
Max T/O: 9500 lb (4309 kg)
Payload: 3880 lb (1759 kg)

Performance:
Max speed: 127 mph
(204 kmh)
Range: 276 nm (511 km)
Power plant: one Textron
Lycoming T53-L-13 turboshaft
Power: 1400 shp (1044 kW)

Armament:
two machine guns in door;
optional rockets and machine
gun pods

Variants:
204 earlier version with
shorter fuselage; gunship;
ambulance; trainer

Notes: Built in huge numbers in the USA between 1959 and 1987, production
continues in Japan. In operational configuration two passengers can be
replaced by a loadmaster and door gunner each with a 7.62 mm M60
machine gun.

Bell Model 212 UH-1N Iroquois (Twin Huey) USA

Type: medium lift helicopter   **Accommodation:** two pilots, 14 passengers

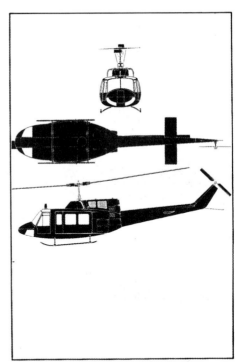

Dimensions:
Length: 42 ft 4 in (12.9 m)
Rotor diameter: 48 ft 2 in (14.7 m)
Height: 14 ft 10 in (4.5 m)

Weights:
Empty: 5997 lb (2720 kg)

Max T/O: 11 200 lb (5080 kg)
Payload: 5000 lb (2268 kg)

Performance:
Max speed: 115 mph (185 kmh)
Range: 227 nm (420 km)
Power plant: one Pratt &

Whitney Canada PT6A-3B turbo twin pack
Power: 1800 shp (1342 kg)

Variants:
412 with four rotor blades; 214ST super transporter; 214C SAR; firefighter

Notes: Originally designed for the Canadian government as the CH-135, the twin Huey was also adopted by the USMC and Navy. It was also produced in Italy. The 412 was designed to reduce noise, vibration and cargo capacity.

439

Bell Model 206 Jetranger USA

Type: light helicopter **Accommodation:** two pilots; three passengers

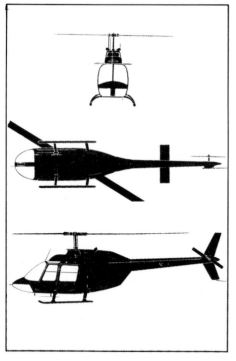

Dimensions:
Length: 31 ft 2 in (9.5 m)
Rotor diameter: 33 ft 4 in
(10.2 m)
Height: 9 ft 6 in (2.9 m)

Weights:
Empty: 1625 lb (737 kg)

Max T/O: 3200 lb (1451 kg)
Payload: 1500 lb (635 kg)

Performance:
Max speed: 140 mph
(225 kmh)
Range: 395 nm (732 km)
Power plant: Allison 250-C20J

turboshaft
Power: 317 shp (236 kW)

Variants:
TH-67 trainer; 206LT
Twinranger

Notes: Over 7000 have been produced since deliveries began in 1971. The Longranger has a stretched cabin to accommodate five passengers or stretchers. A Jetranger was the first helicopter to fly around the world.

Bell Model 206L-4 Longranger USA

Type: light utility helicopter   **Accommodation:** two pilots, five passengers

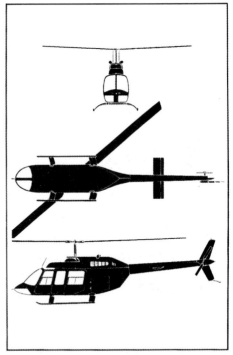

Dimensions:
Length: 34 ft 3 in (10.4 m)
Rotor diameter: 37 ft (11.3 m)
Height: 10 ft 3 in (3.1 m)

Weights:
Empty: 2258 lb (1024 kg)

Max T/O: 4150 lb (1882 kg)
Payload: 2000 lb (907 kg)

Performance:
Max speed: 150 mph (241 kmh)
Range: 360 nm (666 km)

Power plant: one Allison 250-C30P turboshaft
Power: 650 shp (485 kW)

Variants:
air ambulance;

Notes: A stretched development of the standard Jetranger, 1100 have been delivered since it began production in 1973. Its extra length also allows it to carry stretchers.

Bell OH-58D Kiowa USA

Type: light reconnaissance helicopter   **Accommodation:** two pilots side-by-side

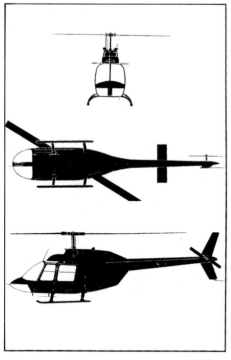

Dimensions:
Length: 34 ft 4 in (10.5 m)
Rotor diameter: 35 ft (10.7 m)
Height: 12 ft 10 in (3.9 m)

Weights:
Empty: 3045 lb (1381 kg)
Max T/O: 4500 lb (2041 kg)
Warload: 2000 lb (907 kg)

Performance:
Max speed: 147 mph
(237 kmh)
Range: 250 nm (463 km)
Power plant: one Allison 250-
C30R turboshaft
Power: 650 shp (485 kW)

Armament:
Kiowa Warrior; Stinger AAMs;
Hellfire AT missiles; gun pods;
rockets

Variants:
Kiowa Warrior armed version;
OH-58A/B/C earlier
observation variants

Notes: All OH-58Ds will be upgraded to Kiowa Warrior standard. A stealth kit is available to reduce the Kiowa Warrior's radar cross section. By using the mast mounted sight to identify and illuminate targets, the Kiowa can control missiles from other helicopters without revealing its location.

Bell Model 222 USA

Type: executive tranport helicopter   **Accommodation:** two pilots, seven passengers

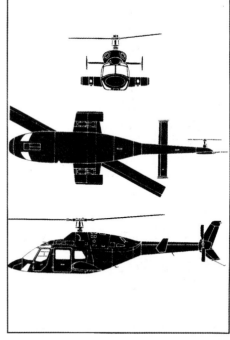

Dimensions:
Length: 42 ft 2 in (12.8 m)
Rotor diameter: 42 ft (12.8 m)
Height: 11 ft 6 in (3.5 m)

Weights:
Empty: 4900 lb (2223 kg)
Max T/O: 8250 lb (3742 kg)

Payload: n\a

Performance:
Max speed: 172 mph
(278 kmh)
Range: 373 nm (691 km)
Power plant: two Textron
Lycoming LTS 101-750C-1

turboshafts
Power: 1368 shp (1020 kW)

Variants:
222UT Utility; Model 230
advanced version

Notes: The utility version is widely used by police forces and as an air ambulance, it can be recognized by its fixed skids instead of the tricycle wheels.

Bell AH-1 Huey Cobra USA

Type: attack helicopter   **Accommodation:** pilot, co-pilot gunner in tandem

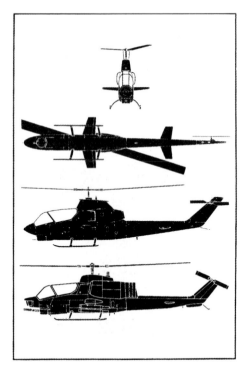

Dimensions:
Length: 45 ft 6 in (13.9 m)
Rotor diameter: 48 ft (14.6 m)
Height: 13 ft 6 in (4.1 m)

Weights:
Empty: 10 200 lb (4627 kg)
Max T/O: 14 750 lb (6690 kg)
Warload: 2466 lb (1118 kg)

Performance:
Max speed: 175 mph (282 kmh)
Range: 343 nm (635 km)
Power plant: one Textron Lycoming T53-L-703 turboshaft
Power: 1800 shp (1342 kW)

Armament:
one three-barrel M197 20 mm gun; four hardpoints; TOW, Hellfire AT missiles; gun pods; rockets

Variants:
single engined AH-1S (US Army); twin engined Sea Cobra; four-blade AH-1W Super Cobra

Notes: The Sea Cobra and Super Cobra can be recognised by their rounder canopies and their twin engine installation. Trials have been carried out with AIM-9 Sidewinders and AGM-65 Mavericks, using a modified Sea Cobra.

Bell/Boeing MV-22 Osprey USA

Type: tilt-rotor transport   **Accommodation:** two pilots, crew chief; 24 troops

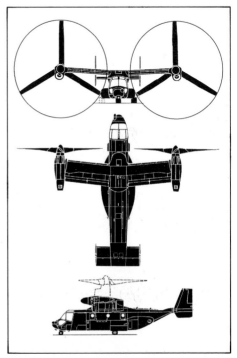

Dimensions:
Length: 57 ft 4 in (17.5 m)
Rotor diameter: 38 ft (11.6 m) each
Height: 17 ft 8 in (5.4 m)

Weights:
Empty: 31 886 lb (14 463 kg)
Max T/O: 55 000 lb (24 947 kg)
Payload: 20 000 lb (9072 kg)

Performance:
Max speed: 345 mph (556 kmh); 115 mph (185 kmh) helicopter mode
Range: 2100 nm (3892 km)
Power plant: two Allison T406-AD-400 turboshafts
Power: 12 300 shp (9172 kW)

Armament:
door-mounted machine guns; ASW versions will be adapted to carry torpedoes and depth charges

Variants:
Proposed SV-22 ASW; CV-22 special ops; HV-22 combat SAR

Notes: V-22 is the first tilt rotor production aircraft. The US Air Force, Navy and Army have also expressed interest in specialist versions.

Boeing/Sikorsky RAH-66 Commanche USA

Type: reconnaissance/attack helicopter   **Accommodation:** two pilots in tandem

Dimensions:
Length: 43 ft 4 in (13.2 m)
Rotor diameter: 39 ft (11.9 m)
Height: 11 ft 1 in (3.4 m)

Weights:
Empty: 7749 lb (3515 kg)

Max T/O: 10 112 lb (4587 kg)
Warload: 2612 lb (1185 kg)

Performance:
Max speed: 204 mph
(328 kmh)
Range: 1260 nm (2344 km)

with external tanks
Power plant: two LHTEC T800-LHT-801 turboshafts
Power: 2688 shp (2004 kW)

Variants:
none

Notes: The first helicopter designed with stealth features, the fuselage is angled and the weapon stations retract into the fuselage to reduce radar cross signature. Designed for nap-of-earth flying the pilots have identical glass cockpits; may also be fitted with the Longbow mast-mounted radar.

Brantly B-2 USA

Type: light helicopter   **Accommodation:** two pilots

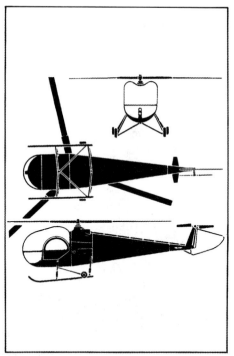

Dimensions:
Length: 21ft 9 in (6.6 m)
Rotor diameter: 23 ft 9 in (7.2 m)
Height: 6 ft 9 in (2.1 m)

Weights:
Empty: 1020 lb (463 kg)

Max T/O: 1670 lb (757 kg)
Payload: 50 lb (22.7 kg)

Performance:
Max speed: 100 mph (161 kmh)
Range: 217 nm (400 km)
Power plant: one Textron
Lycoming IVO-360-A1A piston engine
Power: 180 shp (134 kW)

Variants:
none

Notes: First flown in 1953, the B-2 was put back into production as a cheap helicopter trainer in 1990. Production has again ended, but many remain in service, especially in Japan.

Brantly 305 USA

Type: light helicopter　　　**Accommodation:** two pilots, three passengers

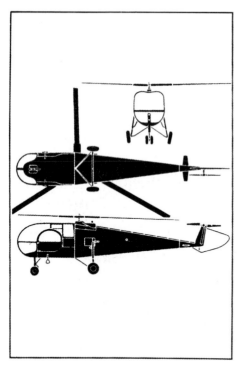

Dimensions:
Length: 24 ft 5 in (7.4 m)
Rotor diameter: 28 ft 8 in (8.7 m)
Height: 8 ft 1 in (2.4 m)

Weights:
Empty: 1800 lb (816 kg)

Max T/O: 2900 lb (1315 kg)
Payload: 250 lb (113 kg)

Performance:
Max speed: 120 mph (193 kmh)
Range: 191 nm (354 km)
Power plant: one Textron Lycoming IVO-540-B1A piston engine
Power: 305 shp (227 kW)

Variants:
none

Notes: First flown in 1964, new production began again in 1993. Basic structure similar to the B-2, with an extended fuselage and more powerful engine.

Boeing Vertol CH-47 Chinook USA

Type: heavy-lift helicopter   **Accommodation:** two pilots, crew chief, 55 troops, 24 stretchers

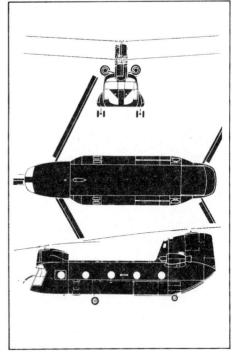

Dimensions:
Length: 51 ft (15.5 m)
Rotor diameter: 60 ft
(18.3 m) each
Height: 18 ft 11 in (5.8 m)

Weights:
Empty: 26 918 lb (12 210 kg)

Max T/O: 54 000 lb (24 494 kg)
Payload: 27 082 lb (12 284 kg)

Performance:
Max speed: 177 mph
(285 kmh)
Range: 613 nm (1136 km)
Power plant: two Textron

Lycoming T55-L-712
turboshafts
Power: 6000 shp (4474 kW)

Variants:
CH-47D with refuelling boom;
MH-47E special ops version

Notes: The Royal Air Force operates a number of standard Chinooks as special forces transports. They are fitted with extra defensive aids, sat comms, extra armour and miniguns. The MH-47E is a more extensive refit with powerful ECM equipment, in-flight refuelling, extra fuel tanks and advanced navigation systems.

Boeing Vertol CH-46 Sea Knight USA

Type: medium-lift helicopter   **Accommodation:** two pilots, crew chief, 25 troops

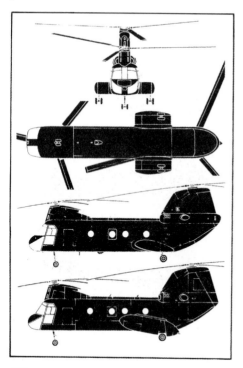

Dimensions:
Length: 44 ft 10 in (13.7 m)
Rotor diameter: 51 ft (15.5 m) each
Height: 16 ft 8 in (5.1 m)

Weights:
Empty: 13 067 lb (5927 kg)

Max T/O: 23 000 lb (10 433 kg)
Payload: 9000 lb (4082 kg)

Performance:
Max speed: 159 mph (256 kmh)
Range: 206 nm (383 km)
Power plant: two General

Electric T58-GE-16 turboshafts
Power: 3740 shp (2788 kW)

Variants:
Model 107 civil version; KV-107 and HKP-2 Rolls-Royce powered and Japanese-built

Notes: Also known by the US Marine Corps as the Frog, the CH-46 first flew in 1958 and is due for replacement by the V-22. Often mistaken for the Chinook, it has a tricycle undercarriage, whereas the CH-47 has four wheels.

Enstrom F-28 USA

Type: light helicopter   **Accommodation:** pilot, two passengers

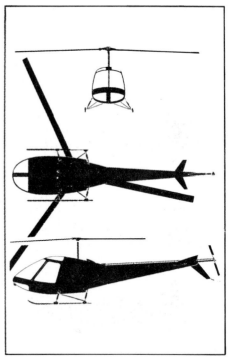

Dimensions:
Length: 29 ft 3 in (8.9 m)
Rotor diameter: 32 ft (9.7 m)
Height: 9 ft 2 in (2.8 m)

Weights:
Empty: 1570 lb (712 kg)
Max T/O: 2600 lb (1179 kg)

Payload: 108 lb (49 kg)

Performance:
Max speed: 117 mph (189 kmh)
Range: 260 nm (483 km)
Power plant: one Textron Lycoming HIO-360-F1AD

piston engine
Power: 225 shp (168 kW)

Variants:
Model 280 advanced version; Sentinel police version; 480 turboshaft powered version

Notes: Used by Chile and Peru for training, over 170 are in service around the world. The 480 is powered by a Allison 250-C20W turboshaft and is faster and longer-ranged.

Eurocopter Tiger France/Germany

Type: attack helicopter   **Accommodation:** pilots (front), weapons operator (rear) in tandem

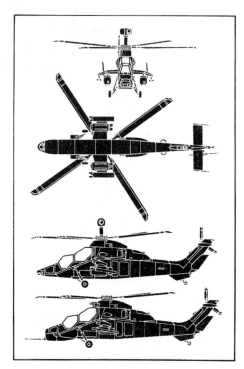

Dimensions:
Length: 45 ft 11 in (14 m)
Rotor diameter: 42ft 7in (13m)
Height: 14 ft 2 in (4.3 m)

Weights:
Empty: 7275 lb (3300 kg)
Max T/O: 12 787 lb (5800 kg)
Warload: n\a

Performance:
Max speed: 174mph (280kmh)
Endurance: 2 hours 50 min
Power plant: two MTU/Rolls-Royce/Turbomeca MTR 390 turboshafts
Power: 2342 shp (1746 kW)

Armament:
(HAP) GIAT AM-30781 cannon;

Matra Mistral AAMs; 68 mm rockets; (UHU/HAC) HOT 2 or Trigat AT missiles; Stinger or Matra Mistral AAMs

Variants:
Tigre HAP French escort; Tigre HAC French anti-tank; UHU German anti-tank

Notes: First flown in 1993, it has been flown in mock-up form of all its different versions. Can be fitted with or without a mast-mounted sight.

EHI EH.101 Merlin Italy/UK

Type: shipborne ASW helicopter   **Accommodation:** two pilots, observer, sonar operator

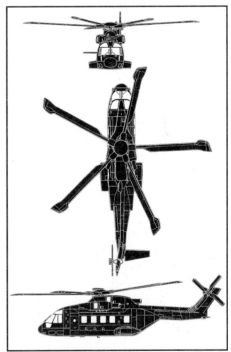

Dimensions:
Length: 74 ft 10 in (22.8 m)
Rotor diameter: 61 ft (18.6 m)
Height: 21 ft 10 in (6.6 m)

Weights:
Empty: 15 700 lb (7121 kg)
Max T/O: 28 660 lb (13 000 kg)
Payload: 8598 lb (3900 kg)

Performance:
Max speed: 192 mph
(309 kmh)
Range: 625 nm (1158 km)
Power plant: three Rolls-
Royce Turbomeca RTM 322
turboshafts (UK); General
Electric T700-GE-T6A (Italy)
Power: 6936 shp (5172 kW) -

5142 lb (3834 kg)

Armament:
ASW torpedoes; Sea Skua
ASMs; depth charges

Variants:
Utility with rear loading ramp;
civil Heliliner

Notes: Primarily designed for anti-submarine warfare the Merlin is being studied as a AEW, ECM and SAR platform. The Heliliner can carry 30 passengers. Utility versions can be fitted with stub wings for rockets, a chin mounted cannon and door guns.

453

Guimbal G2 Cabri France

Type: light helicopter   **Accommodation:** two pilots

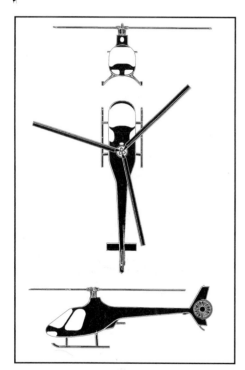

Dimensions:
Length: 18 ft 10 in (5.7 m)
Rotor diameter: 21 ft 4 in (6.5 m)
Height: 6 ft 10 in (2.1 m)

Weights:
Empty: 705 lb (320 kg)

Max T/O: 1212 lb (550 kg)
Payload: n\a

Performance:
Max speed: 124 mph (200 kmh)
Range: 539 nm (1000 km)
Power plant: one Textron

Lycoming O-320 piston engine
Power: 150 shp (112 kW)

Variants:
none

Notes: First flown in 1992, the G2 is a private venture that is still undergoing its test programme.

Kaman SH-2G Seasprite USA

Type: shipborne anti-submarine helicopter   **Accommodation:** two pilots, sonar operator, four passengers

Dimensions:
Length: 40 ft (12.2 m)
Rotor diameter: 44 ft 4 in
(13.5 m)
Height: 15 ft (4.6 m)

Weights:
Empty: 7600 lb (3447 kg)
Max T/O: 13 500 lb (6124 kg)

Payload: 4000 lb (1814 kg)

Performance:
Max speed: 159 mph
(256 kmh)
Range: 478 nm (885 km) with
external tanks
Power plant: General Electric
T700-GE-401 turboshafts

Power: 3446 shp (2570 kW)

Armament:
ASW torpedoes; depth
charges; 7.62 mm door guns

Variants:
SH-2F earlier variant

Notes: First flown in 1959 as a single-engined ASW helicopter (SH-2A), it was put back into production in 1981. The Seasprite is also known as the Light Airborne Multi-Purpose System (LAMPS I).

Kaman K-Max USA

Type: external lift helicopter   **Accommodation:** one pilot

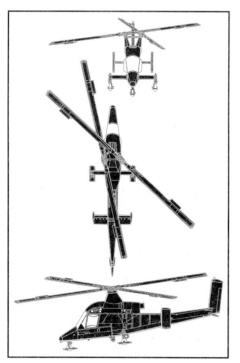

Dimensions:
Length: 52 ft (15.8 m)
Rotor diameter: 48 ft 4 in
(14.7 m)
Height: n\a

Weights:
Empty: 4500 lb (2041 kg)

Max T/O: 11 500 lb (5216 kg)
Payload: 6000 lb (2721 kg)

Performance:
Max speed: 127 mph (204
kmh); 92 mph (148 kmh) with
external load
Range: n\a

Power plant: one Lycoming
T53A-1 turboshaft
Power: 1350 shp (1007 kW)

Variants:
none

Notes: Also known as the aerial truck and air crane, the K-Max is the only modern helicopter using intermeshing rotors. The intermeshing system means that all power is producing lift.

Kamov Ka-25 Hormone Russia

Type: shipborne anti-submarine helicopter

Accommodation: two pilots, (optional) 12 passengers

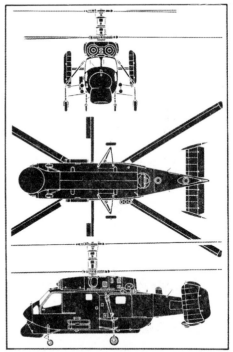

Dimensions:
Length: 32 ft (9.7 m)
Rotor diameter: 51 ft 7 in (15.7 m)
Height: 17 ft 7 in (5.4 m)

Weights:
Empty: 10 505 lb (4765 kg)
Max T/O: 15 873 lb (7200 kg)

Payload: 2866 lb (1300 kg)

Performance:
Max speed: 130 mph (209 kmh)
Range: 351 nm (650 km) with external tanks
Power plant: two Mars GTD-3F turboshafts

Power: 1776 shp (1324 kW)

Armament:
ASW torpedoes; depth charges

Variants:
25Ts special electronic version; 25BShZ minesweeper; 25 PS SAR version

Notes: Built primarily for ASW, the 25Ts carries out over-the-horizon targeting for long-range anti-ship missiles fired from surface ships.

Kamov Ka-126 Hoodlum Russia

Type: general purpose civil helicopter

Accommodation: one or two pilots, six passengers

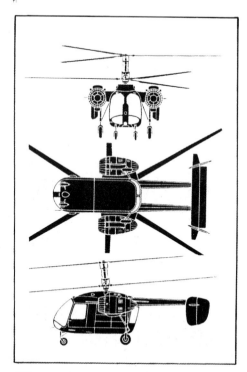

Dimensions:
Length: 25 ft 6 in (7.7 m)
Rotor diameter: 42 ft 7 in (13 m)
Height: 13 ft 7 in (4.2 m)

Weights:
Empty: 4222 lb (1915 kg)
Max T/O: 7165 lb (3250 kg)

Payload: 2205 lb (1000 kg)

Performance:
Max speed: 112 mph (180 kmh)
Range: 384 nm (713 km); 136 nm (235 kmh) with max payload
Power plant: one Mars TV-O-100 turboshaft
Power: 700 shp (522 kW)

Variants:
126 early version with two piston engines; agricultural sprayer; firefighter; 128 re-engined version

Notes: The original Ka-26 first flew in 1965 and the turboshaft version, offering greater range and payload, in 1986. The aircraft consists of the cabin, engines and control surfaces linked by a rigid backbone, various pods can then be fitted in the space below the engines.

Kamov Ka-27 Helix Russia

Type: Shipborne anti-submarine helicopter   **Accommodation:** two pilots, systems operator

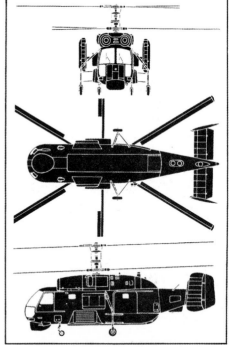

Dimensions:
Length: 37 ft 1 in (11.3 m)
Rotor diameter: 52 ft 2 in
(15.9 m)
Height: 17 ft 8 in (5.4 m)

Weights:
Empty: 14 330 lb (6500 kg)
Max T/O: 24 250 lb (11 000 kg)
Payload: 11 023 lb (5000 kg)

Performance:
Max speed: 168 mph
(270 kmh)
Radius of action: 108 nm
(200 km)
Power plant: (Ka-28) two
Klimov TV3-117BK turboshafts
Power: 4340 shp (3236 kW)

Armament:
ASW torpedoes; depth charges

Variants:
27PS SAR version; Ka-28
export version; Ka-32 civil
firefighter or utility; Ka-32S
civil SAR and ice recce variant

Notes: Built to overcome inability of Ka-25 to operate at night and in adverse
weather, Helix first flew in 1973 but wasn't seen in the West until 1981.

Kamov Ka-29 Russia

Type: assault helicopter   **Accommodation:** two pilots, 16 troops

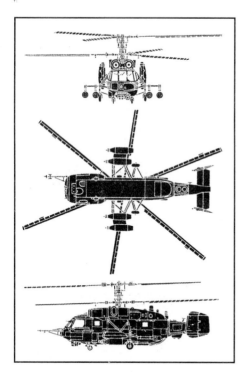

Dimensions:
Length: 37 ft 1 in (11.3 m)
Rotor diameter: 52 ft 2 in (15.9 m)
Height: 17 ft 8 in (5.4 m)

Weights:
Empty: 12 170 lb (5520 kg)
Max T/O: 27 775 lb (12 600 kg)
Payload: 8818 lb (4000 kg)

Performance:
Max speed: 174 mph (280 kmh)
Range: 248 nm (460 km)
Power plant: two Klimov TV3-117V turboshafts
Power: 4380 shp (3266 kW)

Armament:
two 7.62 mm Gatling type machine guns in doors; four hardpoints; AT-6 Spiral AT missiles; 57 mm or 80 mm rockets; 23 mm or 30 mm gun pods

Variants:
29RLD AEW version, now redesignated Ka-31

Notes: In service in 1985 to transport marine units and support amphibous landings. To protect the crew and passengers the cabin and engine bays are heavily armoured. The 29RLD carries a large retractable planar array antenna under the fuselage and is used as a radar picket from aircraft carriers.

Kamov Ka-50 Werewolf (Hokum) Russia

Type: attack helicopter   **Accommodation:** one pilot

Dimensions:
Length: 52 ft 6 in (16 m)
Rotor diameter: 47 ft 7 in (14.5 m)
Height: 16 ft 2 in (4.9 m)

Weights:
Empty: n\a
Max T/O: 23 810 lb (10 800 kg)

Warload: 6610 lb (3000 kg)

Performance:
Max speed: 193 mph (310 kmh)
Endurance: four hours with auxiliary tanks
Power plant: two Klimov TV3-117VK turboshafts

Power: 4380 shp (3266 kW)

Armament:
one 30 mm 2A42 cannon; Vikhr (AT-12) AT missiles; 80 mm rockets; 23 mm gun pods

Variants:
Ka-52 Hokum B two-seater

Notes: A heavily armed and heavily armoured attack helicopter, the Ka-50 is being evaluated by the Russian Army. The only single pilot attack helicopter, the pilot is the only helicopter crewman equipped with an ejector seat.

MBB (Eurocopter)-Kawasaki BK 117 Germany/Japan

Type: multi-purpose civil helicopter   **Accommodation:** one or two pilots, 10 passengers

Dimensions:
Length: 32 ft 6 in (9.9 m)
Rotor diameter: 36 ft 1 in (11 m)
Height: 12 ft 7 in (3.8 m)

Weights:
Empty: 3869 lb (1755 kg)

Max T/O: 7385 lb (3350 kg)
Payload: 2200 lb (998 kg)

Performance:
Max speed: 173 mph (278 kmh)
Range: 292 nm (541 km)
Power plant: Lycoming LTS

101-750B-1 turboshafts
Power: 1100 shp (820 kW)

Variants:
C-1 German version; P5 fly-by-wire prototype

Notes: First flown in 1979 as a joint venture, the BK 117 is also produced in Indonesia by ITPN and assembled in Korea by Hyundai. Like the BO 105 it has clamshell doors in the rear fuselage making the loading of stretchers easier. India is to licence build versions for naval, army and civil roles.

MBB (Eurocopter) Bo 105 Germany

Type: light helicopter   **Accommodation:** two pilots, three passengers

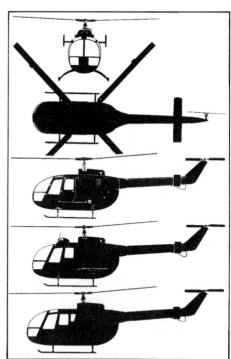

Dimensions:
Length: 28 ft 11 in (8.8 m)
Rotor diameter: 32 ft 3 in (9.8 m)
Height: 9 ft 11 in (3 m)

Weights:
Empty: 2868 lb (1301 kg)
Max T/O: 5511 lb (2500 kg)
Payload: n\a

Performance:
Max speed: 149 mph (240 kmh)
Range: 550 nm (1020 km)
Power plant: Allison 250-C20B turboshafts
Power: 840 shp (626 kW)

Armament:
(PAH-1) HOT AT missiles

Variants:
PAH-1 anti-tank version; Bo 105CBS stretched six-seater; Bo 105M VBH scout; Bo 105ATH anti-tank version for SPain; Bo 105GSH gun-armed recce version for Spain; HKp 9B TOW-armed Bo 105CBS for Sweden

MBB (Eurocopter) Bo EC 135 Germany

Type: light civil helicopter   **Accommodation:** one or two pilots, seven passengers

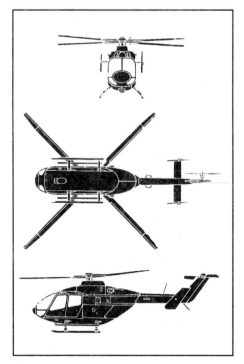

Dimensions:
Length: 32 ft 10 in (10 m)
Rotor diameter: 33 ft 5 in (10.2 m)
Height: 10 ft 7 in (3.3 m)

Weights:
Empty: 2866 lb (1300 kg)

Max T/O: 5511 lb (2500 kg)
Payload: 2646 lb (1200 kg)

Performance:
Max speed: 168 mph (270 kmh)
Range: 432 nm (800 km)
Power plant: Turbomeca

Arrius 2B turboshafts
Power: 918 shp (684 kW)

Variants:
MBB 108 earlier version

Notes: The original Bo 108 was a streched, more powerful development of the Bo 105. The EC 135 is now marketed by Eurocopter, fitted with a New Generation Fenestron. It can also be fitted with a Pratt & Whitney Canada PW206B powerplant.

Mil Mi-2 Hoplite Russia/Poland

Type: light helicopter   **Accommodation:** one or two pilots, eight passengers

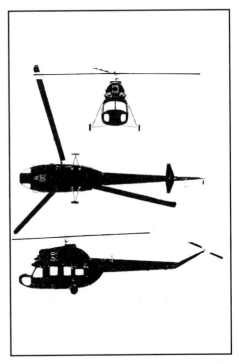

Dimensions:
Length: 37 ft 4 in (11.4 m)
Rotor diameter: 47 ft 6 in (14.5 m)
Height: 12 ft 3 in (3.7 m)

Weights:
Empty: 5295 lb (2402 kg)
Max T/O: 7826 lb (3550 kg)
Payload: 1763 lb (800 kg)

Performance:
Max speed: 124mph (200kmh)
Range: 237 nm (440 km)
Power plant: Two Isotov GTD-350 turboshafts
Power: 800 shp (298 kW)

Armament:
(2RN) 57 mm rockets; gun pods; (2US) one 23 mm NS-23KM cannon; four 7.62 mm machine guns; (2URP) AT-3 Sagger AT missiles; 9M32 Strela 2 AAMs

Variants:
2B upgrade; 2RM naval version; 2RN armed reconnaissance; 2US gunship; 2URP anti-tank version

Notes: Designed and first flown in Russia in 1961, all production switched to PZL Swidnik in Poland in 1965. Over 5250 aircraft of all types have been produced, the airframe also formed the basis of the Polish W-3 Sokol (see separate entry).

Mil Mi-8/-17 Hip Russia

Type: medium-lift multi-purpose helicopter   **Accommodation:** two pilots, optional flight engineer, 24 troops, 12 stretchers

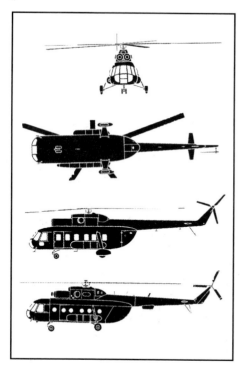

Dimensions:
Length: 60 ft 5 in (18.4 m)
Rotor diameter: 69 ft 10 in (21.3 m)
Height: 15 ft 7 in (4.7 m)

Weights:
Empty: 15 555 lb (7055 kg)
Max T/O: 28 660 lb (13 000 kg)
Payload: 8820 lb (4000 kg)

Performance:
Max speed: 155 mph (250 kmh)
Range: 575 nm (1065 km) with auxiliary tanks
Power plant: two Klimov TV3-117MT turboshafts
Power: 3846 shp (2868 kW)

Armament:
one 12.7 mm machine gun; AT-2 Swatter AT missiles; 57 mm rockets

Variants:
Mi-8 early version; Hip-E and Hip-F armed versions; air ambulance; firefighter; -8MTV converted to -17 standard; Mi-8S civil/military passenger transport with rectangular windows

Notes: Mi-8 flown in 1961, Mi-17 mid-life upgrade replaced Mi-8 in production in 1981. They can be recognised by tail rotor on port side for Mi-17 and starboard for Mi-8.

Mil Mi-8/-17 Hip specialist version Russia

Type: medium-lift EW Helicopter   **Accommodation:** two pilots, mission specialists

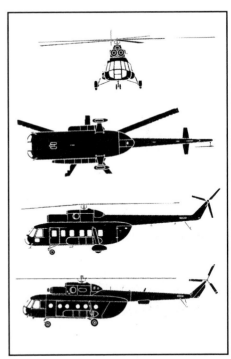

Dimensions:
Length: 60 ft 5 in (18.4 m)
Rotor diameter: 69 ft 10 in (21.3 m)
Height: 15 ft 7 in (4.7 m)

Weights:
Empty: 15 555 lb (7055 kg)
Max T/O: 28 660 lb (13 000 kg)

Payload: 8820 lb (4000 kg)

Performance:
Max speed: less than 155 mph (250 kmh)
Range: under 575 nm (1065 km) with auxiliary tanks
Power plant: two Klimov TV3-117MT turboshafts

Power: 3846 shp (2868 kW)

Variants:
Hip-D comms; Hip-J ECM version; Hip-K (Mi-8PP) comms jamming; 17P ECM comms jammer; Mi-9 airborne control

Notes: Several EW versions are in service with Russia and ex-Warsaw Pact countries. Mi-8PP can be recognized by its star-shaped arrays, the Mi-17P by its flat arrays housing round antennas. Czech EW versions have a large array of cylinders and the Mi-9 has large 'hockey stick' antennae from rear of cabin and tailboom.

Mil Mi-14 Haze Russia

Type: land-based ASW helicopter   **Accommodation:** two pilots, sonar helicopter, MAD operator

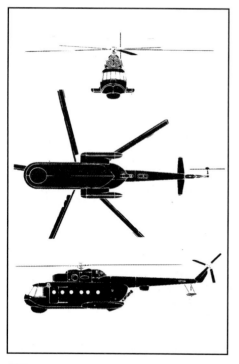

Dimensions:
Length: 60 ft 3 in (18.4 m)
Rotor diameter: 69 ft 10 in (21.3 m)
Height: 22 ft 9 in (6.9 m)

Weights:
Empty: 25 900 lb (11 750 kg)

Max T/O: 30 865 lb (14 000 kg)
Payload: n\a

Performance:
Max speed: 143 mph (230 kmh)
Range: 612 nm (1135 km)
Power plant: two Klimov TV3-117A turboshafts
Power: 3354 shp (2500 kW)

Armament:
ASW torpedoes; depth charges

Variants:
-14BT minesweeper; -14PS SAR version; -14PX Polish SAR

Notes: Developed from the Mi-8 Hip, the Mi-14 first flew in 1969. It differs from the Mi-8 by its boat hull and stability sponsons, retractable undercarriage and under fuselage radar.

Mil Mi-24 Hind Russia

Type: attack/assault helicopter   **Accommodation:** pilot (rear), weapons operator (front), optional flight engineer, eight troops

Dimensions:
Length: 57 ft 5 in (17.5 m)
Rotor diameter: 56 ft 9 in (17.3 m)
Height: 13 ft (3.9 m)

Weights:
Empty: 18 078 lb (8200 kg)
Max T/O: 24 690 lb (11 200 kg)
Warload: 5290 lb (2400 kg)

Performance:
Max speed: 208 mph (335 kmh)

Range: 540 nm (1000 km) with auxiliary tanks
Power plant: Klimov TV3-117 turboshafts
Power: 4380 shp (3266 kW)

Armament:
12.7 mm Gatling type gun in nose; AT-2 Swatter, AT-6 Spiral AT missiles; 57 mm or 80 mm rockets; 23 mm or 12.7 mm gun pods; 30 mm grenade launcher; bombs; chemical weapons; mine

dispensers

Variants:
24A early glasshouse version; 24VP with twin 23 mm cannon; 24P with 30 mm cannon; 24R chemical reconnaissance version; 24K reconnaissance version; Mi-35M upgraded aircraft with Mi-28-type rotor, new avionics and cropped wings

Notes: First seen in the West in 1974, the cabin design was changed in 1977. Since then it has been mainly used in the gunship role, the cabin being used to house reloads.

Mil Mi-26 Halo Russia

Type: heavy-lift helicopter **Accommodation:** two pilots, flight engineer, navigator, 80 troops, 60 stretchers

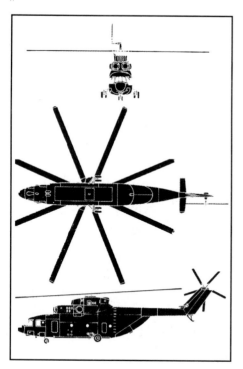

Dimensions:
Length: 110 ft 8 in (33.7 m)
Rotor diameter: 105 ft (32 m)
Height: 26 ft 8 in (8.2 m)

Weights:
Empty: 62 170 lb (28 200 kg)
Max T/O: 123 450 lb
(56 000 kg)

Payload: 44 090 lb (20 000 kg)

Performance:
Max speed: 183 mph
(295 kmh)
Range: 432 nm (800 km)
Power plant: two ZMKB
Progress D-135 free-turbine
turboshafts

Power: 20 000 shp (14 920 kW)

Variants:
26MS medical version; 26TM
flying crane; 26TZ tanker;
26M upgraded version;
firefighter

Notes: The largest helicopter in production, its cargo capacity is similar to that of the C-130 Hercules. Over 300 have been built since it entered squadron service in 1982. The Mi-26TM has a two-man gondola under the fuselage for control during crane operations.

Mil Mi-28 Havoc Russia

Type: attack helicopter   **Accommodation:** pilot (rear) and gunner (front)

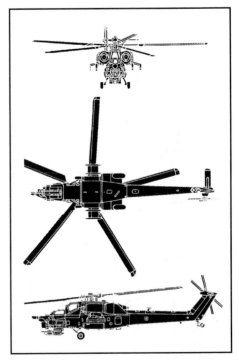

Dimensions:
Length: 55 ft 9 in (17 m)
Rotor diameter: 56 ft 5 in
(17.2 m)
Height: 15 ft 5 in (4.7 m)

Weights:
Empty: 17 846 lb (8095 kg)
Max T/O: 25 705 lb (11 660 kg)

Warload: 4000 lb (1814 kg)

Performance:
Max speed: 186 mph
(300 kmh)
Range: 248 nm (460 km)
Power plant: two Klimov TV3-
117VM turboshafts
Power: 4140 shp (3090 kW)

Armament:
one 30 mm NPPU-28 cannon;
SA-16 Gimlet AAMs; AT-6
Spiral AT missiles; 130 mm or
80 mm rockets

Variants:
28N all-weather version

Notes: In competition with the Kamov Ka-50 for the Russian Army's next generation attack helicopter, the Mi-28 first flew in 1982. Versions for naval duties are also being considered.

Mil Mi-6 Hook Russia

Type: heavy-lift helicopter   **Accommodation:** two pilots, flight engineer, navigator, radio operator, 70 troops

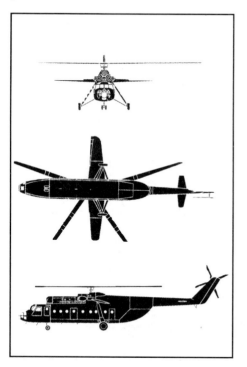

Dimensions:
Length: 108 ft 10 in (33.2 m)
Rotor diameter: 114 ft 10 in (35 m)
Height: 32 ft 4 in (9.9 m)

Weights:
Empty: 60 055 lb (27 240 kg)

Max T/O: 84 657 lb (38 400 kg)
Payload: 26 450 lb (12 000 kg)

Performance:
Max speed: 186 mph (300 mph)
Range: 540 nm (1000 km)
Power plant:

Aviadvigatel/Soloviev D-25V turboshafts
Power: 10 850 shp (8090 kW)

Variants:
6VKP Hook B command post; Mi-22 Hook C developed airborne command post

Notes: When it first flew in 1957 it was by far the largest helicopter in the world. Many of its dynamic parts were used to build the Mi-12, the largest helicopter ever flown. Command versions have numerous antennas along their tail booms and fuselages.

Mil Mi-34 Hermit Russia

Type: light helicopter   **Accommodation:** two pilots, two passengers

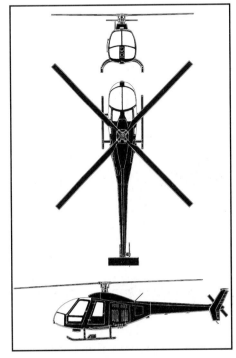

Dimensions:
Length: 28 ft 8 in (8.7 m)
Rotor diameter: 32 ft 9 in
(10 m)
Height: n\a

Weights:
Empty: n\a
Max T/O: 2976 lb (1350 kg)
Payload: n\a

Performance:
Max speed: 136 mph
(220 kmh)

Range: 194 nm (360 km)
Power plant: one VMKB M-14V-26 piston engine
Power: 325 shp (243 kW)

Variants:
Mi-34VAZ twin-engined
version with new rotor head

Notes: Designed as a light transport aerobatic helicopter, Mil claims the Mi-34 can perform normal loops and rolls. Most have been ordered for police and ambulance duties.

McDonnell Douglas Model 500 USA

Type: light utility helicopter   **Accommodation:** one or two pilots, three passengers

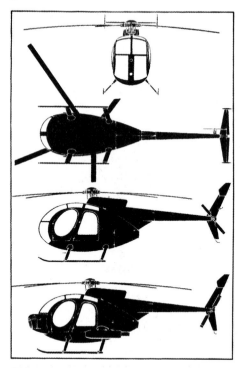

Dimensions:
Length: 23 ft (7 m)
Rotor diameter: 26 ft 6 in (8.1 m)
Height: 8 ft 6 in (2.6 m)

Weights:
Empty: 1320 lb (598 kg)
Max T/O: 3000 lb (1360 kg)
Payload: n\a

Performance:
Max speed: 152 mph (244 kmh)
Range: 325 nm (603 km)
Power plant: Allison 250-C18A turboshaft
Power: 317 shp (236 kW)

Armament:
TOW AT missiles; Stinger AAMs; 30 mm cannon pod; 7.62 mm machine gun pod; rockets

Variants:
OH-6A Cayuse observation helicopter; 500MD Defender military versions; AH-6/MH-6 Special Operations variants (latest are 500/520 hybrids)

Notes: Developed from the US Army's OH-6A Cayuse observation helicopter, the civil version entered production in 1968. The Defender series includes a Taiwanese shipborne ASW version fitted with a large towed MAD detector.

McDonnell Douglas Model 500E USA

Type: light utility helicopter   **Accommodation:** one or two pilots, four passengers

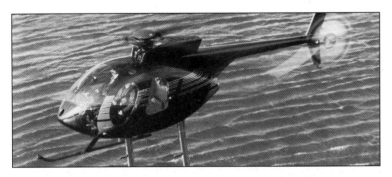

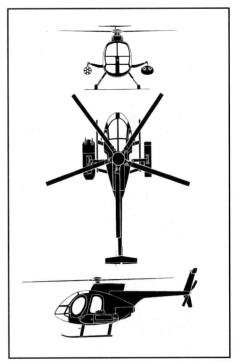

Dimensions:
Length: 24 ft 7 in (7.5 m)
Rotor diameter: 26ft 5in (8.1m)
Height: 8 ft 9 in (2.7 m)

Weights:
Empty: 1445 lb (655 kg)
Max T/O: 3550 lb (1610 kg)
Payload: (530F) 2000lb (907kg)

Performance:
Max speed: 175 mph (282 kmh)
Range: 233 nm (431 km)
Power plant: one Allison 250-C20B turboshaft
Power: 420 shp (313 kW)

Armament:
TOW AT missiles; Stinger AAMs; 30 mm cannon pod; 7.62 mm machine gun pod; rockets

Variants:
530F flying crane; 520N with NOTAR; 530 Defender series

Notes: A development of the 500D series, the E model featured a new engine and re-designed fuselage. Defender versions can be equipped with a mast mounted sight and other have been tailored for special forces requirements. The NOTAR (No Tail Rotor) uses a system of ducted fans to replace the conventional tail rotor.

McDonnell Douglas AH-64 Apache USA

Type: attack helicopter   **Accommodation:** pilot (rear), co-pilot/gunner (front)

Dimensions:
Length: 51 ft (15.5 m)
Rotor diameter: 48 ft (14.6 m)
Height: 12 ft 7 in (3.8 m)

Weights:
Empty: 11 387 lb (5165 kg)
Max T/O: 21 000 lb (9525 kg)
Warload: n\a

Performance:
Max speed: 227mph (365kmh)
Range: 260 nm (482 km)
Power plant: two General
Electric T700-GE-701
turboshafts
Power: 3392 shp (2530 kW)

Armament:
one 30 mm M230 Chain Gun;
Hellfire AT missiles; Stinger or
Starstreak AAMs; 2.75 in
rockets

Variants:
AH-64A early version; AH-64D
Longbow radar equipped
version

Notes: Over 930 Apaches have been built and six countries are now operating them. The British Army and the Netherlands have recently ordered large numbers of the AH-64D Longbow Apache, which can be recognized by its large mast-mounted radar.

McDonnell Douglas MD Explorer USA

Type: light NOTAR utility helicopter   **Accommodation:** one or two pilots, six passengers

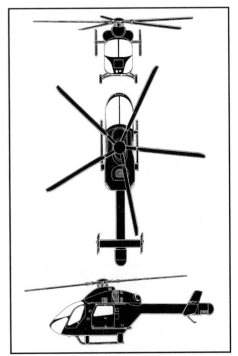

Dimensions:
Length: 31 ft 10 in (9.7 m)
Rotor diameter: 33 ft 10 in (10.3 m)
Height: 12 ft (3.6 m)

Weights:
Empty: 3215 lb (1458 kg)

Max T/O: 6000 lb (2722 kg)
Payload: 2565 lb (1163 kg)

Performance:
Max speed: 184 mph (296 kmh)
Range: 323 nm (599 km)
Power plant: two Pratt &

Whitney Canada PW206B turboshafts
Power: 1258 shp (938 kW)

Variants:
none

Notes: The first helicopter to be designed with NOTAR technology. The MD Explorer first flew in 1992, and over 250 orders have been received.

NH NH90 Italy/Germany/France/The Netherlands

Type: multi-role medium-lift helicopter

Accommodation: two pilots, (NFH) three systems operators, (TTH) 20 troops

Dimensions:
Length: 52 ft 10 in (16.11 m)
Rotor diameter: 53 ft 5 in (16.3 m)
Height: 17 ft 10 in (5.4 m)

Weights:
Empty: 14 741 lb (6428 kg)
Max T/O: 20 062 lb (9100 kg)
Payload: 10 141 lb (4600 kg)

Performance:
Max speed: 186 mph (300 kmh)
Ferry range: 650 nm (1204 km)
Power plant: two RTM 322-01/9 turboshafts
Power: 3084 shp (2300 kW)

Armament:
(NFH) ASW torpedoes; anti-ship missiles; depth charges;

(TTH) 7.62 mm or 12.7 mm door guns

Variants:
NFH shipborne ASW helicopter; TTH transport helicopter

Notes: The NH 90 prototype flew for the first time on 18 December 1995. A very modern design with full nap-of-earth flying and NVG compatible avionics, and many composite parts.

PZL Swidnik W-3 Sokol (Falcon) Poland

Type: medium-lift multi-purpose helicopter   **Accommodation:** two pilots, 12 passengers

Dimensions:
Length: 46 ft 7 in (14.2 m)
Rotor diameter: 51 ft 6 in (15.7 m)
Height: 12 ft 5 in (3.8 m)

Weights:
Empty: 7275 lb (3300 kg)
Max T/O: 14 110 lb (6400 kg)
Payload: 4630 lb (2100 kg)

Performance:
Max speed: 158 mph (255 kmh)
Range: 410 nm (760 km)
Power plant: WSK-PZL Rzeszow PZL-10W turboshafts
Power: 1800 shp (1342 kW)

Armament:
(W-3U) twin 23 mm GSh-23L cannon; Grot AT missiles; 9M32M Strzala AAMs; Mars-2 rockets

Variants:
3A Westernized; 3L Traszka (Newt) stretched version; 3RM Anakonda SAR; 3U Salamandra gunship

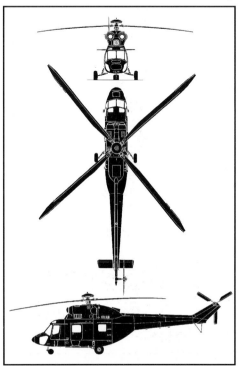

Notes: Two other versions are under development, the W-3WB Huzar gunship equipped with South African weapons and systems, and the W-3U-1 ASW helicopter.

Robinson R-22 USA

Type: light helicopter   **Accommodation:** one pilot, one passenger/pupil

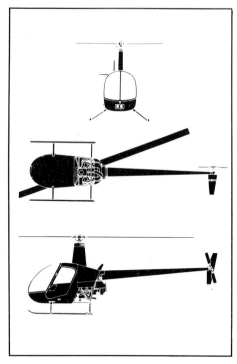

Dimensions:
Length: 20 ft 8 in (6.3 m)
Rotor diameter: 25 ft 2 in (7.7 m)
Height: 8 ft 9 in (2.7 m)

Weights:
Empty: 835 lb (379 kg)
Max T/O: 1370 lb (621 kg)

Payload: 400 lb (181 kg) external

Performance:
Max speed: 112 mph (180 kmh)
Range: 319 nm (592 km)
Power plant: one Textron Lycoming O-320-B2C piston engine
Power: 160 shp (119 kW)

Variants:
R22 Mariner; R22 Police; R22IFR trainer; R22 Agricultural

Notes: One of the smallest and cheapest helicopters in the world at $115 850, the R22 is widely used for training. First flown in 1975, over 2200 have been built.

Robinson R44 USA

Type: light helicopter **Accommodation:** two pilots, two passengers

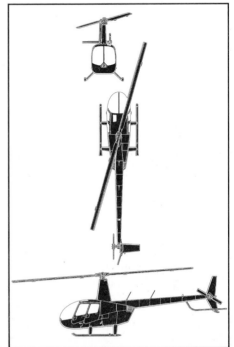

Dimensions:
Length: 38 ft 2 in (11.65 m)
Rotor diameter: 33 ft (10.1 m)
Height: 10 ft 9 in (3.3 m)

Weights:
Empty: 1400 lb (635 kg)

Max T/O: 2400 lb (1088 kg)
Payload: n\a

Performance:
Max speed: 130 mph
(209 kmh)
Range: 347 nm (643 km)

Power plant: one Textron
Lycoming O-540 piston engine
Power: 260 shp (165 kW)

Variants:
none

Notes: Based on many proven concepts of the R22, the R44 has a larger fuselage and more powerful engine.

Rogerson Hiller UH-12E USA

Type: light utility helicopter　　　　**Accommodation:** two pilots, one passenger

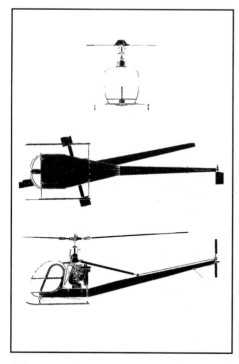

Dimensions:
Length: 28 ft 6 in (8.7 m)
Rotor diameter: 35 ft 5 in (10.8 m)
Height: 10 ft 1 in (3.1 m)

Weights:
Empty: 1759 lb (768 kg)

Max T/O: 3100 lb (1406 kg)
Payload: n\a

Performance:
Max speed: 90 mph (145 kmh)
Range: 316 nm (585 km)
Power plant: one Textron Lycoming VO-540-C2A piston engine
Power: 340 shp (253 kW)

Variants:
Model 360 civil version; H-23 Raven military version

Notes: The original UH-12 first flew in 1948 and the military version entered service during the 1950s. It was put back into production in 1991. Originally a trainer, it is now mainly used for agricultural work.

Schweizer Model 300 (variants) USA

Type: light helicopter   **Accommodation:** two pilots, one passenger

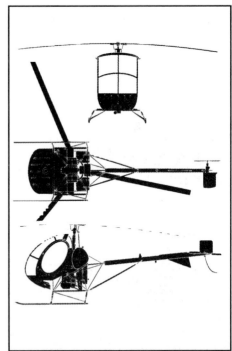

Dimensions:
Length: 30 ft 10 in (9.4 m)
Rotor diameter: 26 ft 10 in
(8.2 m)
Height: 8 ft 8 in (2.7 m)

Weights:
Empty: 1046 lb (474 kg)

Max T/O: 2150 lb (975 kg)
Payload: 100 lb (45 kg)

Performance:
Max speed: 105 mph
(124 kmh)
Range: 194 nm (360 km)
Power plant: one Textron

lycoming HIO-360-D1A piston
engine
Power: 225 hp (168 kW)

Variants:
269 earlier version; 300C
police; TH-300C trainer

Notes: Schweizer acquired the rights to build the Hughes 300 in 1983 and
bought the entire programme in 1986. Hughes built 2800 of all versions,
Schweizer has since sold over 500.

Sikorsky S-58 (CH-34 Choctaw) USA

Type: medium-lift utility helicopter   **Accommodation:** two pilots, crew chief, 16 passengers

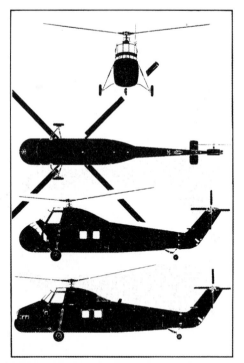

Dimensions:
Length: 47 ft 3 in (14.4 m)
Rotor diameter: 56 ft (17.1 m)
Height: 15 ft 11 in (4.8 m)

Weights:
Empty: 7577 lb (3437 kg)
Max T/O: 13 000 lb (5896 kg)

Payload: n\a

Performance:
Max speed: 138 mph
(222 kmh)
Range: 260 nm (481 km)
Power plant: one Pratt &
Whitney Canada PT6T-3 Twin

Pac turboshaft
Power: 1800 shp (1342 kW)

Variants:
UH-34 Sea Horse USMC
version; Sea Bat minesweeper

Notes: First flown in 1954 powered by a Wright R-1820 piston engine, the S-58 was first fitted with a turboshaft in 1970. Very similar to the Westland Wessex, which was based on it, some of the 1820 built remain in service.

Sikorsky S-62 USA

Type: medium-lift naval helicopter   **Accommodation:** two pilots, 12 passengers

Dimensions:
Length: 44 ft 6 in (13.6 m)
Rotor diameter: 53 ft (16.2 m)
Height: 14 ft 2 in (4.3 m)

Weights:
Empty: 4957 lb (2248 kg)

Max T/O: 7900 lb (3583 kg)
Payload: 2943 lb (1335 kg)

Performance:
Max speed: 101 mph (163 kmh)
Range: 400 nm (743 km)

Power plant: one General Electric CT58-110-1 turboshaft
Power: 1250 shp (932 kW)

Variants:
HH-52A US Coast Guard version

Notes: First flown in 1958, the S-62 clearly shows its lineage in the S-61 family, of which it is the smallest. Built in small numbers mainly for the US Coast Guard, the S-62 was also built in Japan. HH-52As have a small FLIR ball turret in the nose.

Sikorsky S-61 USA

Type: medium-lift naval helicopter **Accommodation:** two pilots, (SH-3) two sonar operators, 26 troops

Dimensions:
Length: 54 ft 9 in (16.7 m)
Rotor diameter: 62 ft (18.9 m)
Height: 15 ft 6 in (4.7 m)

Weights:
Empty: 11 865 lb (5382 kg)
Max T/O: 20 500 lb (9300 kg)

Payload: 8000 lb (3630 kg)

Performance:
Max speed: 166mph (267 kmh)
Range: 542 nm (1005 km)
Power plant: two General
Electric T58-GE-10 turboshafts
Power: 2800 shp (2088 kW)

Armament:
ASW torpedoes; depth charges

Variants:
SH-3G utility/ASW version;
SH-3H ASW version; HH-3A
SAR version; VH-3D VIP
transport

Notes: First flown in 1959, the S-61 has been converted to many tasks including minesweeping and weapon test and evaluation. Also built under licence in Italy, Japan and the UK. Sea King AEW MK illustrated.

Sikorsky S-61N USA

Type: offshore helicopter transport   **Accommodation:** two pilots, 30 passengers

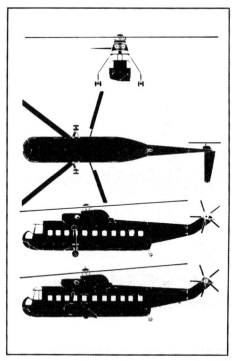

Dimensions:
Length: 72 ft 10 in (22.2 m)
Rotor diameter: 62 ft (18.9 m)
Height: 17 ft (5.2 m)

Weights:
Empty: 12 510 lb (5674 kg)

Max T/O: 22 000 lb (9980 kg)
Payload: 7850 lb (3560 kg)

Performance:
Max speed: 146 mph (235 kmh)
Range: 430 nm (796 km)

Power plant: two General Electric CT58-140-1 turboshafts
Power: 3000 shp (2236 kW)

Variants:
61L early version; Payloader cargo version

Notes: Designed to support the offshore oil industry. The S-61L is non-amphibious and lacks the stability sponsons.

Sikorsky S-61R CH-3 USA

Type: medium-lift transport helicopter

Accommodation: two pilots, 30 troops, 15 stretchers

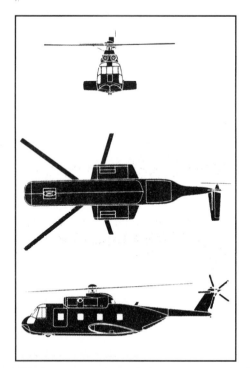

Dimensions:
Length: 57 ft 3 in (17.4 m)
Rotor diameter: 62 ft (18.9 m)
Height: 18 ft 1 in (5.5 m)

Weights:
Empty: 13 225 lb (6010 kg)
Max T/O: 22 050 lb (10 000 kg)

Payload: 5000 lb (2270 kg)

Performance:
Max speed: 162 mph (261 kmh)
Range: 404 nm (748 km)
Power plant: two General Electric T58-GE-5 turboshafts

Power: 3000 shp (2236 kW)

Variants:
HH-3E Jolly Green Giant; HH-3F Pelican US Coast Guard SAR version

Notes: Developed from the standard S-61, the CH-3 differs by the inclusion of a rear loading ramp. The USAF converted 50 into Jolly Green Giant combat search and rescue helicopters, fitting them with an in-flight refuelling boom, drop tanks, armour and several machine guns.

Sikorsky S-64 Skycrane USA

Type: heavy-lift helicopter   **Accommodation:** two pilots, optional third pilot

Dimensions:
Length: 70 ft 3 in (21.4 m)
Rotor diameter: 72 ft (21.9 m)
Height: 25 ft 5 in (7.7 m)

Weights:
Empty: 19 234 lb (8724 kg)
Max T/O: 42 000 lb (19 050 kg)

Payload: 20 000 lb (9072 kg)

Performance:
Max speed: 126 mph
(203 kmh)
Range: 200 nm (370 km)
Power plant: two Pratt &
Whitney JFTD 12-4A

turboshafts
Power: 9600 shp (7158 kW)

Variants:
CH-54 Tarhe US Army
designation, with Air National
Guard

Notes: Designed to carry a variety of cargo pods or underslung loads, the Skycrane set a number of world records, including time-to-height, payload-height and altitude. The pods could carry 45 troops or a complete surgical hospital segment.

Sikorsky S-65A (CH-53 Sea Stallion) USA

Type: heavy-lift transport helicopter   **Accommodation:** two pilots, crew chief, 37 troops, 24 stretchers

Dimensions:
Length: 67 ft 2 in (20.5 m)
Rotor diameter: 72 ft 3 in (22 m)
Height: 24 ft 11 in (7.6 m)

Weights:
Empty: 22 444 lb (10 180 kg)
Max T/O: 37 400 lb (16 964 kg)
Payload: 20 000 lb (9070 kg)

Performance:
Max speed: 186mph (299kmh)
Range: 468 nm (869 km) with auxiliary tanks
Power plant: two General Electric T64–GE–6 turboshafts
Power: 5700 shp (4250 kW)

Armament:
7.62/12.7 mm door guns

Variants:
HH-53B USAF combat SAR; HH-53H Pave Low III special operations; CH-53D improved version; RH-53D minesweeper; VH-53D VIP transport; MH-53J Enhanced Pave Low III Special Ops version

Notes: First flown in 1964, the S-65 was based on many of the proven components of the Skycrane. Special forces versions are equipped with FLIR and radar radomes on the nose and an in-flight refuelling probe .

Sikorsky S-80
(CH-53E Super Stallion) USA

Type: heavy-lift transport helicopter   **Accommodation:** two pilots, crew chief, 55 troops

Dimensions:
Length: 73 ft 4 in (22.3 m)
Rotor diameter: 79 ft (24.1 m)
Height: 29 ft 5 in (8.9 m)

Weights:
Empty: 33 228 lb (15 072 kg)
Max T/O: 69 750 lb (31 640 kg)
Payload: 30 000 b (13 607 kg)

Performance:
Max speed: 196 mph
(315 kmh)
Ferry Range: 1120 nm
(2074 km)
Power plant: three General
Electric T64-GE-416
turboshafts
Power: 13 140 shp (9798 kW)

Armament:
7.62 mm or 12.7 mm door
guns

Variants:
MH-53E Sea Dragon mine
sweeper

Notes: A three-engined development of the Sea Stallion, the S-80 first flew
in 1974. The Sea Dragon can be recognized by its outsize sponsons either side
of the fuselage.

Sikorsky S-70 (UH-60 Black Hawk) USA

Type: medium-lift utility helicopter   **Accommodation:** two pilots, crew chief, 14 troops, (civil) 12 passengers

Dimensions:
Length: 50 ft (15.3 m)
Rotor diameter: 53 ft 8 in (16.4 m)
Height: 16 ft 10 in (5.1 m)

Weights:
Empty: 11 284 lb (5118 kg)
Max T/O: 20 250 lb (9185 kg)
Payload: 8000 lb (3629 kg)

Performance:
Max speed: 184mph (296kmh)
Range: 319 nm (592 km); 1200 nm (2222 km) with max external fuel
Power plant: two General Electric T700-GE-700 turboshafts
Power: 3244 shp (2420 kW)

Armament:
7.62 mm or 12.7 mm door guns

Variants:
UH-60Q Dustoff medical evacuation; EH-60EW platform; VH-60N VIP transport; UH-60L up-engined US Army transport

Notes: First flown in 1974, over 2000 have been delivered. Designed to be air-transportable, the C-5 Galaxy can carry six. Dustoff helicopters have one radar and one FLIR radome on the nose and can be fitted with long range fuel tanks. All versions can be fitted with auxiliary stub wings to carry fuel or weapons.

Sikorsky MH-60 Pave Hawk USA

Type: special operations helicopter   **Accommodation:** two pilots, crew chief, 14 troops, (civil) 12 passengers

Dimensions:
Length: 50 ft (15.3 m)
Rotor diameter: 53 ft 8 in
(16.4 m)
Height: 16 ft 10 in (5.1 m)

Weights:
Empty: 13 000 lb (5896 kg)
Max T/O: 20 250 lb (9185 kg)
Payload: n\a

Performance:
Max speed: 184 mph
(296 kmh)
Range: 319 nm (592 km);
1200 nm (2222 km) with max
external fuel
Power plant: two General
Electric T700-GE-700
turboshafts
Power: 3244 shp (2420 kW)

Armament:
7.62 mm and 12.7 mm
miniguns

Variants:
-60G combat search and
rescue; -60K US Army special
forces aircraft; -60L 'Velcro
Hawk' US Army Special Forces

Notes: The basic Blackhawk has been developed into a number of special operations aircraft, fitted with in-flight refuelling booms and stub wings. They also have FLIR and radar in the nose. A gunship version has also been developed carrying Stinger and Hellfire missiles.

Sikorsky S-70B (SH-60B Seahawk) USA

Type: shipborne anti-submarine helicopter

Accommodation: two pilots, sensor operator

Dimensions:
Length: 50 ft (15.3 m)
Rotor diameter: 53 ft 8 in (16.4 m)
Height: 16 ft 10 in (5.1 m)

Weights:
Empty: 13 448 lb (6191 kg)
Max T/O: 21 884 lb (9926 kg)

Payload: 7829 lb (3551 kg)

Performance:
Max speed: 169 mph (272 kmh)
Range: 319 nm (592 km)
Power plant: General Electric T700-GE-401 turboshafts
Power: 3380 shp (2520 kW)

Armament:
AGM-119B Penguin, Hellfire ASMs; ASW torpedoes; depth charges; 7.62 mm door guns

Variants:
HH-60H naval special operations; HH-60J Jayhawk US Coast Guard version

Notes: To facilitate storage aboard ship the rotors and tail assembly can fold. Also built in Japan by Mitsubishi as the SH-60J. The HH-60H is used to support naval special forces and carry out combat search and rescue. The Jayhawk has a radar in the nose and is used for drug interdiction and rescue duties.

Sikorsky S-76 USA

Type: medium-lift utility helicopter   **Accommodation:** two pilots, 14 passengers

Dimensions:
Length: 44 ft (13.4 m)
Rotor diameter: 44 ft (13.4 m)
Height: 14 ft 5 in (4.4 m)

Weights:
Empty: 6641 lb (3012 kg)
Max T/O: 11 700 lb (5307 kg)
Payload: n\a

Performance:
Max speed: 178 mph
(287 kmh)
Range: 357 nm (661 km)
Power plant: Pratt & Whitney
Canada PT6B-36A turboshaft
Power: 1962 shp (1464 kW)

Armament:
7.62 mm, 12.7 mm or 20 mm
gun pods; Stinger AAMs;
Hellfire, TOW AT missiles; 2.75
in or 5 in rockets

Variants:
76 Eagle military version; Mk
II early version

Notes: First flown in 1977, over 390 have been delivered. Military versions
can be fitted with a wide range of weapons but only the Philippine Air Force
has armed versions. Australia operates a number for SAR.

Westland Scout/Wasp UK

Type: light general-purpose helicopter   **Accommodation:** one pilot, five passengers

Dimensions:
Length: 30 ft 4 in (9.2 m)
Rotor diameter: 32 ft 3 in (9.8 m)
Height: 11 ft 8 in (3.6 m)

Weights:
Empty: 3452 lb (1566 kg)
Max T/O: 5500 lb (2495 kg)

Payload: 1500 lb (680 kg)

Performance:
Max speed: 120 mph (193 kmh)
Range: 263 nm (488 km)
Power plant: one Rolls-Royce Bristol Nimbus 503 turboshaft
Power: 710 shp (529 kW)

Armament:
ASW torpedoes; AS.12 ASMs; depth charges

Variants:
Wasp HAS 1 shipborne ASW version; Scout AH 1 Army version

Notes: First flown in 1958, the Wasp only remains in service with the Royal New Zealand Navy and Malaysian Navy, the Scout is no longer in service.

Westland Wessex UK

Type: medium-lift helicopter   **Accommodation:** two pilots, optional crew chief, 16 troops

Dimensions:
Length: 48 ft 4 in (14.7 m)
Length: 55 ft 10 in (17 m)
Rotor diameter: 62 ft (18.9 m)
Height: 16 ft 10 in (5.1 m)

Weights:
Empty: 12 390 lb (5620 kg)
Max T/O: 21 500 lb (9752 kg)

Payload: 8000 lb (3628 kg)

Performance:
Max speed: 140 mph
(226 kmh)
Range: 214 nm (396 km)
Power plant: two Bristol
Siddeley Gnome turboshaft
(one 112, one 113)

Power: 2700 shp (2013 kW)

Armament:
7.62 mm door guns

Variants:
Mk 2 uprated engine; Mk 5
Commando version; SAR
versions

Westland Lynx UK

Type: light multi-purpose helicopter

Accommodation: pilot, observer/gunner, 10 troops

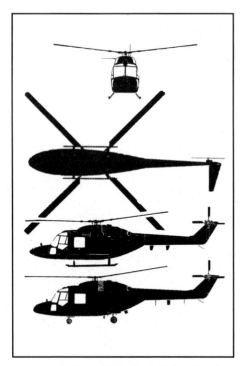

Dimensions:
Length: 49 ft 9 in (15.2 m)
Rotor diameter: 42 ft (12.8 m)
Height: 11 ft 6 in (3.5 m)

Weights:
Empty: 6040 lb (2740 kg)
Max T/O: 10 000 lb (4535 kg)
Payload: 2000 lb (907 kg)

Performance:
Cruising speed: 161 mph (259 kmh)
Range: 340 nm (630 km)
Power plant: two Rolls-Royce Gem 2 turboshafts
Power: 1800 shp (1342 kW)

Armament:
ASW torpedoes; depth charges; Sea Skua or AS.12 ASMs; TOW AT missiles; 12.7 mm or 20 mm gun pods; rockets

Variants:
HAS 3 shipborne ASW version; AH 7 anti-tank version; AH 9 utility version; Super Lynx upgraded version

Notes: Developed in conjunction with France, the Lynx first flew in 1971. Royal Navy aircraft have been seen carrying a number of ECM and self-defence aids for service in the Persian Gulf. Super Lynx has uprated engines and a large 360 deg radar radome under the nose.

DEVELOPMENT AIRCRAFT

Westinghouse YEZ-2A Sentinel 5000 USA

Type: non-rigid Airborne Early Warning airship   **Accomodation:** 10 to 15 crew

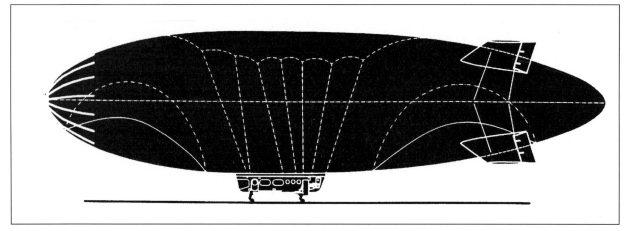

Dimensions:
Length: 425ft (129.5m)
Diameter: 105ft (32m)
Height: 152ft (46.3m)
Volume: 2 500 000 cu ft (70 792sq m)

Weights:
Empty: unknown

Max T/O: unknown
Payload: 60 350lb (27375kg)

Performance:
Max speed: 101mph (163km/h)
Endurance: 30 days with refuelling
Power plant: Combined diesel and gas turbine propulsion system; one General Electric CT7-9 turboprop
Power: 6010shp (4482kW)

Variants:
none

Notes: the largest non-rigid airship ever designed, the US Navy wants an initial fleet of five to carry out autonomous AEW, OTH targeting and communications. First flight is scheduled for 1996. Living accommodation includes a small gymnasium.

GLOSSARY

AAM   Air-to-air missile.

ACLS   Automatic carrier landing system.

ACMI   Air combat manoeuvring instrumentation.

ADAC   Avion de décollage et atterrisage court (STOL).

ADAV   Avion de décollage et atterrisage vertical (VTOL).

ADF   Medium frequency automatic direction finding (equipment).

ADI   Attitude/direction indicator.

AEW   Airborne early warning.

AFB   Air Force Base.

AFCS   Automatic flight control system.

Afterburning   Temporarily augmenting the thrust of a turbofan or turbojet by burning additional fuel in the jetpipe.

AGM   Air-to-ground missile.

ALCM   Air-launched cruise missile.

anhedral   Downward slope of wing seen from the front, in direction from root to tip.

ANVIS   Aviator's night vision system.

APFD   Autopilot flight director.

approach noise   Measured 1nm from downwind end of runway with aircraft passing overhead at 370ft (113m).

APU   Auxiliary power unit.

ASI   Airspeed indicator.

ASIR   Airspeed indicator reading.

ASM   Air-to-surface missile.

aspect ratio   Measure of wing (or other aerofoil) slenderness seen in plan view, usually defined as the square of the span divided by gross area.

ASPJ   Advanced self-protection jammer.

ASV   Air-to-surface vessel.

ASVW   Anti-surface vessel-warfare.

ASW   Anti-submarine warfare.

ATA   Air Transport Association of America.

ATC   Air traffic control.

ATDS   Airborne tactical data system.

attack, angle of (alpha)   Angle at which airstream meets aerofoil (angle between mean chord and free-stream direction) Not to be confused with angle of incidence (which see).

augmented   Boosted by afterburning.

autogyro   Rotary-wing aircraft propelled by a propeller (or other thrusting device) and lifted by a freely running autorotating rotor.

avionics   Aviation electronics, such as communications radio, radars, navigation systems and computers.

AWACS   Airborne warning and control system (aircraft).

bearingless rotor   Rotor in which flapping lead/lag and pitch change movements are provided by the flexibility of the structural material and not by bearings. No rotor is rigid.

bladder tank   Fuel (or other fluid) tank of flexible material.

BLC   Boundary-layer control.

bleed air   Hot high-pressure air extracted from gas turbine engine compressor or combustor and taken through valves and pipes to perform useful work such as pressurisation, driving machinery or anti-icing by heating surfaces.

blown flap   Flap across which bleed air is discharged at high (often supersonic) speed to prevent flow breakaway.

BVR   Beyond visual range.

bypass ratio   Airflow through fan duct (not passing through core) divided by airflow through core.

C3   Command, control and communications.

C3CM   Command, control, communications and countermeasures.

CAA   Civil Aviation Authority (UK).

canards   Foreplanes, fixed or controllable aerodynamic surfaces ahead of CG.

CAR   Civil Airworthiness Regulations.

carbonfibre   Fine filament of carbon/graphite used as strength element in composites.

CAS   close air support.

CBU   Cluster bomb unit.

CEAM   Centre d'Expériences Aériennes Militaires.

CEAT   Centre d'Essais Aéronautiques de Toulouse.

CEP   Circular error probability (50/50 chance of hit being inside or outside) in bombing, missile attack or gunnery.

CFRP   Carbonfibre-reinforced plastics.

CG   Centre of gravity.

chaff   Thin slivers of radar-reflective material cut to length appropriate to wavelengths of hostile radars and scattered in clouds to protect friendly aircraft; also known as window.

clean i) In flight configuration with landing gear, flaps, slats etc retracted.

ii) Without any optional external stores.

COIN Counter-insurgency.

comint Communications intelligence.

composite material Made of two constituents, such as filaments or short whiskers plus adhesive, forming binding matrix.

CSRL Common strategic rotary launcher (for the B-52, B-1B and B-2 bombers).

DARPA Defense Advanced Research Projects Agency.

databus Electronic highway for passing digital data between aircraft sensors and system processors, usually MIL-STD-1553B or ARINC 419 (one way) and 619 (two way) systems.

derated Engine restricted to power less than potential maximum (usually such engine is flat rated, which see).

DF Direction finder or direction finding.

DGAC Direction Générale à l'Aviation Civile.

dihedral Upward slope of wing seen from front, in direction from root to tip.

disposable load Sum of masses that can be loaded or unloaded, including payload, crew, usable fuel, etc; Max MTO minus operating weight empty.

dogtooth A step in the leading-edge of an

aircraft wing.

Doppler Short for Doppler radar which measures speed over ground to detect moving vehicles over static ground.

DRA Defence Research Agency, Farnborough.

drone Pilotless aircraft, usually winged, following pre-set programme of manoeuvres.

ECCM Electronic counter-countermeasures.

ECM Electronic countermeasures.

ehp Equivalent horsepower, thrust from turboprop engine including residual jet thrust.

ELF Extreme low frequency.

elint Electronics intelligence.

EMP Electromagnetic pulse of nuclear or electronic origin.

EO Electro-optical.

EPU Emergency power unit (part of aircraft, not used for propulsion).

ESA European Space Agency.

ESM i) Electronic surveillance (or support) measures.

ii) Electronic signal monitoring.

EW Electronic warfare.

EWSM Early-warning support measures.

FAA Federal Aviation Authority.

FAI Fédération Aéronautique Internationale.

fence a projection on the surface of a wing used to modify the distribution of pressure.

fenestron Helicopter tail rotor with many

slender blades rotating in short duct.

ferry range Extreme safe range with zero payload.

flaperon Wing trailing-edge surface combining functions of flap and aileron.

flat rated Propulsion engine capable of giving full thrust or power for take-off to high airfield height and/or high ambient temperature (thus, probably derated at S/L).

FLIR Forward-looking infra-red.

fly-by-light Flight control system in which signals pass between computers and actuators along fibre optic leads.

fly-by-wire Flight control system with electrical signalling (i.e. without mechanical interconnection between cockpit flying controls and control surfaces).

Fowler flap Moves initially aft to increase wing area and also deflects down to increase drag.

free turbine Turbine mechanically independent of engine upstream, other than being connected by rotating bearings and the gas stream, and thus able to run at its own speed.

g Acceleration due to mean Earth gravity, ie of a body in free fall; or acceleration due to rapid change of direction of flight path.

glove Fixed portion of wing inboard of variable sweep wing.

GPS Global Positioning System.

gunship Helicopter designed for battlefield

GLOSSARY

attack, normally with slim body carrying pilot and weapon operator only.

hardpoint Reinforced part of aircraft to which external load can be attached, eg weapon or tank pylon.

HMD Helmet-mounted display; hence HMS = sight.

hot and high Adverse combination of airfield height and high ambient temperature, which lengthens required TOD.

hp Horsepower.

HUD Head-up display.

IFF Identification friend or foe.

ILS Instrument landing system.

incidence Strictly, the angle at which the wing is set in relation to the fore/aft axis.

INEWS Integrated electronic warfare system.

IR Infra-red.

IRST Infra-red search and track.

JASDF Japan Air Self-Defence Force.

JATO Jet-assisted take-off (actually means rocket-assisted.

JGSDF Japan Ground Self-Defence Force.

JMSDF Japan Maritime Self-Defence Force.

J-STARS US Air Force/Navy Joint Surveillance Target Attack Radar System in Boeing/Northrop Grumman E-8A.

JTIDS Joint Tactical Information Distribution System.

Kevlar Aramid fibre used as basis of high-strength composite material.

km/h Kilometres per hour.

kN Kilonewtons, the metric unit for measuring power output of jet engine.

knot 1 nm per hour.

kW Kilowatts, the metric unit for measuring power output of a propeller driven engine.

LANTIRN Low-altitude navigation and targeting infra-red, night.

LBA Luftfahrtbundesamt (German civil aviation authority).

lb Pounds of static thrust, the measurement of a jet engine's static thrust.

LLTV Low-light TV (thus LLLTV, low-light-level).

loiter Flight for maximum endurance, such as supersonic fighter on patrol.

longerons Principal fore-and-aft structural members (eg in fuselage).

low observables Materials and structures designed to reduce aircraft signatures of all kinds.

LRMTS Laser ranger and marked-target seeker.

m metre(s), the metric unit of length.

M or Mach number The ratio of the speed of a body to the speed of sound (at 1116 ft: 340 m/s in air at 15 degC) under the same ambient temperature.

MAD Magnetic anomaly detector.

MFD Multi-function display.

MMS Mast-mounted sight.

MO Maximum permitted operating Mach number.

mph Miles per hour.

MaxTO Maximum take-off weight.

NAS US Naval Air Station.

NASA National Aeronautics and Space Administration.

nm Nautical mile, 1.15152 miles (1.8532 km)

NOE Nap-of-the-Earth (low-flying in military aircraft using natural cover of hills and trees etc).

NVG Night Vision Goggles.

OCU Operational Conversion Unit.

omni Generalised term meaning equal in all directions (as in omni-range, omni-flash beacon).

optronics Combination of optics and electronics in viewing and sighting systems.

OTH Over the horizon.

pallet Rigid platform for freight for handling by forklift or conveyor.

phased array Radar in which the beam is scanned electronically in one or both axes without moving the antenna.

port Left side, looking forward.

propfan A family of new technology propellers

characterised by multiple scimitar-shaped blades with thin sharp-edged profile.

pulse Doppler   Radar sending out pulses and measuring frequency-shift to detect returns only from moving target(s) in background clutter.

pylon   Structure linking aircraft to external load (engine nacelle, drop tank, bomb etc).

radius   The distance an aircraft can fly from base and return without intermediate landing.

RAI   Registro Aeronatico Italiano.

RAM   Radar absorbent material.

rigid rotor   see bearingless rotor.

RLD   Rijksluchtvaartdienst (Netherlands Civil Aviation Department).

RPV   Remotely piloted vehicle.

ruddervators   Flying control surfaces, usually a V tail, that control both yaw and pitch attitude.

SAR   i) Search and rescue.
     ii) Synthetic aperture radar.

saw-tooth   Same as dog-tooth.

semi-active   Homing on to radiation reflected from target illuminated by radar or laser energy beamed from elsewhere.

service ceiling   Usually height equivalent to air density at which maximum attainable rate of climb is 100ft/min.

shp   Shaft horsepower, measure of power transmitted via rotating shaft.

sidestick   Control column in the form of a short hand-stick beside the pilot.

sigint   Signals intelligence.

signature   Characteristic "fingerprint" of all electromagnetic radiation (radar, IR etc).

single-shaft   Gas turbine in which all compressors and turbines are on common shaft rotating together.

SLAR   Side-looking airborne radar.

stabiliser   Fin (thus, horizontal stabiliser = tailplane).

stalling speed   Airspeed at which wing lift suddenly collapses.

starboard   Right side, looking forward.

STOL   Short take-off and landing.

supercritical wing   Wing of relatively deep, flat-topped profile generating lift right across upper surface instead of concentrated close behind the leading-edge.

t   Tonne, 1 Megagram, 1000kg.

taileron   Left and right tailplanes used as primary control surfaces in both pitch and roll.

tailplane   Main horizontal tail surface, originally fixed and carrying hinged elevator(s) but today often a single 'slab' serving as a control surface.

tilt-rotor   Aircraft with fixed wing and rotors that tilt up for hovering and forward for fast flight.

T-O   Take-off.

ton   Imperial (long) ton == 1.016t or 2240lb, US

(short) ton = 0.9072t or 2000lb.

transponder   Radio transmitter triggered automatically by a particular received signal as in civil secondary surveillance radar (SSR)

turbofan   Gas-turbine jet engine generating most thrust by a large-diameter cowled fan, with small part added by jet from core.

turbojet   Simplest form of gas turbine comprising compressor, combustion chamber, turbine and propulsive nozzle.

turboprop   Gas turbine in which as much energy as possible is taken from gas jet and used to drive reduction gearbox and propeller.

turboshaft   Gas turbine in which as much energy as possible is taken from gas jet and used to drive helicopter rotors.

UAV   Unmanned air vehicle.

variable geometry   Capable of grossly changing shape in flight, especially by varying sweep of wings.

VTOL   Vertical take-off and landing.

VISTOL   Vertical/short take-off and landing.

winglet   Small auxiliary aerofoil, usually sharply upturned and often sweptback, at tip of wing.

zero/zero seat   Ejection seat designed for use even at zero speed on ground.

Acknowledgements:

Photo credits
All photographs via Jane's Information Group except:
Aviation Picture Library: 288, 304, 333, 345, 350, 362, 371,
372, 375, 380, 381, 382, 383, 386, 387, 388, 394, 395, 404, 410,
418, 427, 437, 482, 398, 479, 448 (Mark Wagner), 483, 492,
M-Slides: 194, 202, 206

Design: Rod Teasdale

HarperCollinsPublishers
PO Box, Glasgow G4 0BN

First published 1996

Reprint
1 3 5 7 9 10 8 6 4 2

© Jane's Information Group 1996

ISBN 0 00 4709802

Printed in Italy by Amadeus S.p.A. Rome